THE CINEMA OF CANADA

First published in Great Britain in 2006 by
Wallflower Press
6a Middleton Place, Langham Street, London W1W 7TE
www.wallflowerpress.co.uk

A catalogue for this book is available from the British Library

ISBN 1-904764-60-6 (paperback)
ISBN 1-904764-61-4 (hardback)

Printed by Replika Press Pvt Ltd., India

THE CINEMA OF
CANADA

EDITED BY

JERRY WHITE

 WALLFLOWER PRESS LONDON & NEW YORK

24 FRAMES is a major new series focusing on national and regional cinemas from around the world. Rather than offering a 'best of' selection, the feature films and documentaries selected in each volume serve to highlight the specific elements of that territory's cinema, elucidating the historical and industrial context of production, the key genres and modes of representation, and foregrounding the work of the most important directors and their exemplary films. In taking an explicitly text-centred approach, the titles in this list offer 24 diverse entry-points into each national and regional cinema, and thus contribute to the appreciation of the rich traditions of global cinema.

Series Editors: Yoram Allon & Ian Haydn Smith

OTHER TITLES IN THE **24 FRAMES** SERIES:

THE CINEMA OF LATIN AMERICA *edited by Alberto Elena and Marina Díaz López*

THE CINEMA OF THE LOW COUNTRIES *edited by Ernest Mathijs*

THE CINEMA OF ITALY *edited by Giorgio Bertellini*

THE CINEMA OF JAPAN & KOREA *edited by Justin Bowyer*

THE CINEMA OF CENTRAL EUROPE *edited by Peter Hames*

THE CINEMA OF SPAIN & PORTUGAL *edited by Alberto Mira*

THE CINEMA OF SCANDINAVIA *edited by Tytti Soila*

THE CINEMA OF BRITAIN & IRELAND *edited by Brian McFarlane*

THE CINEMA OF FRANCE *edited by Phil Powrie*

FORTHCOMING TITLES:

THE CINEMA OF THE BALKANS *edited by Dina Iordanova*

THE CINEMA OF AUSTRALIA & NEW ZEALAND *edited by Geoff Mayer and Keith Beattie*

THE CINEMA OF RUSSIA & THE FORMER SOVIET UNION *edited by Birgit Beumers*

THE CINEMA OF NORTH AFRICA & THE MIDDLE EAST *edited by Gönül Dönmez-Colin*

CONTENTS

NOTES ON CONTRIBUTORS

MICHAEL BRENDAN BAKER is in the PhD Communication Studies programme at McGill University. His research interests include the intersection of documentary film and popular music. He was recently awarded the Film Studies Association of Canada's Gerald Pratley Award, given for outstanding research on Canadian or Quebec cinema.

WILLIAM BEARD is Professor of Film Studies in the Department of English and Film Studies at the University of Alberta. He is the author of *Persistence of Double Vision: Essays on Clint Eastwood* (2000) and *The Artist as Monster: The Cinema of David Cronenberg* (2001), and co-editor of *North of Everything: English-Canadian Cinema Since 1980* (2002).

MARIAN BREDIN is Associate Professor and Chair of the Department of Communications, Popular Culture and Film at Brock University. Her main research interests are postcolonial theory, cultural politics, Aboriginal and minority media, Canadian communications and cultural policy, local heritage and popular memory in the Niagara region. Her work has been published in the *Canadian Journal of Communication*, the *Canadian Journal of Native Studies* and elsewhere.

DAMIEN DETCHBERRY has been an active member of www.cine-courts.com, the first French website dedicated to the promotion and broadcast of short films, since its creation in 1999. He is also a regular contributor to the revue of aesthetics Eclipses. After graduating from La Sorbonne with an MA in Film Studies, he is now specialising in Film Distribution at the French film school La fémis.

AMY FUNG graduated from the University of Alberta with a double concentration in English Literature and Film Studies. She writes and researches on visual and aural media and urban design, and has written on film and media for the Edmonton weekly magazines *See* and *Vue*. She is currently on the staff of *The Works*, an arts festival in Edmonton.

PETER HARCOURT has published in magazines such as *Sight and Sound, Film Quarterly, The Canadian Forum* and *CineAction*, and is the author of several books on filmmaking, including *Six European Directors* (1974) and *Jean Pierre Lefebvre: Vidéatse* (2001), as well as the memoir *A*

Canadian Journey: Conversations with Time (1994). He was inducted into the Order of Canada in 2004.

FARBOD HONARPISHEH studies and teaches part-time in the Mel Hoppenheim School of Cinema at Concordia University, Montreal. Born in Iran, his current interests include cultural theory, Middle Eastern, First Nations and Diaspora cinemas. Farbod has curated a number of film-related academic and public events. His publications include *The Soviet Phantasmagoria of Production and Its Filmic Orient* (2006).

COLLEEN IRWIN is a PhD candidate in Comparative Literature at the University of Alberta, where she taught for several years. Her research relates to strategies of reconstructing Aboriginal heritages, an area of study that encompasses contemporary Native novels, autobiography and film.

ANDRÉ LAVOIE has been a film and television critic for the Montreal newspaper *Le Devoir* since 1998 and is also a long-time contributor to the film magazine *Ciné-Bulles*. He also works frequently on television as researcher, writer and film critic, mostly for Radio-Canada, Télé-Québec, ARTV and la Chaîne culturelle de Radio-Canada. He recently served on the jury for the Toronto Film Festival's Top Ten Canadian Films of 2005.

ANDRÉ LOISELLE teaches Film Studies at Carleton University, Ottawa. He is author of *Scream from Silence/Mourir à tue-tête* (2000), *Stage-Bound: Feature Film Adaptations of Canadian and Québécois Drama* (2003) and *À l'image d'une nation: le cinéma de Michel Brault et l'histoire du Québec contemporain* (2005). He is also the co-editor of the anthology *Self Portraits: The Cinemas of Canada Since Telefilm* (2006).

BRIAN MCILROY is Professor of Film Studies at the University of British Columbia. His most recent book is *Shooting to Kill: Filmmaking and the Troubles in Northern Ireland* (2001). He guest edited a special issue of the *Canadian Journal of Irish Studies* on Irish Cinema (2003), and is currently embarked on a project on Irish film genres.

JAMES MISSEN is a part-time lecturer on artists' film, video and new media at Carleton University in Ottawa. In February 2005 he was appointed Interim Policy Advisor at the Canadian Conference of the Arts. He is active as a programming member of the Available Light Screening Collective and also sits on the board of the Independent Media Arts Alliance.

CRAIG MOYES was Director of Studies in French at Christ's College, Cambridge University, before moving to King's College, University of London in 1999. His principal teaching and research interests are in seventeenth- and eighteenth-century French and comparative literature, and is currently working on a monograph on the literary city under Bourbon Absolutism. He has also lectured on Québécois cinema.

MARSH MURPHY is the Executive Director of Metro Cinema, a cinematheque in Edmonton. He has also been Vice-President of FAVA (a media production co-op in Edmonton), and chief technician of the Global Visions Documentary Film Festival. He also writes about the media arts, and when he finds the time, he makes his own videos and animations.

JODI RAEMER is a PhD candidate at Concordia University, Montreal, where she is researching images of the female flâneur in Montreal film and culture. She has taught courses on Women and Cinema, and has has various essays published in the online film journal *Synoptique*. She works on the Hollywood women's picture of the 1930s and 1940s, specifically examining concepts of affect and glamour.

ADAM ROSADIUK has a Master's degree in Film Studies from Concordia University, where he wrote a thesis on Terrence Malick and philosophy's place in Film Studies. He is one of the founders of *Synoptique*, an online film journal (www.synoptique.ca), and is also a freelance website designer.

GWENN SCHEPPLER is a PhD candidate in Comparative Literature and Film Studies in a trans-Atlantic doctoral programme shared with Université de Montréal and Université Lyon 2. He is writing a dissertation about the inscription of Pierre Perrault's films in the social and cultural context of Quebec.

JASON SILVERMAN is the former artistic director of the Taos Talking Pictures festival, publications editor for the Telluride Film Festival and a contributing writer for *Wired News*. He has also written for the *Austin Chronicle*, *Time Out New York* and the Berlin Film Festival. As a curator, he has built programs for the Smithsonian National Museum of the American Indian, SITE Santa Fe and the Center for Contemporary Arts, Santa Fe. He is also a contributor to *Contemporary North American Film Directors: A Wallflower Critical Guide (second edition)* (2002).

MONIQUE TSCHOFEN is Associate Professor at Toronto's Ryerson University who works on English- and French-Canadian film and literature. She has written on Canadian literature and film, in both English and French. She is the editor of book on Icelandic-Canadian writer Kristjana Gunnars (2004) and co-editor of *Image and Territories: Essays on Atom Egoyan* (2006).

DARRELL VARGA is Canada Research Chair in Contemporary Film and Media Studies at NSCAD University (The Nova Scotia College of Art and Design) in Halifax, Nova Scotia, where his research addresses the question of regional cultural production in the context of globalisation. He is is co-editor of *Working on Screen: Representations of the Working Class in Canadian Cinema* (2006).

PIERRE VÉRONNEAU has worked at the Cinémathèque Québécoise since 1973, and is currently their Conservateur du cinéma québécois et canadien. He is Adjunct Professor at Université de Montréal and Université du Québec à Montréal, and also teaches at Concordia University. He is the author of many books on cinema and television in Québec and Canada, including *Résistance et affirmation: la production francophone à l'ONF – 1939–1964* (1987) and *David Cronenberg: la beauté du chaos* (2003).

JERRY WHITE is Assistant Professor of Film Studies at the University of Alberta. He is co-editor of *North of Everything: English-Canadian Cinema Since 1980* (2002) and author of *Peter Mettler: Towards Global Cinema* (2006). He writes for academic publications, contributes to film magazines such as *Cinema Scope* (Toronto) and *Dox* (Copenhagen), and regularly reviews books for the *Edmonton Journal and Books in Canada*.

LYSANDRA WOODS is a graduate of Concordia University's MA programme in Film Studies. She is a freelance writer, has worked for the Telluride Film Festival, and is currently working in film distribution in Montreal. Her work has also appeared in *Synoptique*, the anthology *North of Everything: English Canadian Cinema Since 1980*, and *Contemporary North American Film Directors: A Wallflower Critical Guide (second edition)* (2002).

ACKNOWLEDGEMENTS

I want first of all to thank all of the contributors; this book belongs to them. A special note of thanks is due to the translators here as well: Lynn Penrod, Christa Polley, Kathy Durnin and Vivian Bosley. Many thanks also to Celia Nicholls who compiled the bibliography, filmography and index, and did a crackerjack job on all three.

Thanks to Shirley Cheechoo for the loan of tapes, and for providing images from *Bearwalker*.

Cinematheque Ontario provided the stills for *The Learning Path*, *Dead Man* and *Atanarjuat: The Fast Runner*. Many thanks to Eve Goldin at Cinematheque Ontario for her help on this.

Cinémathèque québécoise provided the stills for the following films: *Thirty Two Short Films About Glenn Gould*, *Churchill's Island*, *Le confessionnal*, *Earth*, *En pays neufs*, *Exotica*, *La Forteresse*, *Foster Child*, *I've Heard the Mermaids Singing*, *Kahnasatake: 270 Years of Resistance*, *Mourir à tue-tête*, *Nobody Waved Good-bye*, *On est au coton*, *Pour la suite du monde*, *Sonatine* and *The Winds of Fogo*. The photograph from *Le Déclin de l'empire américain* is © Bertrand Carrière/Cinémathèque québécoise, and is used with permission. Many thanks to Manon Viens at the Cinémathèque québécoise for her help on this.

The Canadian Filmmaker's Distribution Centre provided the still for *Reason Over Passion*. Many thanks to Ana Barajas for her help on this.

George Stoney came through in the clutch on a still related to *You Are on Indian Land*, and I am very grateful to him.

Further to all this, all photos are reproduced in the spirit of promoting the films they illustrate.

PREFACE

Recently, I presented my film, *The Sweet Hereafter* (1997), to a group of high school students in Toronto. The screening was coordinated under the auspices of 'Reel Canada', an exciting and absolutely essential new programme designed to introduce students to the rich legacy of Canadian films. The students got to choose which films they wished to watch, and filmmakers were then invited to attend the screening to speak to the teenagers afterwards. For most of these students, it would be the first time they would have seen a Canadian film.

I entered Marc Garneau Collegiate Institute suddenly aware that I hadn't set foot in a public high school since I graduated from Mount Douglas Senior Secondary in Victoria, British Columbia, almost thirty years earlier. At that time, the only way to see a Canadian film was to rent a 16mm projector from the local branch of the National Film Board. In this way, the first Canadian feature I ever saw was Don Owen's *Nobody Waved Good-bye* (1964), one of the films included in this collection. Yet I remember being more impressed with the extremely cool idea of projecting a movie in the basement of my house than by registering the film's national identity.

What would the idea of a 'Canadian film' have meant to me at that point? Certainly, like most of my peers, I was raised on a staple of American media culture, from movies to television to music. I was aware of famous Canadian writers, as well as knowing that some of my favourite bands were Canadian. I was certainly aware of the Canadian Broadcasting Corporation, and understood that much of the television I watched was being generated from within my borders.

But movies were the domain of the big screen. Movies had big stars. Movies transported you to exciting new places full of glamour and action. And here I was in the basement of my house, watching a scratched black and white print of my first Canadian feature film. Thinking about this seminal moment in my cultural evolution, I wonder what had brought me to borrow that projector from the National Film Board, what had compelled me to bring home the three metal reels of film? Again, in all honesty, I was probably more excited by the sheer novelty of controlling what I could watch than by the subject matter of the product. My search for 'identification' – if this is what it actually was – was based on common teenage angst rather than any lofty idea of cultural consciousness.

And now, thirty years later, I was addressing a group of students who could watch whatever they wanted when they wanted. From the movies they could rent on DVD, to the product they could illegally download on their computers, this was a generation for which the sheer manual effort of lugging three heavy metal canisters and a projector for entertainment would seem ridiculous. As I walked down the busy hallway to the classroom, I was also immediately struck by the student demographics. While I was an anomaly at my high school – someone born somewhere else with a difficult last name – forty per cent of the students at this high school were recent arrivals, having been in Canada for five years or less. Well over half were Muslim, many of the girls wearing traditional hijabs. They were Urdu, Tamil, Chinese, Bengali, Arabic, Turkish – students from over seventy different countries. This was a very different Canada than the one in which I was raised. Of course, Victoria is a much smaller and more culturally homogenous place than Toronto – we were the only Armenian family in the country's western-most city – but I was in a state of shock. What would such a culturally diverse bunch of kids make of a film that told the story of a small Canadian town in which a bus crash takes the lives of its white-skinned kids?

In retrospect, this was a ridiculous and embarrassing thought. The rest of the world had embraced the film. It had been successfully shown at festivals in many of the same countries from which these students had emigrated. Why would I expect that this multicultural assembly wouldn't be able to relate to *The Sweet Hereafter* as something that emanated from the culture in which they were now living? I came to realise this anxiety was a complete reversal of a feeling with which I had grown up. For most of my childhood, I tried to prove to everyone else that I was just like them. And now, having made a film that was set in the most Canadian of environments, I was projecting my sense of cultural displacement back onto this group of students.

But these kids were very different from me. They were completely comfortable in their skins. They were under no social pressure to assimilate. They were proud of where they were from, and spoke a variety of different languages to each other in the hall. And what made this particular situation so Canadian was the complete absence of racial tension. I asked the teachers about this later on. While there were sometimes fights within the groups, they were rarely directed against each other. What is it about Canada that allows for this almost alarming degree of tolerance?

In English Canada – I can't profess to represent the other two 'traditions' referred to in Jerry White's introduction to this volume – this tolerance comes from a surprising lack of obvious cultural chauvinism. English-Canadians are not raised with any sense of the superiority of their own distinct identity. As a boy growing up in Victoria, a city which many used to consider the last bastion of the British Empire, I was taught to love the Queen and sang English hymns and read George Orwell's essay 'England Your England' as though he were talking about me. This colonial attitude is laughably out of date – it probably was at the time – but it defined who I was. In fact, when I asked the man at the National Film Board if there were any feature films I could play at home, I would have taken anything he would have given me.

The fact was he gave me *Nobody Waved Good-bye* which – if memory serves me – was the only English-Canadian feature they may have had. While I honestly can't recall what my response to Don Owen's film was at the time, I do remember a tremendous excitement over the short experimental films of Norman McLaren. I'll never forget the feeling of holding up a strip of *Boogie Doodle* (1940), his hand-drawn animated short, and realising that the marks I was seeing were an exact replica of the physical marks McLaren had made on the celluloid.

This artisan-like approach to filmmaking would have a huge effect on my development. From the low-budget features of Jean-Pierre Lefebvre to the experimental traditions of Michael Snow, Bruce Elder, Barbara Sternberg, Phil Hoffman and Michael Hoolboom to the work of my Toronto colleagues Bruce McDonald, Peter Mettler and John Greyson, the idea of the 'handmade' film was essential to what I came to identify as Canadian. I understand the omissions of the above works in this study – given the essay format concentrating on individual films it's impossible to be completely inclusive. This collection does, however, include an essay on Joyce Wieland's film *Reason Over Passion* (1969) and essays on other, very different kinds of artisan-like or 'handmade' films like Fr. Maurice Proulx's *En pays neufs* (1937) or Micheline Lanctôt's *Sonatine* (1983).

But I do believe that the idea of a 'triangular reality' (English, French and Aboriginal) used as an assumption of Canadian identity is problematic. The inclusion of an essay on Deepa Mehta's *Earth* (1998) under the umbrella of an anglophone film points to the forced notion of this construct. The country is clearly moving away from John Ralston Saul's idea of Canada as an anglophone-francophone Siamese twin and needs a new controlling metaphor. White's introduction here mentions both Charles Taylor's discussion of 'deep diversity' and George Melynk's use of the 'Metis model' as competing visions for Canadian identity. In an essay on Canadian film for the programme of the 40th Karlovy Vary Film Festival, Tom McSorley also offers the image of the Hydra, a fabled creature with multiple and rapidly multiplying heads. McSorley suggests that our filmmakers are currently 'engaged in the search for this newly forming, constantly shifting Canadian-ness in an open-ended set of narrative possibilities and cinematic expressions'.

The idea of 'three distinctive cinematic traditions' will certainly become more diffuse as the multicultural fabric of Canada becomes a permanent feature of its artistic production. Indeed, this fabric has always been a crucial part of Canada's artistic production and is even visible here, with films like *Earth* as well as *La Forteresse* (1947), directed by Russian immigrant Fédor Ozep, and *Atanarjuat: The Fast Runner* (2001), where the Inuit media community that the film is a part of is made up of Inuit as well as Québécois and American immigrants. In the years to come we will see more and more Canadian films that speak of the experiences I had in the school that day. Not only were these students excited to see films like *The Sweet Hereafter*, they were thrilled with *Double Happiness* (1994), *Khaled* (2001) and *Bollywood Hollywood* (2002) – films that not only validated the idea of Canadian cinema, but also helped to validate their own experience of growing up in this country.

Atom Egoyan
April 2006

INTRODUCTION

Writing the introduction to an anthology on Canadian cinema is a treacherous undertaking. Notions of what should constitute 'cinema' have become awfully hard-fought these days (should we include television? video? new media? computer games? flipbooks?). This plagues everyone who tries to survey some area of 'cinema', including all the editors in this *24 Frames* series. But the notion of 'Canada' is also a particularly contentious area, and this presents problems that are not faced by the editors of the other volumes in this series in quite the same way.

A great deal of my thinking about Canadian identity has been influenced by John Raulston Saul, a political philosopher and novelist (and the husband of the former Governor General of Canada, Adrienne Clarkson). In his 1997 book *Reflections of a Siamese Twin*, he writes of Canada that 'its strength – you might even say what makes it interesting – is its complexity; its refusal of the conforming, monolithic nineteenth-century nation-state model. That complexity has been constructed upon three deeply-rooted pillars, three experiences – the aboriginal, the francophone and the anglophone. No matter how much each may deny the others at various times, each of their existences is dependent on the other two.' Saul calls this 'a triangular reality', and it is one of the assumptions that gives *The Cinema of Canada* its form; I have sought to create a triangular portrait of the cinemas of Canada.

It goes without saying that there are other highly compelling visions of Canadian identity. George Melnyk's vision of 'radical regionalism' (enunciated in his 1983 book of that name) is particularly important for Westerners struggling to come to grips with Canadian distinctiveness. He sees in particular the Metis, the nation born of the intermarriage between Europeans (mostly French) and Aboriginals (mostly Cree) as being a crucial metaphor for Western Canada and Canadian identity generally; he writes that 'the Metis model of a Western society is a white immigrant civilisation that has adapted to native elements. This is a far cry from the thrust of Canadian nationalism which is still based in Ontario'. Renowned philosopher Charles Taylor (who for many years was the Chichele professor of Moral Philosophy at Oxford University) also has a longstanding engagement with the complexities and contradictions at work here, particularly visible in his 1993 collection *Reconciling the Solitudes*. There he writes of 'second-level or "deep diversity", in which a plurality of ways of belonging would also be acknowledged' (he uses Italian and Ukrainian immigrants and their descendants as examples) as being crucial for a sustainable Canadian identity. But the Saul schema is appealing to me because it acknowledges a myth of the sort that all nations have, at the same time that it posits that myth as interdependent and compound. 'Smaller or more recently arrived groups … have nothing to gain by attempting to deny the three-legged foundation and the long experience', Saul goes on to write, seemingly in answer to thinkers like Melnyk or Taylor (or Atom Egoyan, writing in this book's preface). 'These merely set out the principal defining lines of the Canadian experience which, unlike those of most countries, permit an inclusive rather than an exclusive mythology.'

Within Canadian film studies, the 'national cinema question' represents a long-standing argument, and it is in some ways connected to the kinds of tensions that Saul identifies. A number of English-language books treat Canadian cinema as a single national cinema, comprised of English and French elements. This was particularly the case with the first generation of Canadian books written in English. Book-length studies in French tended to be a bit more aware of the divisions between the linguistic groups, or a bit more sceptical of the validity of thinking of 'Canadian Cinema' as something unitary (Pierre Véronneau's 1991 anthology *À la recherche d'une identité: Renaissance du cinéma d'auteur canadien-anglais* is a good example here). Recent books in English tend to more or less uphold this assumption that 'Canadian Cinema' is the relevant organisational category, as opposed to 'Quebec Cinema' or 'English Canadian Cinema'. Bill Marshall's 2001 book *Quebec National Cinema* and Scott MacKenzie's 2004 book *Screening Québec* are notable exceptions; it bears mentioning that both are based at universities in Scotland. Indeed, many English-Canadians remain heavily invested in the notion of a unified country, although some have also become insecure in that investment and easily bothered by even modest challenges to Canadian federalism.

This is, of course, a reasonable investment to make, and so the reasons for this insecurity are not hard to understand. Quebec separatism has been a major aspect of the political life of Canada since the 1970s, and that itself is a reflection of tensions between the francophone and anglophone communities that, as Saul, Melnyk and Taylor all know, go back to their very earliest presence on the North American continent. A 1980 referendum on 'Sovereignty-Association' for Quebec failed roughly 60/40, but a 1995 referendum (one that was more vaguely phrased still: 'Do you agree that Quebec should become sovereign after having made a formal offer to Canada for a new economic and political partnership within the scope of the bill respecting the future of Quebec and of the agreement signed on June 12, 1995?'), failed by less than one half of one percent (50.58 per cent to 49.42 per cent). The late 1980s and early 1990s saw seemingly endless wrangling over the Canadian constitution and the place of Quebec (and to a lesser extent Aboriginal communities) within it. This wrangling has still not been resolved; to this day, Quebec has never formally signed on to the Canadian constitution, and the rest of Canada has never formally recognised Quebec as a 'distinct society' (a term now sure to inspire shivers of anxiety in most Canadians, regardless of mother-tongue).

More and more, though, people interested in Canadian film studies find themselves between various camps of these arguments, seeing how Quebec cinema probably is distinctive, but wanting also to hang on to some sense that these three cinematic traditions are connected in ways that are meaningful, if not always entirely clear. Melnyk's own book *100 Years of Canadian Cinema* spells out the contemporary ambiguity quite explicitly: 'The entrenched division in the two non-communicating national cinemas should be viewed as a major barrier for building a sustained critical mass for the nation's cinema.'

What I have tried to do here, then, is to give a sense of the three distinctive cinematic traditions that have emerged in the nation-state we call Canada. Whether Quebec or Aboriginal communities are locations of national identity that can exist apart from, or can supersede, Canadian identity is a question that I (coyly, I suppose) want to avoid as much as I can, in this introduction anyway. I have instead tried to build this book on two assumptions: that Canada is a nation-state (it issues passports, stamps and money; it has an Olympic team and an army; and so on); because of this, it provides a reasonable way to organise a cinematic inquiry; and that Canada has within it three groups whose cohesiveness go back to its foundation as a nation-state and remain very much part of its contemporary experience. English-Canadian, Québécois and Aboriginal cultures, like their films, never really existed as monolithic groups anyway, as Saul acknowledges in his discussion of the 'triangle' metaphor. He writes that 'after all, in both languages we were dealing in large measure not with English and French, but with Scots and Irish and Bretons and Normans' – in other words, as Saul says, perpetual losers in power struggles between the marginal regions (where you did not usually hear much English, or much French) and the metropolitan centre, and, not coincidentally, perpetual migrants. And of course, 'Aboriginal' refers to a group of peoples indigenous to this continent whose linguistic and cultural diversity is truly mind-blowing. But despite these complexities, it seems reasonable to organise a book in a way that reflects this sense of belonging.

I have therefore chosen to break the book into three parts. The anglophone, francophone and Aboriginal traditions get eight films each. I have conceived of these traditions in as broad a way as I can. Not all of the anglophone films are only in English: Deepa Mehta's *Earth* (1997) is in English, Hindi, Parsee, Punjabi and Urdu; I include it partially because Mehta lives in the majority-anglophone province of British Columbia and represents Canadian cinema's trans-national reality. Not all of the francophone films are only in French; Fédor Ozep's *La Forteresse* (1947) also exists in an English-language version called *Whispering City*; I include it because it is an important part of Quebec's early, mostly French-language feature film industry. And not all of the Aboriginal films are directed by people with Aboriginal ancestry. To explain the most seemingly eccentric entry of the book, *Dead Man* (1996), directed by the white American Jim Jarmusch, is included because it stars Gary Farmer (Cayuga), a figure who has been important in the promotion of Aboriginal cultural practice both in both the USA and Canada and who collaborated closely with Jarmusch on the creation of the film (the chapter, really, is about Farmer). *Dead Man* can (and in this case I hope does) identify a continental understanding of Aboriginal culture – one that seeks to transcend the borders of colonially-imposed nation-states.

One problem that is faced by the other editors in this series, though, is the selection of specific films, and the inevitable sense that they are creating a canon of films for the area under their consideration. Of course this is not what we are trying to do with this series, so I would like to explain what, exactly, my slightly eccentric choice of films is meant to illustrate about Canadian cinema.

One aspect of Canadian cinema that crosses linguistic or national divides is the importance of documentary. I have therefore included documentaries in each part of the book: two in the English section, three in the French section, five in the Aboriginal section. Altogether, documentaries account for just shy of half of the films under consideration. To a certain extent this reflects the importance of the National Film Board of Canada/Office National du Film du Canada (NFB/ONF). This body, founded in 1939 under the leadership of John Grierson, was originally mandated to produce wartime propaganda. Its current official mandate is to 'interpret Canada to Canadians and the world', and its films have made a major impact on the way that Canadians visualise themselves. But the NFB has also been home to an enormous amount of cinematic innovation; this is not widely known in Canada, where NFB films are often thought of as being dry or overly-didactic, if heart-warmingly patriotic. Essays on films from each group, however, illustrate the degree to which the NFB was a host to innovative approaches to both documentary film practice and cultural politics. And all three sections also discuss fiction films which are heavily influenced by documentary film practice; *Nobody Waved Good-bye* (1964), *Mourir à tue-tête* (*Scream from Silence*, 1979) and *Atanarjuat: The Fast*

Runner (2001) all illustrate the degree to which fictional and non-fictional modes interact with, and creatively corrupt, one another.

Another important aspect of Canadian cinema from anglophone, francophone and Aboriginal traditions is the way in which all three cinemas have been the site of attempts to sustain the production of low-budget but still semi-commercial fiction film. Quebec has clearly been the most successful here, both in terms of the size of its local audience and of the accomplishment of local filmmakers; chapters on films as different as *La Forteresse, Sonatine* (1983), *Le Declin de l'empire américain* (1988) and *Le confessionnal* (*The Confessional*, 1995) make this quite clear. English Canada has also seen the production of modestly-conceived and reasonably successful (both in terms of audience size and artistic accomplishment) films like *I've Heard the Mermaid Singing* (1987), *Thirty Two Short Films About Glenn Gould* (1993), *Exotica* (1994) and *Earth*, which, like the Quebec films just mentioned, depended on public subsidy to be produced, but which have helped to build a small, reasonably secure local film culture. Aboriginal directors have also begun to make inroads into this form, as films like *Atanarjuat: The Fast Runner* or *Bearwalker* (2002), both of which were similarly dependent on public subsidy for their production, illustrate.

The history of that public subsidy is an important part of understanding the tensions that have long been at work in Canadian cinema. Although there was some Canadian film production in the pre-NFB period (and the seminal history of this is Peter Morris' book *Embattled Shadows*), a lot of this was restricted to 'Quota Quickies', produced to satisfy the quota of Empire films on British screens. A sustainable, indigenous Canadian cinema was born of government intervention via the aforementioned creation of the NFB, and that set the stage for the country's cinema overall. Although Grierson had explicitly rejected the idea of a commercial industry in his 1944 essay 'A Film Policy for Canada', there remained a fair bit of popular desire for just such an industry.

Quebec had begun to develop the infrastructure for film production in the 1940s and 1950s (which André Loiselle's chapter on *La Forteresse* hints at). The ground started to look even more fertile when the NFB moved to Montreal from Ottawa in 1956 and the Quebec government established the Office du film du Québec in 1961 (the latter was born of the former Service de ciné-photographie, established by the Quebec government in 1941). The Canadian government shortly followed suit, establishing the Canadian Film Development Corporation in 1967 with the mandate to support a Canadian, semi-commercial feature film industry. Again, Quebec reciprocated in 1975 via its Loi sur le cinéma, which established the Institut québécois du cinéma (also meant to fund feature-length filmmaking) and changed the Office du film du Québec into the Direction générale du cinéma et de l'audiovisuel (DGCA).

At about this time the Canadian government was instituting the Capital Cost Allowance programme, which provided tax shelters for film production in Canada. The relatively fluid definition of a Canadian film meant that the primary beneficiaries of this policy were Hollywood productions looking for an easy way to save some cash; this ended up being the policy that led to the production of Canadian masterpieces like *Meatballs* (1979) and *Porky's* (1982).

Although this was not a particularly happy experience for Canadian film policy, it was not fatal. Via the transformation of the CFDC into Telefilm Canada in 1984 (which is still in existence) and the emergence of funding agencies in Quebec such as the Société générale du cinéma du Québec (SGCQ, created in 1983), the Société générale des industries culturelles (SOGIC, created in 1987) and the Société de développement des enterprises culturelles (SODEC, created in 1995 and still in existence) a publicly-supported, semi-commercial cinema, the likes of which is very common in Europe, still exists in Canada and Quebec. Aboriginal cinema tends to rely on the funding infrastructure of one of these two national cinemas, although this is changing.

The real failure of Canadian film policy is that it has not been able to address the debilitating problem that is the lack of screen space for Canadian films (and this is also a well-known experience for many Europeans). Canadian films are, to a great extent, foreign films in their own country (and, until relatively recently, many video store owners in Canada believed this literally to be true, filing Canadian films under 'Foreign' or 'International' sections while Hollywood films, which are, of course, *actually* foreign, were front and centre, presented as simple 'movies'). Although most Canadian films will enjoy some theatrical release in Toronto, Montreal and Vancouver, outside of these three cities access is very spotty indeed. Indeed, as I write this sitting in Edmonton – the capital city of the province of Alberta, a city with a population of approximately 800,000 – *not a single Canadian film is playing within the city limits.* Any attempts to impose quotas for Canadian films on Canadian screens – the likes of which have been extremely successful, if not indispensable, in building a Canadian music industry – have been met with furious resistance from the Motion Picture Association of America (MPAA), resistance which has in turn been met by almost instant capitulation from the Canadian government. Quebec had some success on this front starting in 1983 by regulating distribution (the Loi sur le cinéma de 1983 sought to mandate first Canadian ownership, and then, via amendments, Quebec headquarters, as a requirement for engaging in film distribution in that province), but the MPAA managed to negotiate exemptions to the law for its members.

The Canadian government's failure to defend screen space was the subject of a bitter 1984 article by Sandra Gathercole called 'The Best Film Policy This Country Never Had' (itself an updated version of an article first published in 1978). Twenty-one years later, after a round of nationwide consultations from policymakers, little had changed, with the journalist Kate Taylor writing in the *Globe and Mail*, on 24 September 2005, that 'It's official: the Federal film policy isn't working … The goal was for Canadian films, never popular with Canadian audiences, to earn a meagre 5 per cent of the domestic box office so utterly dominated by Hollywood. Many in the industry said it couldn't be done and have been proved more or less right.' She goes on to observe that the situation in Quebec is far better, since Quebec films account for around 25 per cent of the province's box office. Indeed, it is often remarked informally that if Canada has a 'real' cinema, then it is clearly in Quebec. This sometimes comes as a shock to anglophone observers (especially in the US), who all too often assume (as a result of a narcissism painfully common to English speakers worldwide, I think in my less charitable moments) that of course the real action must be in English. This is not the case in Canada.

Again, this problem of access to local screens is a common difficulty in European countries, many of whom are well-acquainted with the breathtakingly arrogant and unapologetically crass cultural imperialism embodied by the MPAA. It is especially familiar in 'small countries' like Belgium or Switzerland, and to my mind it is these countries that provide the most relevant point of comparison for Canada. Alas, much of Canada remains pre-occupied with comparing the country to the United States; this is hardly surprising, given the combined issues of proximity and geopolitical weight (the late Prime Minister Pierre Trudeau famously compared bordering the United States to sleeping with an elephant). That said, there has been some recent re-aligning of allegiances on this front. At the moment policy makers are involved in an informal alliance with France, trying to press the case for an international 'cultural exception' to global trade policies; a joint statement from then-Foreign Minister Bill Graham dated 22 May 2003 read that 'Our two countries support UNESCO's development of a legally binding international convention that sets out clear rules and enables all countries to implement policies for promoting cultural diversity from a perspective of international openness'. South Korea, a country with a long history of restrictive regulations on film imports and (not coincidentally) the home of a vibrant film industry, has since joined this coalition. All this is for the good, for Canadian cinema, like Canadian culture generally, is not well-served by a constant anxiety about not measuring up to, or being able to resist the lure of, powerful Americans.

There are a number of exclusions from this book that are likely to raise eyebrows among devotees of Canadian cinema, but I have also tried to include material that will lead to some sort of re-framing of cinema in Canada. That the English section includes no films from either David Cronenberg or Guy Maddin is the most obvious omission. I exclude these two because their films, although widely seen and sometimes interesting, do not offer the opportunity for re-appraisal that I think English-Canadian cinema desperately needs. The feature-narratives included here all illustrate the development of a feature narrative cinema at the same time that they 'rhyme' nicely with the non-narrative films included. *Nobody Waved Good-bye* thus connects with *The Winds of Fogo* (1969) via the seminally Canadian genre of the docu-fiction; *Reason Over Passion* (1969) rhymes with *I've Heard the Mermaids Singing* via their shared, tricky connections with both Canadian identity and conceptual art; *Exotica* connects nicely with *Thirty Two Short Films About Glenn Gould* via their shared engagement with memory and their shared restlessness with, and yet inability to abandon, narrative form. And I like very much that the earliest English-Canadian film (the World War Two propaganda documentary *Churchill's Island*, 1941) is, in some ways, a British film, while the latest English-Canadian film (Deepa Mehta's *Earth*) is, in some ways, an Indian film. That shift in definitions of transnational connections speaks volumes about the evolution of English-Canadian culture over five decades. Given these sorts of connections, I do not feel that the exclusion of either Maddin or Cronenberg is a fatal loss.

Something similar is going on with the first and last of the Aboriginal films. *Asivaqtiin/The Hunters* (1977) is made by Inuit filmmaker Mosha Michael; it is in some ways part of the *ancien regime*, being produced as part of an NFB programme operating in the Northwest Territories, which was then a gargantuan, sparsely populated and nearly ungovernable territory taking up a third of Canada. The last is Zacharias Kunuk's *Atanarjuat: The Fast Runner*, a film made in the new territory of Nunavut (carved from the eastern half of the Northwest Territories in 1999 as part of a 'Home Rule'-style agreement with the Inuit) by Kunuk's independent production company. Like the shift from British to Indian references of the English-Canadian section, the shift from the Northwest Territories to Nunavut speaks volumes about the transformation of Aboriginal politics over the course of two decades. In between these two films, I have tried, as with the English section, to choose films that connect with each other in interesting ways. *You Are on Indian Land* (1969) and *Dead Man* are both made by outsiders (Americans!)

committed to collaborating with their subjects and pushing against the conventions of their chosen forms (documentary and narrative, respectively) in order to do that; *Foster Child* (1987) and *The Learning Path* (1991) both use essayistic documentary to examine the complex web of allegiances that Aboriginal Canadians have created; *Bearwalker* and *Kahnasatake: 270 Years of Resistance* (1993) both draw on the emotional power of carefully-crafted drama to give a sense of their territories' cultural conflicts that is as highly detailed as any conventional documentary. Aboriginal cinema is not well-known outside Canada, but given the degree to which it intersects with the broader concerns of filmmaking here and makes contributions that move the conversations about these concerns forward in significant ways, it clearly requires a third of this book.

As I have said, Quebec cinema is the most domestically successful of these three cinemas. André Loiselle's chapter on *La Forteresse* gives a sense of the degree to which a self-sustaining pop culture has long existed and continues to exist in that majority-francophone province. But until the 1960s, Québec was known as a conservative and rigidly Catholic society. That began to change in 1960, the beginning of the period known as the 'Quiet Revolution', the name given to Quebec's period of modernisation and secularisation. The period between 1936–59, on the other hand, is known as 'La Grande Noirceur', 'the Great Darkness', marked by the rule of the anti-Semitic and corrupt regime of Maurice Duplessis as Premier (Duplessis was out of power briefly during World War Two). The earliest francophone film in the book, then, is a film that is made just before the dawn of the Duplessis era, *En pays neufs* (1937) a documentary commissioned by the government to promote its colonisation scheme in the west of Quebec; the latest film in this group is *Le confessionnal*, a re-consideration both of the Duplessis era and the legacy of modernisation that supposedly redeemed it, shot in a style of high artifice that rejects Quebec's legacy of realist filmmaking which, in the 1960s, became synonymous with radical filmmaking. The francophone films are similarly engaged with crucial formal and thematic issues that have preoccupied Quebec's cinema. *Pour la suite du monde* (*Of Whales, the Moon, and Men*, 1962) and *On est au coton* (*Cotton Mill, Treadmill*, 1970) are both early examples of *cinéma vérité* (a term commonly used in France and some of the anglophone world; the terms *cinéma direct* or direct cinema are often heard in Quebec and the USA; despite the occasional attempts by critics and historians to distinguish between them, they are all used rather interchangeably); but both are also highly manipulated films, constantly moving back and forth between subjectivity and the search for a new truth about Quebec life; *Sonatine* and *Mourir à tue-tête* are similarly gripped with a desire to re-frame the truth of women's lives in post-Quiet-Revolution Quebec, but both do so by combining naturalism and artifice in equal measure; *Le confessionnal* and *Le Declin de l'empire américain* both seem to ask what kind of cultural and emotional work a straightforwardly narrative practice can perform during periods of transition in Quebec's evolution. The cinema of Quebec has certainly earned its reputation as highly engaged with the evolution both of film aesthetics and its domestic culture; what I have tried to acknowledge here is that it is very closely linked, via its engagement with issues of realism, narrative and cultural identity, with its sister cinemas in English and Aboriginal Canada.

I do feel, then, that it is time to take a look at Canadian cinema in a way that takes account of recent, well-known achievements (as I do here with chapters on *Exotica, Thirty Two Short Films About Glenn Gould, I've Heard the Mermaids Singing, Le Declin de l'empire américain, Le confessionnal, Atanarjuat: The Fast Runner*), and of lesser-known and often more formally eccentric works that readers might not know much about but which offer important insights into Canadian cinema (indeed, most of these films are relatively easy to find on video; mail-order options are given for each film in their entry in the filmography). Studies of Canadian cinema are in danger of calcification because of their tendency to focus again and again on a fairly specific group of films. I hope that my work here as editor of this anthology will help, in some small way, to open up the discussion, to suggest that there are lots of parts of the national cinemas of Canada that are not widely known but which are, in various ways, as interesting as the better-known work.

So while I have tried to be historically responsible, I have also tried to offer a view of Canadian cinema that is *interesting*. The three traditions that have given shape to the majority of filmmaking (more or less) within the borders of the Canadian nation-state have a tremendous amount to offer to our understanding of world cinema. These 24 films provide a necessarily incomplete view of Canada's three national cinemas, but they provide a view that, hopefully, will inspire greater interest in the cinematic complexities that can be found north of the 49th parallel.

Jerry White

EN PAYS NEUFS

MAURICE PROULX, 1937

To write the history of film, even to write about a single film, one must know and understand not only the context of a work's production and its process of creation, but also the socio-political context surrounding its conception and even its later use. This is all certainly necessary for an analysis of *En pays neufs* by Maurice Proulx (1902–88), a full-length feature documentary made in 1937 that remains a model testimonial from one participant in the last period of colonisation in Quebec and, like all films of this filmmaker, illustrates a very specific religious or political system with a very straightforward ideology.

En pays neufs and its twenty-minute epilogue, *Ste-Anne-de-Roquemaure* (1942), prove to be useful films for those who already have a general knowledge of the history of Quebec. There are numerous ways of approaching these films, for they resonate in multiple ways, allowing each viewer to discover or choose a specific interest (cultural heritage, regional history, artisanal techniques, agriculture, social history, and so on); the same can be said for the majority of his films. Here it is a matter of distinguishing between the historical value of a film (flowing from research, perspectives or points of view, critical and scientific thought, and so on), its historiographic or historico-cinematographic value, and the historical value of its images that serve both to document a time and place as well as to illustrate an idea in another film.

The films of Proulx fit within the context of regional Canadian film production, whereby films were made by people who were not permanent residents of the region in which the films were shot. No matter when the film was made or for what purpose, the point of view turns out almost always to be external. The catalogue of the National Film Board of Canada (NFB) is packed with such works, works that served the purpose of interpreting Canada to Canadians, as much for establishing a sense of identity as for political or pragmatic objectives. It was not until the 1970s that regions would demand the right to an indigenous cinema appropriate for expressing a feeling of local belonging or that the NFB would set up its regional studios.

It should never be forgotten that Proulx was one of the best 16mm filmmakers in Quebec during the period of 1935 to 1955. Unlike filmmakers who were limited by the problems of the cost of film (saving on film stock), Proulx never paid attention to film stock cost and always took the time to use a variety of long takes of any subject he was filming. The advantage of this practice is that it allowed filmed action to continue for as long as possible, which in turn gave greater latitude to the editor in framing them and more time for the viewer to see, understand and appreciate the action. Moreover, Proulx, who was also an excellent photographer, had a sense of framing that often gives an interesting dynamism to his images. He does not hesitate to vary his camera's point of view, which later allows him to do a more lively and dynamic job of editing. The subsequent use of his films by other filmmakers flows in part from the quality of their filming.

Let us go back now to 1935, back to the time when Proulx took his first steps in cinema. The Great Depression that followed the Stock Market Crash of 1929 was at its height. It struck both urban and rural areas. Measures for 'helping the poor' were everywhere. One of the solutions put forward by the religious and civil authorities in Quebec consisted of recruiting men to volunteer to colonise uninhabited land in regions deemed to have potential for such activity. Up until that time the Liberal government of Quebec, under the leadership of Louis-Alexandre Taschereau (in power from 1920 to 1936), had not demonstrated a strong inclination to undertake the economic and social reforms that Quebec needed. Defender of the interests of big business, particularly those of foreign origin, the government refused to institute measures of ongoing social welfare that would have eased the population's difficulties. On the other hand, it did not turn its back on more traditionally motivated actions. Thus it authorised the new Minister of Colonisation, Irénée Vautrin, to put in place an assistance plan to help the settlers. Known as the 'Vautrin Plan' its official launch took place in October 1934, during an important conference on colonisation held at the parliament building. Cardinal Rodrigue Villeneuve, Archbishop of Quebec City, Lieutenant-Governor Esioff-Léon Patenaude, and several other important dignitaries attended the opening session.

The practice of colonisation was a well-established one in Canada for the settlement of territory. For hundreds of years, and especially during the nineteenth century, companies had been established specifically to undertake the promotion and coordination of immigration and colonisation. Each time it became a question of attracting potential settlers with a set of incentives, then transporting them to the designated area and finally supporting them in their new settlement environment. Indeed this was the essence of the Vautrin Plan, a plan that gave thousands of victims of the great economic crisis an opportunity to return to the land. The Catholic Church supported this project since it saw in it the application of its own social doctrine. In fact, the Church had not waited for the government's decision before going ahead with the establishment of colonisation societies in several dioceses. As a member of the Oblates of Mary Immaculate, an order with a missionary vocation, even Cardinal Villeneuve himself could not help but be attracted to this enterprise. Accordingly, in 1933 he had set up in his own diocese a Society for Colonisation. In order to develop it, he directed the Catholic Action Committee of each parish in his diocese to form a colonisation sub-committee named by the parish priest.

So it came to pass that a young priest, Father Maurice Proulx, began working for this Society for Colonisation. Ordained in 1928, he had decided to pursue his studies in agriculture at Cornell University (in New York), where he obtained his doctorate in 1933. Just prior to returning to Canada he purchased a 16mm Kodak camera (K model), which he gradually learned to use. He returned to Ste-Anne de La Pocatière (a small town located on the south bank of the St Lawrence, east of Quebec City) in 1934 to teach at the School of Agriculture. Father François-Xavier Jean, Secretary of the diocesan Society for Colonisation, was working there as well, which perhaps explains why this town's parish became one of the most active in contributing to the work of colonisation.

In August of 1933 a dozen settlers selected from the counties of Kamouraska and L'Islet had founded Ste-Anne-de-Roquemaure, the first parish to be sponsored by the Diocesan Society of Quebec City and located right in the middle of a heavily forested area. In a little over a year the population grew to several hundred inhabitants. Necessary staff members were sent out in order to provide essential services (a priest, an agronomist and a nurse), a fact demonstrating the availability of this type of person to go live in very difficult circumstances. Like all new parishes, Roquemaure needed not only manpower but clothing, provisions, household goods and ploughing equipment as well. From time to time the priest-coloniser would make the rounds of his diocese of origin in order to gather contributions, but it was really necessary to rely on the work of the local members of the Society and on the propaganda tools they required.

This explains why, shortly after the launching of the Vautrin Plan, Father Jean asked Proulx to accompany him to Roquemaure and to bring along his 'cinematographic machine' in order to record images that would be useful, in the words of Cardinal Villeneuve, for building a groundswell of favourable public opinion. He was reimbursed for his travel costs and the costs of film stock, and once in Abitibi he lived with the priest-colonisers. The two priests returned in September of 1935, and the next two years as well. It would appear, however, that during these years, Proulx did not often show his films, which probably remained unedited, a fact that somewhat contradicts the immediate propagandistic objective for which they could have been used.

The fact remains, however, that in the summer of 1937, after having finished the editing of his material and having shot the titles, Proulx and Maurice Montgrain (a musician and radio personality, at that time working in the public affairs section of the Department of Agriculture) arrived in New York for the purpose of recording the film's narrative commentary and producing a version complete with soundtrack.

The reason Proulx could allow himself this extraordinary expense was that the Quebec government had decided that it would be a good idea to show the film in the Colonisation Pavilion at the Provincial Exhibition scheduled for September 1937. This would be the first Québécois (and first Canadian) feature-length sound documentary (marking the beginning of a cinema career that lasted until 1961, during which Proulx made some fifty films). Two Departments, Colonisation and Agriculture, sponsored the film, which explains why both Ministers were there to introduce it. The first day of the fair more than two thousand people attended the screening of the film.

Both Quebec City and Montreal newspapers greeted the film enthusiastically. In this response evidence can be seen for the validity of the entire enterprise of colonisation, whose successes with the new parishes were held up as shining examples of the energy and courage of French Canadians. In the words of *L'Action Catholique* (9 September 1937): 'The film makes us see the real life of settlers from the time they leave the city and a life of unemployment behind and go forth to brave the uncultivated forestland ... The greatest merit of this film is its truthfulness ... The work of Abbé Proulx is the filmed history of the beautiful and glorious epic being written by our own people in Abitibi ... This film carries a significant lesson of far-reaching importance that will preserve for years to come the unique illustration of the courage of our settlers, the initiative of our farmers, and the perceptiveness and foresight of our government'. *La Presse* (13 September 1937) was similarly impressed: 'As an intelligent, mature, and experienced filmmaker, Maurice Proulx has discovered how to capture the most gripping point in every scene he has filmed, thus avoiding the danger common to such shots – banality, or worse, vulgarity. Moreover, he has thought of every way possible to educate viewers while entertaining them at the same time.'

How did Proulx organise his material? Chronological construction was a necessity imposed on him since he went to Abitibi for four successive years and needed to make the evolutionary dimension of the setting up and establishment of colonisation visible (which explains the regular use of titles within the film identifying the year in question). At the same time he creates a sort of fiction in which a narrator (speaking in the first person) accompanying a group of settlers goes off to explore the countryside and holds forth on everything he observes. In the first section of the film, Proulx describes and comments on the life of an Indian tribe living on the banks of Lake Abitibi from a 'white' point of view. This native theme will not be picked up later in the film (nor even later in Proulx's other films, unlike other priest-filmmakers), but it does allow him right from the outset to establish in a comparative mode two different ways of taking possession of land, although both are under the leadership of a missionary or priest-coloniser. He shows that the configuration and the extent of the space are linked to the socio-cultural origins of the occupiers, to their resources (of all kinds), and to the variety of situations they can control. After this section begins the chronicle of colonisation. This earns film viewers a train trip from Quebec City to La Sarre as well as numerous sequences shot at Ste-Anne-de-Roquemaure itself. As the years go by, we follow the evolution of colonisation, the gradual retreat of the forest thanks to the hard work of the inhabitants; the consolidation of the parish, families and land; the improvement in the life of settlers and the professional and economic support they have available to them. Recurring images provide evidence of progress: a new church replaces the chapel or wooden houses replace log camps, the situation of the nurse and the agronomist improve, children seem happy. Everything is constructed so as to lead to the film's optimistic conclusion: 'A day will come when the time of the tree trunks will be forgotten forever. With this vision of prosperity, let us leave Abitibi, land of the future…' One would have liked to know, but there are no data available as to whether the propaganda of the film actually succeeded in convincing city dwellers to come settle in the Abitibi region.

The success Proulx had with his first film since the 100-foot-long reels he had produced up until then cannot really be categorised as films encouraged him to buy a more advanced, sophisticated and powerful camera, the Ciné-Kodak Special. With this purchase, the filmmaker further established his professional status and evidenced a desire to enjoy greater latitude in terms of cinematographic expression. Proulx benefited as well from another Kodak innovation: colour film. Always wanting to be on the technical cutting-edge, he first experimented with the Kodacolor lenticular process, which he found proved to be of mediocre quality, and which also did not allow for the making of duplicate prints. The arrival of Kodachrome in the middle of the 1930s changed the situation, however, since this reversible film allowed him to move forward with the work he had been doing up until that time. Thus he returned to Abitibi to add an epilogue in colour to his Nordic saga that would prove better than black and white for showing the beauty of the region and the impressiveness of the settlers' accomplishments. With *Ste-Anne-de Roquemaure*, Proulx brings out the progress achieved by the settlers, progress illustrated by the establishment of a cooperative union, the construction of a parish hall, a school and a post office and, for some people, the purchase of an automobile. The film even shows Cardinal Rodrigue Villeneuve proudly visiting the parish. It is not surprising that this film is much more explicit in its reflections relating to the French-Canadian nation, land and family.

The images of *En pays neufs* and *Ste-Anne-de-Roquemaure* were, in some ways, already organised before Proulx ever set eyes on them. The two films establish a certain number of facts relating to the colonisation process but do not criticise its implementation. One finds in them very little information relating to the social organisation of the colonisation villages, on the relations among people (except in the case of the priest, the nurse or the agronomist, or in the presentation of the cooperative), or on the economic aspects of the settler's life (his level of income and wealth, his property, and so on) or similar information about the professionals working in the milieu.

The film carries a hint of the kind of 'agriculturalism' that at the time a number of Quebec elites were very taken with, and it acts as the mouthpiece for the conservative ideology that makes use of the four pillars of 'country life, family, religion and French language' as the basis for nationalist thought. However, it does not show the city, urbanisation or industrialisation as threats. The presentation of Val d'Or and its mines, and of all the burgeoning little towns nearby, is one indication of this. Yet it is always the rural countryside in the shadow of the church steeple that remains dominant. Furthermore, it is remarkable that each new year reported in the film and the presentation of each new establishment begins with the image of the church flanked by its presbytery.

In its commentary or in its images there is no hesitation, not a single negative feature. The major portion of the narration remains mostly informative, commenting upon and filling in what is seen in the on-screen images. The voice-over is ever-present but it is frequently interrupted. The first-person plural 'we' that refers to Proulx and his hypothetical visitors as well as the third-person (both singular and plural) and neutral pronouns are very frequently employed interchangeably. At regular intervals the voice-over questions the spectator using a second-person formal 'you' or verbs in the second-person plural. This preponderance of narration actually weakens the poetry of the images a great deal. While the commentary expresses the ideological biases of the period quite clearly, it is the images that give the film its ethnological flavour through the documentary recording of events and practices, conferring upon them an 'objective' descriptive weight in contrast to the subjective content of the narrative text.

Their interpretations converge only insofar as they reaffirm the official discourse of their sponsors. Moreover, the commentary proves to be rather poor in terms of information. Its greatest value is for those interested in historiography and the history of ideologies in Quebec. Because of the diachronic structure that Proulx gives to his film, he appears to be presenting viewers with evidence of the soundness or appropriateness of the colonising enterprise and of the vision of those who initiated it. But every real shot does not in and of itself produce truth nor does it prevent cinematographic documentary orchestration. Although Proulx presents us with a certain number of trees that have grown in the Abititi region, he does not really let us see much of the forest, nor does he help us understand how the forest has taken root and grown. He is more the surveyor of colonisation rather than its geometer.

Although the film presents material and factual elements that document the colonisation enterprise, it does not provide an explanation of the history behind it. On the contrary, the film is presented as a set of facts surrounded by certain discursive elements that then give it meaning. Proulx's cinema has as its starting point the revelation of the politics of colonisation adopted by the Quebec government and its clerical backing. The use of these images and these sounds as testimonials of the time can prove to be accurate so long as one does not take them as proof. Reality should not be confused with what is true, just as the true does not always come down to what is real. In the case of colonisation, further accounts, evidence and facts are required. To this day, this is the only aspect of Proulx's work that has interested historians and filmmakers. But his work cannot be reduced to this single subject. For example, Proulx, who was an agronomist himself, does not hesitate to use plants or flowers in close-ups, emphasising their marvellous beauty and poetry while at the same time fighting the botanical ignorance of the population. In the same way, he remained interested in the rural practices of both the past and present. This was a leitmotif of his work.

In the world of cinema, all regions did not benefit from the same appeal or the same advantages as Abitibi. In this respect, Abitibi turned out to be a much-favoured region, thanks to the pioneering work of Proulx and the other NFB filmmakers who were interested by it, not to mention local filmmakers who emerged during the 1970s. But let us limit ourselves to the ones who had some kind of link to Proulx. His two films, like the works that later make use of them, are historic constructions that propose their own interpretation of the facts. They make up the richest stock shots on the Abitibi region of the 1930s, and have attracted virtually everyone who is interested in the region or who wants to make films that feature it. The first of these was Bernard Devlin. Devlin had a major interest in the Abitibi region and in colonisation (he was the Grandson of Charles Ramsay Devlin, Minister of Colonisation, Mines and Fisheries from 1907 to 1914). He is responsible for the fact that with the exception of Montreal and Quebec City, the Abitibi region is the most often filmed region by NFB cinema from 1950 to 1964. Devlin had already tackled the subject of colonisation to some extent in his *Horizons de Québec* (1948, 30 mins) just as he already had to his credit both the scenario and the narrative commentary of the English-language film *Abitibi* (David Bairstow, 1949, 22 mins), which focuses primarily on the urban and mining aspects of the region. But he wanted to develop the problematic of colonisation (which, in actual practice, had lasted just barely fifteen years) in greater depth. In the context of his research on the subject, he brought Proulx's two films to Ottawa and showed them to the staff of the NFB, after which he forwarded their reactions on to Proulx, in a letter of 12 September 1949: 'Everyone without exception was unanimous in saying that these films were great film documents. I'll quote you several remarks: "This [film] has an aura of mysticism, of the land, nature, men and their courage", "This film made me aware of a new aspect of the French-Canadian character that I had never even thought of before", "Comparable to the great film *Triumph of the Will*".

In contrast to Devlin, the great Quebec filmmaker Pierre Perrault (director, with Michel Brault, of *Pour la suite du monde* (*Of Whales, the Moon, and Men*, 1962); see Gwenn Scheppler's chapter in this volume) proposes a completely different ideological perspective. Thus Perrault's use of large extracts from *En pays neufs* in his own hour-long film, *Le retour à la terre* (1976), allows him to give Proulx's images a status of truth that he then contrasts with contemporary accounts (contemporary to the 1970s), which he invests with an equal status of truth in order to allow his own conclusion that the colonising enterprise had been a failure. But Perrault's discourse is about history itself; he is not using his discourse to try to spur further and deeper investigation and interpretation. Such an interpretation was already in place, even before he began filming or selecting images from Proulx's films.

Perrault concentrates on a population to whom a kingdom has been promised but a population that has been betrayed and finds itself, less than forty years later, disillusioned by the results of its collective adventure. The fact remains that if the colonisation enterprise proved to be the source of numerous failures, this was because the setting up of an agricultural enterprise on land that was truly barren, located in a Northern region with a harsh climate and distant from consumer markets could only lead, in the medium-term, to abandonment, even if in the immediate perspective as the propagandistic optimism of Proulx shows the harvests did allow families to subsist. Like Proulx, Perrault proposes an ideological reading of events. Where Proulx saw in colonisation the metaphor of the birth of a nation, Perrault sees in the Abitibi region another metaphor of the Quebec people who had been stripped of their dream and uprooted. Moreover, whereas Proulx expresses himself through his film's narrative commentary, Perrault's self-expression comes through the dialectic of his editing and the actual speech of his protagonists. Instead of the political-clerical nationalism that emerges from Proulx's film, Perrault substitutes a neo-nationalism that finesses the reasons for the failures in the history of the development of the territory of Quebec, whether economic or simply scientific in nature. One shows history in the act of being made, the other explains this same history as it is coming apart rather badly, and at the same time has no plan for remaking it save for the possibility of an independence to be acquired or a country to be made. Both Proulx and Perrault are, each in his own way, men of hope who have built that hope on a failure, the Great Depression in the case of Proulx and the failure of agricultural Abitibi in the case of Perrault. How ironic the conclusion of *En pays neufs* seems ('We who have faith in the success of Abitibi, we see in these truly marvelous fields the realisation of the greatest of hopes') when it is juxtaposed with the speeches of Perrault's characters.

En pays neufs and its epilogue are part and parcel of the reinforcement of a certain French Canadian mythology concerning the pioneer construction of the nation under the aegis of the Roman Catholic religion. But one must not simply reduce them to their ideological function. These two films allow us most importantly to better know and understand the final phase of intensive colonisation in the Quebec territory. The importance of the subject, along with the quality of Proulx's work, explains the films' central position in the history of regional cinema in Quebec and in the history of Quebec cinema as a whole, as well as their special fate in later productions by other filmmakers. Of all the images of Quebec that remain from the 1930s these are probably the most striking, the most revealing, the ones that allow the Quebec nation to better see the road that has been traveled from colonisation to modernisation. Their meaning comes from history, but it is history that has justified their impact. Did Abbé Proulx have any idea that at scarcely thirty years of age he was in the process of creating a piece of history?

Pierre Véronneau

Translated from French by Lynn Penrod

CHURCHILL'S ISLAND

STUART LEGG, 1941

At first glance, *Churchill's Island* (Stuart Legg, 1941) appears to be a film like many others produced by the National Film Board of Canada (NFB) during World War Two. Making use of the wealth of footage both shot by the Allies and captured from the Axis during the opening years of the war, the film epitomises the dominant documentary form of the era with its skilful compilation of pre-existing material and a rhetorically motivated design. *Churchill's Island* proves, however, to be one of the most significant and lasting entries in the canons of Canadian and world documentary. As the winner of the very first Academy Award for Documentary, it would set the standard against which all other war-era short subjects from the NFB would be compared and as such left an indelible mark upon the face of Canada's rich documentary tradition. But the special status this Oscar win afforded *Churchill's Island* should not be over-valued, as it came at a time of great change in North American-British political relations. The devastating impact of Japan's attack upon Pearl Harbour was fresh in the minds of Academy voters in the early spring of 1942, and the complicated reality of American involvement on numerous warfronts was only just revealing the need for the public to support the Allied effort unconditionally.

Churchill's Island, produced in September and October of 1940 during the height of the German Blitz-attacks on England, was released on Friday 27 June 1941 following a special screening at the Imperial Theatre in Toronto. It was only one of over a dozen films director-producer Stuart Legg was directly involved in as part of the *Canada Carries On* series he helped establish and execute under the auspices of film commissioner John Grierson, launched in April 1940. Legg was an Englishman who had in Grierson a friend, former colleague and staunch supporter. Grierson called Legg over to the NFB late in 1939 with the express intent of setting the documentarian to work on a series of films that would focus on current events at home and abroad, illustrate the war effort and elucidate Canada's role amongst the Allies. Legg's experience with the Empire Marketing Board and General Post Office film units in Britain made him a prized and ideal recruit for the fledgling NFB, his celebrity in the documentary world secured with the commentary he recorded for the John Grierson-produced *Night Mail* (Basil Wright & Harry Watt, 1936).

Under Legg's direction, *Canada Carries On* and its companion series, *The World In Action* (established in January 1942), were the twin engines that drove NFB production throughout the early-to-mid 1940s. While the series was never exclusively the domain of war-themed films, *Canada Carries On* was a critical component of the NFB's wartime production schedule. The series was intended by Grierson to be a programme that would introduce and explain domestic and international events to Canadian citizens. Those films that were selected for international distribution were reassigned under the *World In Action* moniker and enjoyed great success, particularly within the United States (which had only recently entered the war). *Churchill's Island* was the second film to be distributed under the *World In Action* banner and its critical and commercial success was unmatched.

Offered by the NFB as a presentation of the strategy of the Battle of Britain, *Churchill's Island* illustrates the role of the Royal Air Force, the Royal Navy and its coastal defence system, and stresses the ever-important significance of the citizens' perseverance and commitment to the total war effort. This is the period following Churchill's ascendance to power at the height of Germany's air raids, a time when the spirit of Britons was challenged nightly and the agenda of the Allies was to bring the United States of America into the war. The film was described by the distribution wing of the NFB as 'a picture of life on an island faced by imminent annihilation. The spirit of the time is recreated in scenes of attacks by Nazi bombers, subs and long-range guns contrasted with others of the RAF in action, work of the home guard, coastal defences and arrival of troops from the dominions.' *Churchill's Island* stresses both the domestic face of the war (specifically those who risked their lives simply going about their day-to-day business under the constant threat of German attacks) and the participation of the dominion as a whole. Led by narrator Lorne Greene's now unmistakable voice, one noted for its dynamic balance of power, sensitivity and authority, the film's function as propaganda was always clear in the mind of Grierson and the NFB. The tone of *Churchill's Island*, however, transcends the rigid didacticism that generally characterises the compilation form. It sets itself apart from many of the films from the era with several innovative flourishes and a flair for making the action exist outside of the closed shell of history, instead crafting a text that captures the present-tense, the immediacy, of the subject matter presented.

Churchill's Island's structure is fairly routine. Words and images work in cooperation to ensure the narration shapes and contextualises the pre-existing footage so that it serves to illustrate the central thesis of the film. Dynamic action and graphic displays of air power and ground artillery are balanced by sober reflections upon the cost of war. Green's commentary (written by Legg) is rhythmically clipped, kinetic and propulsive in a manner akin to the pulp and noir literature that had established itself during the era. While Nazi tactical efforts and their mechanical superiority are stunningly illustrated with captured footage of Hitler's rally speeches, submarine attacks and airborne raids of the Luftwaffe, Green's clinical accounts of these German gains are always quickly countered by the presentation of Allied victories intended to illustrate the path to the Axis' ruin has been laid. The use of this material to introduce a German point of view is not only compelling but is offered as an approximation of journalistic objectivity. Legg ensures the Axis' fight never appears completely hopeless by balancing the booster-ism of Green's voice-over narration with evidence of their control of numerous battlefronts. While the Axis material was not unique to the films of the NFB, Ottawa's central role in the control, distribution and warehousing of the captured footage offered Canadian filmmakers the special opportunity to screen the material and mark footage for use in the *Canada Carries On* and *The World In Action* series.

The literary quality of the narration in tandem with the assured and insightful compilation process results in a complex of meanings and significance. Ernest Borneman, a film editor at the NFB involved with both series, wrote in an unpublished manuscript from the era that the artistic accomplishment of the *Canada Carries On* and *The World In Action* films could be accurately located in the tripartite structuring of meaning, image and sound working to create a third level of signification. This Eisensteinian formulation of film form has grown appreciably more apparent and significant as these films age, although their ingenuity is no longer so markedly ground-breaking or emotionally stirring: 'Since visual, music and effects tracks were running side by side in a highly complex three-part counterpoint, and since the visual by itself constantly skipped from place to place all over the globe, it became doubly important for the commentary to draw the two other tracks and the visual together into a single continuity, and this had to be done in such a manner as to make its points through the spectator's subconscious as well as through his conscious.' Borneman notes that active verbs and pseudo-quotations ('The experts say that…') work in conjunction with metaphors and similes as a means of charging the images with significance and formulating the appearance of an empirically-informed speaking position.

The most notable aspects of *Churchill's Island* are three instances of synchronised speech, an ambitious technological leap for any short subject of the time, which is to say nothing of the logistics involved in filming the exchanges in the war-torn United Kingdom. Two interviews are with Allied servicemen in the field and serve to illustrate and amplify claims made on the soundtrack by Green's narration. A third scene appears as an epilogue to the film. All serve as early examples of the use of the 'talking head'.

Synchronised sound, tremendously cumbersome and unreliable in the field, appeared only sparingly in documentaries prior to the late 1940s and the use of a prepared text ensured speaking subjects did not complicate shooting schedules or inflate production costs with misspeaking or unwanted editorialising. Presented as unscripted interviews, these sequences are in actual fact tightly scripted exchanges performed for the camera. Technical limitations of the period point towards such assumptions, and in the case of *Churchill's Island,* production files can be used to confirm them. Their appearance in *Churchill's Island* at such an early stage of development, however, is significant and a brief examination of these 'talking heads' illuminates how the device would function both formally and ideologically for decades to follow.

The first speaking subject appears midway through the first reel; an Allied auxiliary fire serviceman is shown reclining on a stone-walled overlook above a civilian area. He explains how one recognies and prepares for incoming German fire:

> I can usually hear Gerry leaving the other side. We watch out for him, and as for the shells – well, we see a flash, count sixty, and there she is.

The serviceman points over his shoulder and a matching cut takes us to footage of bombed buildings that serve as the disregarded backdrop to citizens resuming their daily routines; the voice-over narration stirs the viewer's response to their steely resolve. In this case, the serviceman functions as an expert whose own first-hand experience of recognising enemy fire both explains the images presented by the filmmakers and validates the claims made by Green's commentary. With its roots in the British documentary tradition (within which both Grierson and Legg played pivotal roles), the hastened development of this call-and-response system of testimony and validation is further articulated in the work produced by the Office of War Information in the United States following its creation in 1942.

As the outlook of *Churchill's Island* becomes optimistic and assured, so too does the tone of the speaking subjects recruited to elaborate upon the successes of Britain's defence. Members of an AA gun crew are shown resting on a piece of naval machinery and support the voice-over's declaration that Germany's war cannot be won in light of Britain's unrivalled coastal defence:

We've pulled more Gerries out of the drink than I ever knew existed, in fact – fat 'uns, thin 'uns, small 'uns. You'd be surprised. We're getting fed up with it.

The matter-of-factness of the soldier's reaction to the rescue and capture of enemy soldiers is intended to secure the alleged imminence of Britain's victory but contrasts uncomfortably with the footage of corpses, not prisoners of war, to which the soldier is made to refer.

A third and final instance of synchronised speech appears during the film's epilogue. Brigadier M. A. Pope of the Canadian Military Headquarters in England is photographed in an office environment. Solemnly he states, 'I have just come back from England. I have seen with my own eyes what you have just seen in this film.' His ominous tone parallels aspects of Green's narration and is designed to lend bombast to the preceding film, serving to ratify the embedded claim of a realistic summary of the Battle of Britain. *Churchill's Island* is offered as a penetrating look at the network of military and civilian systems that served as the foundation of Britain's proud defence and deserved victory, and it is the relationship of voice and image that establishes the transparency of this claim.

As the 'arsenal of democracy', Roosevelt's United States were glad to supply armaments to the Allies but had no interest in formally joining the fight – with the start of American involvement in the war following the events at Pearl Harbour, the need for an informed and supportive population had been greatly underscored and Hollywood was officially involved in the campaign. It would thus seem prudent to search for the seeds of *Churchill's Island*'s critical success in the months preceding its ground-breaking Oscar win at the 14th Academy Awards on 26 February 1942. It was the year of John Ford's *How Green Was My Valley* (winning Best Picture at the expense of Orson Welles' *Citizen Kane*) and it would be the first time the Academy recognised productions in the documentary field. Truth be told, public accolades for the NFB film did not rain down until after its historic win and it was the vociferous support of critics from the United States that affirmed *Churchill's Island*'s stature as a beacon of documentary filmmaking.

In the weeks following *Churchill's Island*'s prestigious win, critics in the United States turned their attention towards the prints still in circulation through United Artists and referenced the Oscar as the reason for its significance and cause for further celebration. Generally speaking, these reviews sought to validate its contribution to the war effort. The point, it seems, was to stress that *Churchill's Island* and *The World In Action* were an efficient way of staying informed of the events of the war as US forces debated their involvement. Few talked specifically about the content of the film, but those that did offered penetrating insights into the perceived significance of the documentary's cinematic accomplishment.

Critics believed the realism of the film was confirmed through its compilation structure – 'newsreeling', as the *New Republic* referred to it in its 23 March 1942 issue – and its photography. That the film conveyed 'war as it really is' was offered as evidence of its intellectual insight and the quality of its journalistic perspective, a point agreed upon by both the *New York Post* and *New Yorker* in March 1942. 'Realism' was a term bandied about quite often, with the 11 April 1942 edition of the *Motion Picture Herald* positing that *Churchill's Island* 'achieves a realism as yet unapproached by US newsreels. This is a straightforward documentary on the war … captured Nazi newsreels clearly show the victory effort is necessary'. Few discussed the bias of the government body responsible for producing the film, while others fed the growing legend of Grierson at the expense of properly acknowledging Legg and Green's central role in the success of the film. Those reviews that did discuss *Churchill's Island*'s function as propaganda use that fact as the reason for its excellence; the 11 March 1942 *Variety* review goes so far as to say it is 'socko war stuff' and would serve to 'answer the plea for "Wake Up America"'. Quite often, however, simplistic descriptions of the film and the general tone of particular reviews suggest the coverage was sparked by its Oscar win as opposed to a genuine editorial interest in the material or its message.

The most sycophantic review to be found is an editorial piece written by Florence Fisher Parry from the *Pittsburgh Press* on 26 April 1942 – precisely a month after Churchill declared Allied victory was secured and the very same day Hitler announced the war would be won by Germany before the summer's end. In a pronouncement that seems rooted in a frenzy brought about by the terror of a repeat of the events at Pearl Harbour, the author argues *Churchill's Island* is a tool with which the complete unification of the Allies will be secured. She moves forward to claim that *Churchill's Island* is reason to think the documentary short has finally proven its usefulness as a cinematic form:

> To me, this short … is the very best motion picture we have had out of the war, and provides the healthiest and most stirring kind of propaganda. No editorials, no government effort, no radio blast, could have hoped to do more to cement our two countries than was accomplished by this one single picture.
>
> It should be shown in every theatre; it should reach our whole population. We do *not* understand the British people … It is terribly important that we *do* like them; that

we work together with the closest harmony and sympathy. A picture such as *Churchill's Island* provides the most effective solution to this difficult and dangerous problem.

The World in Action is a series of twelve such pictures … Watch for them. Make a great effort to see them. If the others attain the high excellence of these first two, then indeed can we assert that the short takes its place alongside the most meritorious propaganda as Weapon for Victory in this war.

Once again, the propagandistic purpose of the film is given as cause for its celebration, specifically its role in US-British relations. It is curious, however, to hear Ms Fisher Parry opine that 'no government effort' could have played a bigger part in this alliance – unless she refers to diplomatic or military 'effort', it would seem that the NFB's institutional authority was momentarily overlooked. No formal features of the film are addressed, nor are any specifics offered with regard to how *Churchill's Island* 'provides the most effective solution' to the task of fostering American sympathy to the war effort. But in an echo of Lorne Greene's triumphant declaration of the Allies' assured success at the conclusion of *Churchill's Island*, Fisher Parry's reaction encapsulates the popular reception of the film by applauding its propagandistic value while subtly allowing that the NFB's artistry and command of the form are the principle reasons behind its success.

While Lorne Greene boldly announces it is the inner strength of the British people – their 'stubborn calm which bomb and fire and steel cannot pierce' – that assured an Allied victory, it is, in fact, the structure of the film and its pointed commentary in unifying the images that empowers both its silent and speaking subjects. Metaphorically speaking, it is the compilation form, under the informed and intelligent guidance of Stuart Legg and John Grierson, which allows Britain to win the battle. The NFB are willing collaborators in designing a fight that would resonate with viewers and convince audiences, both domestic and international, that the war was not only winnable but inevitably so.

It was the popular and critical success of *Canada Carries On* and *The World In Action* (and the achievement of *Churchill's Island* specifically) that put Canadian documentarians and the work of the National Film Board of Canada on the map of global cinema. The combination of committed government funding and an influx of talent from across the provinces within Grierson's highly organised environment would lay the foundation for further artistic and technical achievements of the 1950s and 1960s. With an Oscar win under their belts and the eyes of the world cast upon them, the NFB announced its arrival as a filmmaking nation with a film about the resolve of its allies across the Atlantic. That it came with the help of a patriotic whirlwind in a United States that had hitherto regarded Canadian and British war films as a news service chronicling events far removed from their domestic sphere is a fact that was surely not lost on Legg and Grierson.

Michael Brendan Baker

LA FORTERESSE WHISPERING CITY

FÉDOR OZEP, 1947

In its hundred-year history, the Quebec film industry has enjoyed a few periods of genuine commercial success during which locally produced films often managed to surpass Hollywood blockbusters at the box office. The late 1960s and early 1970s, as well as the 1990s and early 2000s, witnessed a number of highly lucrative domestic productions, such as Denis Héroux's *Valérie* (1968), Claude Fournier's *Deux femmes en or* (1970), Jean-Claude Lord's *Bingo* (1974) and, more recently, Alain Chartrand's *Ding et Dong: Le Film* (1990), George Mihalka's *La Florida* (1993), Louise Saia's *Les Boys* tetralogy (1997–2005) and Jean-François Pouliot's *La Grande Séduction* (2003). These movies might not have been the most critically acclaimed works to come out of Quebec, but they attracted huge crowds to the cinemas of the province. The first time French-Canadian spectators started flocking to the theatre to see themselves on screen was in the mid-1940s. Fédor Ozep's *La Forteresse*, from 1947, was among the movies that triggered this first boom in French-Canadian film history.

The boom began in 1944, in part due to the lack of French films being produced under Nazi occupation. By 1940, films from France occupied about 10 per cent of the market in Quebec. The shortage of French-language films resulting from the war encouraged French-Canadian entrepreneurs, such as Alexandre DeSève and Paul L'Anglais, to produce home-grown features. Furthermore, a number of French film artists had left Europe at the beginning of the Nazi invasions and now formed a sizable community of experienced, French-speaking directors and actors who could offer their expertise to the burgeoning Quebec film industry. Fédor Ozep, a Russian filmmaker who moved to France in 1932 and then to North America in 1940, directed *Le Père Chopin* which marked the beginning of the boom in 1944. Well over a dozen films were made in the next ten years, some by European filmmakers in Canada, like Ozep, Paul Gury and René Delacroix, and others by Canadian filmmakers, like Jean-Yves Bigras, who gave up documentary practice at the National Film Board of Canada (NFB) to make fiction films in the private sector.

By and large, the films made during this period reflect the traditional French-Canadian values that have become associated with the Maurice Duplessis regime, now characterised as 'La Grande Noirceur' or 'The Great Darkness'. Duplessis was the charismatic leader of the conservative provincial party Union nationale and autocratic premier of Quebec from 1936 to his death in 1959, with a brief interruption during World War Two. A rural lifestyle and respect for the Catholic Church were the cornerstones of Duplessis' brand of French-Canadian nationalism and most films made in the 1940s and 1950s – either fiction features or documentaries produced by priests like Albert Tessier and Maurice Proulx – supported more or less explicitly his ideology. The heroes of these films were rugged lumberjacks, as in *Le gros Bill* (René Delacroix, 1948), country priests, as in *Le Curé de village* (Paul Gury, 1949) and humble farmers as in *Le Père Chopin*, while villains were those who embodied foul sins like misery or dishonoured such revered social roles as motherhood. One of the best-known villains was Séraphin, a despicable miser first made famous in a radio drama and brought to the big screen in *Un homme et son péché* (1949) and its sequel, *Séraphin* (1950), both directed by Paul Gury. The miser was brought back to life recently in a big-budget remake of *Séraphin: Un homme et son péché*, directed by Charles Binamé, that became the top-grossing Quebec film of 2002.

Another famous villain was the evil stepmother in *La Petite Aurore, l'enfant martyre* (Jean-Yves Bigras, 1951), the most commercially successful Canadian film of the 1950s (which was also recently remade into a 2005 box-office hit by Luc Dionne). Based on real-life events and an equally successful play, the film shows the life and death of 10-year-old Aurore, who suffered atrocious physical abuse at the hands of her stepmother and father. Sociologists such as Christine Tremblay-Daviault (author of the seminal history of these films) have argued that French-Canadian audiences strongly identified with the martyr child, who is silenced by her stepmother by having her tongue burnt with a hot iron. As the malevolent woman tells the child 'je vais te brûler la langue', she points the iron directly at the camera thus emphasising the degree of identification. That the word 'langue' means both tongue and *language* suggests a clear connection between bodily torture and cultural (that is, linguistic) persecution.

Audiences also flocked to see Gratien Gélinas' *Tit-Coq* (co-directed with René Delacroix, 1952), based on his famous play. Universally recognised as the first major piece of the French-Canadian national dramaturgy and perhaps as the first true artistic achievement of Quebec's fiction film industry, Gélinas' work focuses on an orphan soldier nicknamed Tit-Coq, or Cocky, who is torn between the desire to settle down with a nice woman and have a normal family, and the burden of having to live a life of lonely wandering because of the stigma attached to his illegitimate origins. Wishing to fit in but constantly persecuted by oppressive societal forces epitomised by the Church, Tit-Coq eventually elects to leave his girlfriend and go on living his rootless, aimless, but free existence. One of the most enthusiastic responses to the film came from René Lévesque who declared, years before becoming the first sovereigntist premier of Quebec, that with the production of *Tit-Coq* 'le cinéma canadien sort de l'âge des cavernes' ('Canadian cinema emerges from the stone ages') – this is recounted in Pierre Véronneau's 1979 book *Cinéma de l'époque duplessiste*. The film's atypical criticism of the Church and indirectly of the Duplessis regime was an early sign of the changes that had already started to affect traditional French Canada. The radical artistic manifesto *Refus Global*, signed by painters, actors, poets and musicians in 1948, and the 1949 Asbestos strike, which rallied workers, journalists and intellectuals against the government, were other vocal oppositions to the Duplessis regime. The resistance expressed in *Tit-Coq*, *Refus Global* and the growing union movement in the late 1940s and 1950s would culminate in the Quiet Revolution of the 1960s, which saw one of the most significant movements of modernisation in the province's history.

Shortly after the success of *Tit-Coq*, however, feature films ceased to be made in Quebec. As much as individual films attracted sizeable audiences, the box-office receipts were never large enough to maintain the infrastructure necessary for a mass production film industry. The small size of the French-Canadian market, compounded with the arrival of television in 1952 and the American control over distribution and exhibition, meant that even a 'big success' still did not guarantee much profit. Quebec films always had limited release because the language issue made it difficult, if not impossible, to attract audiences beyond the province's borders. Paul L'Anglais, founder of Quebec Productions Corp., tried to find a solution for this problem by producing a film that could *at once* attract local French-speaking spectators *and* reach much larger English-speaking audiences throughout North America. What L'Anglais did was to produce simultaneously two versions of the same story: one in French, *La Forteresse,* starring local celebrities; the other, *Whispering City,* in English with American actors Mary Anderson, who played Maybelle Merriwether in *Gone with the Wind* (Victor Fleming, 1939), Paul Lukas, who won an Oscar in 1943 for his performance in *Watch on the Rhine* (Herman Shumlin, 1943) and Helmut Dantine in leading roles, and French-Canadians playing smaller parts.

According to Véronneau's entry on him in Michel Coulombe and Marcel Jean's *Dictionnaire du cinéma québécois*, L'Anglais clearly wanted to take advantage of Quebec's bilingual character and create a Canadian film industry that would attract interests from France, England and the United States. In theory, this project should have enjoyed the best of both worlds. On the one hand, the French-language version would build on the growing nationalist sentiments of a homogeneous population eager to recognise itself in various artistic and cultural forms.

On the other, the English version would capitalise on the province's combination of European exoticism and Anglo-American environment. To achieve his dual goal, L'Anglais hired the seasoned director Fédor Ozep who, with *Le Père Chopin*, had proved his ability to make films that French-Canadians would enjoy. But L'Anglais chose to move away from the conservative, rural themes of Ozep's previous work and elected instead to produce a Hollywood thriller. He bought a story by American writers Michael Lennox and George Zuckerman, who went on to pen the screenplay for Douglas Sirk's *Written on the Wind* (1956), and hired Leonard Lee and Rian James, of *42nd Street* (Lloyd Bacon, 1933) fame, to develop a script. But to avoid making merely a Hollywood clone, L'Anglais transposed the action from the original New York location to Quebec City.

Produced for an astounding $750,000 (which, according to D. J. Turner's *Canadian Feature Film Index*, remained the highest budget for any Canadian production until the 1970s), *La Forteresse/Whispering City* tells the story of Marie Roberts (played by Nicole Germain in the French-language version and Mary Anderson in the English-language film), a reporter investigating a twenty-year-old murder. In the process, she uncovers the machinations of nefarious lawyer Albert Frédéric (Jacques Auger and Paul Lukas), an art lover whose patronage of promising talents has a tendency to end up in someone's death. Frédéric blackmails one of his protégés, the brilliant but unstable composer Michel Lacoste (Paul Dupuis and Helmut Dantine), into killing the journalist when her probe threatens to expose him. But Marie and Michel become romantically involved and in the end the evil Frédéric is deservedly punished.

While the plotline is not particularly innovative, several aspects of *La Forteresse/ Whispering City* are surprisingly progressive and clearly meant to put Quebec cinema on par with its American and European counterparts. First, given the conservatism of Quebec society up to 1960, the cigarette-smoking, smart-dressing, sharp-witted 'girl reporter' (Roly Young always uses this expression in his many articles on *La Forteresse/Whispering City*) in the leading role is in striking contrast with the devoted mothers and innocent young girls of most French-Canadian films at the time. Furthermore, the Quebec City setting brings a degree of urbanism generally absent from rural-oriented post-World War Two Quebec cinema. Most importantly, L'Anglais' choice to produce a thriller shows a definite desire to be in synch with Hollywood at a time when what would eventually be known as *film noir* was in the process of becoming American cinema's most critically respected genre.

L'Anglais also tried to emulate the excitement of a Hollywood premiere with celebrities and dignitaries parading on the red carpet on their way to the first screening of *La Forteresse* on 23 April 1947 at His Majesty's Theatre. Reviewers extolled the premiere as one of the most important cultural events in Montreal's 'artistic history', an evening that could rival the brilliance of Hollywood galas, with crowds applauding their favourite stars. After its successful premiere, the French version opened on 2 May at the Orphéum. Francophone audiences responded very positively to the film's perfect combination of local content and Hollywood style, and they packed the theatre during the film's lucrative six-week run (the film played until 12 June). Nicole Germain, a well-known media personality who had been voted 'Miss Radio 1946', was deemed excellent in her first screen appearance as the assertive heroine Marie Roberts. Also praiseworthy were the two other stars, Jacques Auger, an experienced stage actor (who played Frédéric) and Paul Dupuis (who played Lacoste), a dashing young man who enjoyed a brief acting career in the British film industry during the war before returning to work in Montreal in 1946. The music, written by André Mathieu, a local musical prodigy, also attracted flattering comments, and reviewers congratulated cinematographer Guy Roe for the striking quality of the image. In sum, as one observer in the 17 May 1947 issue of *La Presse* declared, *La Forteresse* was 'un succès complet, auprès du public' ('a complete success with the public').

While the French version was as successful as L'Anglais could have anticipated, the English version failed to attract anglophone spectators either in Canada or in the US. Premiered in Mary Anderson's hometown of Birmingham, Alabama on 20 November 1947, released in Montreal in January 1948, in Toronto in February and in New York in May, *Whispering City* did receive some positive reviews. For instance, Jack Karr of the *Toronto Star* wrote on 21 February 1948 that 'putting it alongside any melodramas produced in Hollywood or London, it stands up under the comparison excellently'. And one could read in *Variety* that 'this first Canadian feature film to attract attention in the US is a melodrama of considerable suspense'. But other critics saw the film as a commonplace bore, with average American actors doing a competent job but nothing more. The review in *The New York Times* reads: 'Count as novelty the fact that *Whispering City* was turned out in Canada, but apparently that is as far as the novelty, or, for that matter, the excitement goes. For the melodrama … is lethargic, garrulous and for the most part obvious fare which takes a tediously long time to tell a transparent and none too impressive story'. The review in the 22 January 1948 issue of *Le Devoir* also criticised the English-language film for its banal story, the clichéd ending, the inadequate editing and the uneven performance of Dantine as Michel. Audiences were equally unimpressed with the movie and *Whispering City* quickly died at the box office. It played for a week in Montreal and a week in Toronto, after which it made a few sporadic appearances in theatres as a second feature in double bills. It seems to have vanished completely from the screens after about a dozen screenings. Browsing through the film ads of the *Toronto Star*, *Whispering City* seems to have played in various venues from August 1948 to December 1950, before disappearing.

The success of the French-language version in contrast to the failure of its anglophone counterpart might be explained in part by the fact that the former had the advantage of featuring local stars performing in a Hollywood-style story and thus enjoyed the best of both worlds, as it were. The film was at once familiar, with home-grown celebrities and recognisable locations, and significantly different from other French-Canadian films with its emphasis on a suspenseful story unfolding in an urban setting. The English-language version, on the other hand, was merely an average thriller with nothing to distinguish it from dozens of other thrillers made in the US at roughly the same time, except for its Canadian location. But even then, with other thrillers such as *The Iron Curtain* (William A. Wellman, 1948) and *Dangers of the Canadian Mounted* (Fred C. Brown & Yakima Canutt, 1948) released at the same time, exotic Canadian settings were becoming increasingly commonplace.

When compared with Alfred Hitchcock's *I Confess* (1953), a *noir* that uses the looming Quebec City background, especially its churches and heritage buildings, to mirror expressionistically a priest's guilt-ridden psyche, *Whispering City* comes across as a bland exercise in stylistic understatement. Except for a handful of scenes, such as a brief confrontation between Marie and Frédéric in a cemetery, which creates an evocatively gloomy atmosphere, most of the film lacks the more striking elements of *noir* (extreme low-key lighting, destabilising camera work, threatening urban space, a sense of moral decay) that characterise the best examples of the genre. For instance, when Michel wanders aimlessly in the city, haunted by the belief that he has killed his wife, any sense of doom or existential angst is undermined by the beautiful post-card cinematography used to trace his movement throughout Vieux Québec's picturesque streets. Unlike francophone spectators who felt that they were watching a *film noir* of their own, anglophone spectators saw instead a mediocre by-product of a Hollywood genre.

The divergent fortunes of *La Forteresse* and *Whispering City,* it could be argued, embody the difference between Quebec cinema and the English-Canadian film industry as it still exists today. Like *La Forteresse,* many recent Quebec genre films enjoy great success at home because the Hollywood formulas they adopt are fully integrated in the local culture. These films, however, remain virtually unknown in the rest of North America precisely because their box-office appeal stems from their uncanny ability to cater to French-Canadians' taste for Quebec-made Hollywood-style entertainment. Conversely, like *Whispering City*, English-Canadian films might enjoy a small degree of success in Canada and the US but they are generally engulfed by a marasmus of inane American movies. Only clearly distinctive English-Canadian voices sometimes manage to rise above the anonymous mass of irrelevant flicks produced in North America each year.

There is of course the possibility that if *La Forteresse* was more successful than *Whispering City* it is simply because it is a better film. This is what Roly Young thought when he saw both versions together at a special screening in Toronto in May 1947. For Young the all-Canadian French version is 'considerably superior' to the English version, which relies on American actors. In Montreal, English-speaking audiences also seem to have preferred the French version. The two films being virtually identical, it is difficult to determine with certainty what would make one better than the other. There are a few dissimilarities that might make *La Forteresse* a slightly more satisfying viewing experience. For instance, the framing device – the plot of the film is an anecdote related by a sleigh driver to a couple of tourists – is somewhat more elaborate in *La Forteresse*, having both opening and closing chats between the driver and his clients. *Whispering City* has only a few words spoken by the driver at the beginning and there's no closing exchange at the end. Rather, a single shot of the sleigh moving towards the city's old fortifications signifies the return to the narrative frame, but the driver's story is denied closure. Thus the logic of the framing narrative is more evident in the French version. Furthermore, by giving more importance to the driver's recollection of the story 'whispered' to him by the city, *La Forteresse* conveys to the audience a better sense of place. It allows the city to evoke, however briefly, the many secrets it confides in the driver, which helps create a '*noirish*' atmosphere of urban mystery. The cinematography of the French version also looks lower key than that of the English version, giving the film a darker or '*noirer*' tone. This difference, however, might be due more to the quality of the prints that have come down to us than to any actual distinction between the two films.

Interestingly, for Young, it is literally the fact that *La Forteresse* is in French that gives it 'a good deal more animation in the unfolding of the story'. For him, the tendency of French speakers to gesticulate more than anglophones adds liveliness to each scene. This might very well be true, but Young's sense that the French film is more animated probably has less to do with gesticulation then with the fact that *La Forteresse* is edited at a slightly quicker pace than *Whispering City*. In the last 10 minutes of the two films, from the gloomy cemetery scene to the moment when the police shoot Frédéric and the final embrace of Michel and Marie, the exact same actions are depicted with 79 cuts in *Whispering City*, and 87 cuts in *La Forteresse*. Similarly, the first 5 minutes of *Whispering City*, from the beginning of the driver's story to the end of the deathbed revelation of a murder twenty years earlier, which triggers Marie's investigation, are composed of 23 cuts. The same sequence in *La Forteresse* numbers 30 cuts. What exactly led Leonard Anderson and his assistant editors to use a few more inserts and shot/reverse-shots in the French version remains unclear. Perhaps the gestures of the francophone actors dictated a greater number of cuts. In any event, the rhythm of *La Forteresse* is somewhat more animated than that of *Whispering City*.

But all of these differences are so minor that one must ultimately conclude that what explains the success of *La Forteresse* and the failure of *Whispering City* are cultural rather than stylistic or aesthetic reasons. The former, as a French-Canadian thriller enjoyed the best of both worlds, as it capitalised on both the insular character of Quebec's culture and its status as merely another subdivision of Hollywood's domestic market. *Whispering City* on the other hand, suffered from the *worst* of both worlds as it proved to be neither a particularly good Hollywood film nor a distinctly Canadian work. Sadly, much of English-Canadian cinema suffers from the '*Whispering City* syndrome'. By trying to reach both Canadian and American audiences it ends up appealing to neither.

André Loiselle

POUR LA SUITE DU MONDE OF WHALES, THE MOON, AND MEN

PIERRE PERRAULT, MICHEL BRAULT AND MARCEL CARRIÈRE, 1962

04

Pour la suite du monde (*Of Whales, the Moon, and Men*) was the first Canadian feature film to be presented at the Cannes Film Festival in May 1963, where it gained international recognition uncommon for '*cinéma vérité*'-style documentaries. The film was released in Canada on 4 August 1963, for the opening of Montreal's International Film Festival. It is a kind of précis of the direct cinema movement, and of an emergent Quebec cinema, being made collaboratively by some of the most important figures of both traditions: Marcel Carrière, Bernard Gosselin, the great cameraman Michel Brault, and, of course, Pierre Perrault. It is the first in a trilogy made about, and to some extent by, the residents of l'Île-aux-coudres, a tiny island in the St Lawrence river where Perrault made many films (including the other two instalments of this trilogy, 1967's *Le Règne du jour* and 1969's *Les Voitures d'eau*). Innovative not only through its poetic visual form, but also because of the use of colloquial speech and orality (Perrault would probably say 'living speech'), this film is a subtle interrogation of the Québécois identity through its people and language.

In 1961, the small island of l'Île-aux-coudres, situated in the middle of the St Lawrence, was cut off from modern life, ignored by the cities and spared by the wars. Apart from agriculture, the island's economy has depended on the river; the construction of schooners, freight and fishing has been especially important. But every resident keeps the memory of the mythical porpoise hunting that was practised by generations of islanders, and which was abandoned at the turn of the last century for largely economic reasons.

In 1960, some filmmakers from the National Film Board of Canada (NFB) thought that the time had come to revive an ancient epic and to put tradition into practice; they went to the island and tried to convince the inhabitants to recover the now-abandoned tradition of beluga hunting. For one year, under the watchful eye of Pierre Perrault and Michel Brault, who shared in the lives of the islanders, everyone organised themselves to 'tend to the fishing'. The filmmakers went to the island's elders, in search of their wisdom, but also went to the young for their strength and dynamism. Before long, the community began to live according to the rhythm of fishing and hunting and in hopes of successful expeditions.

Apart from fishing and hunting proper, the filmmakers were particularly interested in the cultural life of the community. Parties, stories and the daily life of the farmers and fishermen of the island give the film as much form as the attempt to catch a whale. Three characters in particular attract the attention of the filmmakers: the old man Alexis Tremblay, who is a kind of living memory for the island, likes to recite the travel narratives of Jacques Cartier (who set foot on the island in the name of the King of France in 1534); the son of Alexis, Léopold Tremblay, whose desire to perpetuate the tradition 'for future generations' makes it possible to convince even the most reluctant (he is also a valuable liaison between the filmmakers and the islanders); and Grand-Louis Harvey, the witty old man, the joker and comedian who always keeps his listeners engaged.

Pour la suite du monde came about because of the meeting of two men: Pierre Perrault, the man of speech, and Michel Brault, the man of images. These two dimensions are essential for understanding what makes this film so unique. Michel Brault was one of the NFB's chief cameramen; an inventive director, he was the leader of the direct cinema movement, which had a kind of heart of the NFB. Brault had worked with Jean Rouch and Mario Ruspoli in France; he knew how to film people in action, to follow them where they go, always with an eye for that 'decisive moment' so beloved both of Henri Cartier-Bresson and of the NFB filmmakers who idolised him. He knew how to catch the depth and the hidden aspects of expressions, and how to compose a subtle, resonant image. He was also bold as an editor. Despite the fact that many of the film's critics pay attention only to the cinematography, the editing of *Pour la suite du monde*, in collaboration with Werner Nold, is very complex. Brault was also one of the principal innovators of the revolutionary techniques around lightweight cameras' ultra-sensitive microphones and synchronisation; his innovations helped make cameramen independent (and not connected by wires between camera and sound recorder) and so capable of following the subjects through every situation, while concealing themselves within the setting and only rarely appearing on screen. Brault completed this technical revolution through a parallel ethical revolution. He insisted that the benefits of freedom offered to the filmmaker must allow him to mix with the people he films without disturbing their activities, in order to push them to speak naturally. He was always searching for a reciprocal relationship with his subjects, and tried to avoid the distance common to television news or mainstream documentaries.

Pierre Perrault was, in 1961, not yet a true 'filmmaker'. He had written the text for a series of searching documentaries (*Au Pays de Neufve-France*, 1958–59), and was also a dramatist, an essayist and an all-around man of letters. He was a poet possessed of a 'vision of Quebec', but was also capable of listening to men and of discovering within them the potential for a natural drama, and of sensing the situation where this potential will reveal itself. He was, in a word, an intercessor. He also knew how to speak of Quebec, and how to make the inhabitants of l'Île-aux-coudres speak of and play out their stories and their lives (in this context the term 'play' is quite inadequate, because there is no production, no staging). He assumes that the inhabitants of the island can reveal themselves more deeply and significantly than do their social roles. He also knows how to go beyond the simple shooting of reality, by rightly joining myth and everyday life. Lastly, he understands how to provoke and capture speech and dialogue.

In 1961, having already known the island dwellers for some time, Perrault had the occasion to record and to film crucial parts of the island's life, such as fishing and hunting expeditions and the meetings of those who hold shares in those expeditions, the festival of masks, the stories of Jacques Cartier as told by Alexis. These elements that he had spent years getting to know were seen in *Pour la suite du monde* for the first time. He presented several versions of documentary projects to the NFB and to Radio-Canada, where he insisted on two particular aspects: the basing of the film entirely on the stories of Alexis Tremblay, and the necessity for the team to be as discrete and restrained as possible.

Perrault also wrote a proposal for Radio-Canada entitled 'Argument pour un télé-théâtre filmé', a mix of documentary and fiction film. He seemed to be flirting with Radio-Canada's expectations, although he never really fulfilled them. This first version of the proposal contains the main elements of *Pour la suite du monde*; beluga hunting, the mi-carême carnival, the omnipresence of Alexis Tremblay (standing in for the living memory of the island), and so on. Roger Roland, the programme director of Radio-Canada, recommended that Perrault work on the project with Michel Brault and the NFB. In order to do that, Perrault submitted a documentary proposal to the NFB, titled 'Projet du film à l'Île-aux-coudres'. In that proposal, we find no more discussion of a pre-written script, although we do find in this document an accurate description of what the final film will be. Perrault had to await Brault's return from France, where he was working with Jean Rouch on his celebrated 1960 film *Chronique d'un été*. When he did come back to Canada, both he and Perrault agreed on the uselessness of a pre-written script. They also guaranteed that the film could be built around the speech and stories of Alexis Tremblay. The producer wrote that:

POUR LA SUITE DU MONDE

We plan to centre a film on a particular person who actually lives on l'Île-aux-coudres (Alexis), who has practised porpoise fishing and who, for sentimental reasons, would die to take it up again. It is he who will receive the command ... and who will see to convincing the parish to carry out the work necessary for its re-enactment. Much will depend on this character. The testimonies of the 'screenwriter' (Pierre Perrault) and of the director (Michel Brault) on the subject are formal; this is an extremely interesting man, intelligent and agreeable enough to risk building the film around him.

Pour la suite du monde is the first example of 'lived cinema', or *le cinéma vécu*, as Perrault has called it. This concept of cinéma vécu is not solely the question of a new aesthetic made possible through the clarification of new material, but rather of a new approach to reality, more 'fabricated' than any other documentary film, but structured by speech, and by speech in all its diversity (stories, conversations, speeches, discussions, sermons, prophecies, and so on). Speech is the driving element of the film, its structure and its goal: Perrault wants to make Québécois speech, *la parlure*, heard.

The arrival of lightweight camera and sound equipment, along with the technology needed to synchronise it, gave direct cinema more freedom of movement. In turn, this period saw a transformation of documentary aesthetics. The cameraman, now much more mobile, no longer thought of space as a function of possible camera placements. He no longer organised the action along a pre-established screenplay, but could instead follow the real action in order to provide an 'internal' point of view, and consider the organisation of space once the shooting is complete. That old chestnut of documentary, the interview, which remained static and was usually directed by the filmmaker, was replaced by 'speech in action', which was spontaneous and unrestrained by the set up. The cameraman no longer found himself on the margins, but was instead at the heart of the action where speech took place, where action was unfolding. Sound and image interact with one another in a way that is very different from a 'classic' documentary. The difference in relations to space and to speech offered by the direct shooting allow for meaningful structures to be created during the editing process: between the character and his surroundings, between space and time, between reality and the imaginary. *Pour la suite du monde* presents to the spectator interactions between *space* and *speech* that are the crucial, defining tensions throughout the entirety of the film.

When the film begins, we are on a *voiture d'eau*, a small watercraft, before the winter. In several different shots, we see three self-enclosed spaces: the river, the continent and the island where, says one of the characters, 'there is nothing to do but wait for winter'. The river is seen as a place of work that is transformed into a wall of ice between the island and the continent. The continent becomes inaccessible and the island a dismal prison.

During the film, the river is *conquered* by the inhabitants of the island, and the latter will in return be contaminated by the river, since the one and the other, at the end of the film, form a unitary, 'insular' place. This re-conquering of the river by the inhabitants of the island is the primary meaning within the film, a meaning that evokes a 'contamination' of spaces, a complexity ordered by sound and speech.

At the beginning of the film, the St Lawrence is anonymous, a place where all the boats pass without stopping, a barrier between the island and the continent. By the intervention of the founding story of Cartier and the beluga hunt, it will become a 'topographic' place; it becomes a *named* place. It thus takes on the value of a testing ground, where a performance (capturing a porpoise) endows its subjects with new qualities (the 'genius' of the porpoises, the 'genius' of the Aboriginals who first practiced the hunt, the courage to confront the cold, the capacity to organise the community to strive for a common goal and for it to be reached). Then, it 'prolongs' the island which, week after week, conquers and lets itself be invaded by its myths. It becomes a centre of activity, and of redefinition, for the island's people. Finally, it becomes a *space-link*: through fishing and hunting, New York (where the porpoise captured by the island-ers winds up) and l'Île-aux-coudres become linked.

The space constituted by the river thus re-defined corresponds to the definition of the frontier that Michel de Certeau lays out in his book *L'invention du quotidien:* 'the frontier is not that which separates two spaces, but that which serves to link two spaces, it is what they share in common'. For the transformation of the river, the inhabitants' return is fundamentally modified. At the beginning of the film, the island is excluded from the world, but by the end it takes a place in the cultural space of the North American economy by expressing its particularity as a francophone island. In this sense, *la suite du monde*, the continuation of the world, becomes effectively possible.

One sequence of the film clearly illustrates the process of contamination of spaces through speech as a device; we see contamination of one space by another, but also of one time by another, of a reality by an imaginary. Alexis Tremblay relates to his son Leopold the discovery of the island by Cartier. At the same time as the story begins, we leave the forge where they are working; images of the river appear, illustrating what the patriarch says, seemingly showing the island four hundred years beforehand. The shots of the river and of the forge develop along a progressively accelerating rhythm. The sequence ends once the images of the river become familiar and we recognise the individuals on the island. The images which seem to illustrate the story reveal themselves against another sequence of the film, recorded at a separate shooting. But when the temporality, the reality of the images, inserts itself, things become more complex once again.

The camera's gaze is common in most 'direct cinema' productions, but in *Pour la suite du monde* it constitutes a cinematic *option*; the filmmaker/actor relationship is reclaimed and returned. This camera's gaze is always different, depending on the person who is doing the gazing; all this is consistent with Perrault's investment in and his conception of the film he is in the process of making. The gaze of Grand-Louis is the means by which the cameraman becomes a kind of public accomplice, a collaborator with the filmed subject. It is primarily a matter of assigning roles, or assigning places to those who are present and to those who are watching the film. We also hear the disembodied voice of Alexis, prior to or following the apparition of his face fixing itself on the camera; his gaze addresses both the spectator and an invisibLe confidant, the cameraman who silently observes him.

This device leads the spectator to read the speech of Alexis as prophetic. Alexis does not look at anything in the *present*, nor does he really look at the space; he looks at his *past*, and also at what Cartier should have seen. He attempts to see the spectator who will see the film long after his own death, as if he seeks to find through his writing Jacques Cartier, gone for four centuries. In fact, in the face of the camera, he seems to become aware of the potential of the cinema to create a trace of real life, a trace of the living. The camera's eye (a specifically documentary-eye) becomes an element of cinematic tale, a *récit cinématographique*.

One sequence, where we see the meeting of the shareholders in the porpoise hunting exhibition, is very interesting for the way that it shows us the attitudes of Michel Brault's 'participant' camera, and shows us the way that camera functions. Each phase of this sequence is accompanied by a corresponding ambiance. The camera not only follows and integrates itself with those it films (the camera is in the middle of the rows of chairs), but it also provides a visual account of the emotional ambiance.

At the beginning of this sequence the people are listening to Leopold Tremblay. The camera is amidst the rows of chairs (giving us fixed shots of the listeners), and on the platforms (staring at Leopold from a low-angle shot). The camera's movement is minimal, apparent only in some long shots of the assembly in the room. The sound is clear and from a single source. The cameraman films the reactions of the public. But once the debates start the bearing and position of the camera changes. The shots are cut in full motion and a sort of visual confusion reigns, a confusion that is intensified by the editing. The sound reflects the state of things: a confused brouhaha. Excitement and nervousness take hold of the cameraman, preventing him from correctly framing the shot, incessantly distracting him, as though he was following the discussion rather than filming it.

At the end of the meeting, a spontaneous crowd surrounds Grand-Louis. The camera rests at the same distance from the crowd as from Grand-Louis, and alternates between shots of both, itself becoming part of the crowd. Grand-Louis does not look at the camera, but he communicates with a third person, which we neither hear nor see. This second person makes himself all the more present through the camera's insistence to not show him. By this 'censorship', the camera becomes an entity responsible for the frame, claiming it, incarnating it.

The participant camera is as much an approach to shooting (it corresponds to a position in reality, and to a positioning of this reality) as it is to editing. The effect produced by the participant camera is always reinforced and completed by the editing. Indeed, the editor assembles the shots taken *in the middle* of groups of characters, and the shots taken of the characters from a distance: this back-and-forth style of imagery, this free-form shot/reverse-shot, provokes a mirror effect in the spectator, where they are invited to enter the image while being artificially 'watched' by those they watch as well as by the camera.

This is all a matter of a *participation* cinema, where the filmmakers not only organise what they see but also invest themselves in what they film. Filming is still part of a process of simple recording, but is also becomes an *action* that, in part, permits participation in the film, a participation that is also, then, valuable for the spectators. The distance between characters and filmmakers is annihilated, the goal being to expose the bonds that unite them, the very real bonds between those that film and those who are filmed. It is a matter of transporting *to the film itself* the act of enunciation that produced it.

The viewer thus feels him or herself to be within the film that is unfolding before their eyes. The viewer is no longer simply a member of the audience, this position being eliminated through the impossibility of identifying oneself with either characters or cameraman. The viewer becomes a witness to the film. This approach, aimed at eliminating traditional conceptions of the audience as a passive consumer as well as the distance between filmmaker, character and audience, is *a cinema of participation*.

A film that does not conform to any one genre because of its polyvalent essence, *Pour la suite du monde* was, for Perrault, the materialisation of a political and poetic project, ripened

POUR LA SUITE DU MONDE

over several years. It was also a sort of matrix of his future films as well as his meditation on the nature of the Quebec nation. For Michel Brault, it was his first fully realised piece of direct cinema. For the entire francophone team at the National Film Board, the film was a realisation of their struggle to get their work recognised. It was also a feature film in the (then emerging) tradition of films that sought to investigate and affirm Québécois identity. *Pour la suite du monde* is thus a film that reflects a particular conception of Quebec society at the dawn of the Quiet Revolution, the period of Quebec's modernisation that began when long-serving Premier Maurice Duplessis died in office in 1959. That period saw an insular francophone community searching for a means of cultural continuity; a community existing between a difficult mythical past and a present that risks being forgotten, dissolved in an international economic system. That community had to be re-discovered from its roots, from its specificity; it had to dig deep in order to participate in the evolution of the world without losing its soul. Finally, then, *Pour la suite du monde* reflects Perrault's own interpretation of the Quiet Revolution.

Gwenn Scheppler
Translated from French by Christa Polley

NOBODY WAVED GOOD-BYE

DON OWEN, 1964

> I really don't know where I want to go, and what I want to do, but I can tell you … I can tell you without a minute's hesitation what I don't want to do. I don't want to get into the kind of rut that my parents are in.
>
> – Peter Mark, *Nobody Waved Good-bye*

With these words, *Nobody Waved Good-bye* (1964) declares itself to be a film about adolescent rebellion; Peter Mark rejects his parents' values, but offers nothing to replace them. This theme of adolescent rebellion is mirrored in a parallel narrative, the story of Don Owen the filmmaker, who defied the National Film Board of Canada (NFB) and made a feature film. The theme can be read a third time, using *Nobody Waved Good-bye* as an example of Canadian films in general, moving away from their childhood as government-sponsored documentaries, but still informed by that heritage.

Peter Mark (played by Peter Kastner) is a teenager who lives with his parents in suburban Toronto. He is contemptuous of his family's materialism and middle-class values, and constantly argues with his parents. He borrows his father's new car without asking, and takes his girlfriend Julie (Julie Biggs) out for a joyride. They are picked up by the police for dangerous driving, and his father, not sure how to deal with him, lets him spend the night in jail. Peter is then required to see a probation officer, but his behaviour is unchanged. Coming home late one night, he fights with his mother, and ends up moving out of the house. He tries to find work, but without a high school diploma, the job market finds him unappealing. He finally gets a job as a parking attendant, where his employer teaches him how to short-change the customers. Julie does well on her end-of-school exams, but Peter fails some of his. His parents offer to pay for a tutor if he will move back home and stop seeing Julie, but Peter refuses. When he and Julie want to go away together, Peter asks his father for money, but his father turns him down. Angry, Peter steals money and a car, and drives off with Julie. When she realises what he's done, Julie begs him to stop, but he does not. She tells him she is pregnant, and cannot raise a child on the run. Peter leaves her on the side of the road, and drives away crying.

To understand *Nobody Waved Good-bye*, we need to understand the role the National Film Board played in the birth of a new documentary practice. In the late 1950s and early 1960s, documentary filmmakers in several countries began working in a style sometimes known as *cinéma vérité*, sometimes as direct cinema. Armed with quiet, lightweight 16mm cameras and portable sync-sound equipment, these filmmakers left the confines of the studio to film the world as it was unfolding, live and unscripted.

The movement erupted in several places simultaneously, and key figures helped spread the ideas by moving from job to job. In the French Unit of the NFB, Michel Brault and Gilles Groulx made the pioneering *Les raquetteurs* (1958), about a snowshoeing festival in rural Quebec. In Paris, Jean Rouch and Edgar Morin made *Chronique d'un été*, about Paris in 1960. In America, Drew Associates made a number of films, including the groundbreaking *Primary* (1960), about the Wisconsin Democratic primary between John F. Kennedy and Hubert Humphrey. Back in Montreal, in the NFB's Unit B, filmmakers such as Wolf Koenig, Roman Kroitor and Terence Macartney-Filgate worked on the *Candid Eye* series, which included *The Days Before Christmas* (1958), about the Christmas season, and *Lonely Boy* (1963), which followed Paul Anka.

Large and well-funded, the NFB was a natural incubator for this new method of production. Their technical division built the specialised cameras and sound equipment that their filmmakers required. Their large budgets meant they could afford the film stock demanded by the high shooting ratios. They had skilled editors and mixers on staff, who helped filmmakers through the long and vital editing phase. Ideas and techniques spread quickly, both inside and outside the Film Board. Filmmakers from Unit B and the French Unit worked on each other's projects, as well as on films from other countries; Michel Brault was a cinematographer on *Chronique d'un été* (see Gwenn Scheppler's chapter in this volume), and Terence Macartney-Filgate shot *Primary* with Richard Leacock and Albert Maysles.

Into this environment walked Don Owen, a young poet from Toronto who had worked for the Canadian Broadcasting Corporation (CBC) before moving to Montreal. Owen joined Unit B, and trained under Roman Kroitor and Tom Daly. He worked as a cameraman on two of the French Unit's multi-camera shoots: *La lutte* (1961) and *À Saint-Henri le cinq septembre* (1962). He also directed two short documentaries of his own; the first, *Runner* (1962), was a formally constructed documentary about long distance runner Bruce Kidd. With his second film, *Toronto Jazz* (1964), Owen began to reflect the vérité work going on around him.

Owen was not content to stay shackled to non-fiction; he had left poetry behind because he was tired of writing for small audiences, consisting only of 'other poets and a few librarians', as he told the *Montreal Star* on 11 August 1964. Owen wanted to speak to a wider audience; he wanted to make a feature. He wanted to combine the techniques of John Cassavetes and the French New Wave with the direct cinema techniques he had learned at the NFB to make an improvised feature film.

This was not a secret – his colleagues in Unit B were well aware of Owen's feature aspirations. All he needed was the opportunity, which came with his next assignment. Sent out to make a half-hour documentary about juvenile delinquency, Owen rebelled against his parents at the NFB, and kept on shooting. Armed with thirty paragraphs of notes, he kept the camera rolling, and gave scenarios to his young actors, rather than a script. As he told the *Montreal Star* on 15 August 1964, when the film was released, 'We improvised. This way we got terribly close to reality … Our first takes were always the most spontaneous, because the actors didn't know what the others were going to do.'

In that same interview, Owen bragged that the Film Board 'didn't know [that he was shooting a feature] until it was all shot', and that 'they couldn't touch [him]'. The media loved the story, and repeated it widely. Don Owen became the stuff of legend in the Canadian film world: he was the rebel auteur, the plucky kid who bucked the system, the guy who snuck a feature through the Film Board with the old boys none the wiser.

This account of Don Owen's secret feature is disputed by the Film Board. Everyone in the chain of command, from Roman Kroitor, his producer, all the way up to Guy Roberge, the film commissioner, has denied Owen's claims of independence.

As Owen headed into production on *Nobody Waved Good-bye*, he did so on the shoulders of the NFB's massive support system, which was so helpful that good filmmakers could make great films, and in the words of an anonymous NFB producer it meant that 'an idiot could make a reasonably good documentary film here'.

Owen's was the first film to be shot completely with the Film Board's new gear, a quiet little camera and Nagra sync-sound recorder, built to spec by the Camera Division, and perfected during the shooting of *Stravinsky* (1965) by Kroitor, Koenig and Marcel Carrière. These specialised tools enabled Owen to shoot some very tricky scenes on location; especially the poignant dialogue between Peter and Julie in the park, in the mall and in the subway station. In those scenes, the Nagra is hidden in Julie's shoulder bag.

As Owen's project grew from a short documentary into an improvised feature, he requested more time, more money and more film stock, which were all approved by his superiors. Tom Daly, the head of Unit B, had begun his career as an editor, apprenticing under John Grierson and Stuart Legg. Daly reviewed Unit B rushes with an editor's eye, and was hesitant to approve a film unless he could imagine how it would be edited. Daly was taken with the engaging quality of Owen's rushes, and despite some misgivings about the improvised scenes being overlong and under-structured, he felt that the film would respond well to editing. Daly championed the film to Grant McLean, Director of Production, who agreed to provide the extra funds.

However, Daly's misgivings proved accurate, and the editing process was quite challenging. In the course of improvisation, Owen sometimes shot twenty or thirty takes of a single scene, and both Owen and Kroitor have talked about how difficult the film was to edit. They finally brought in Donald Ginsberg, an editor from Toronto, to pull it all together. Kroitor says that fully half of the story was built in the editing room.

Owen may have assumed that the vérité technique of building the story in the editing room would work as well for improvisation as it did for vérité. However, as D. B. Jones points out in *Movies and Memoranda*, 'pre-production is to fiction what post-production is to documentary'. When editing actuality footage, you have a rich block of material that can be shaped into a story through judicious cutting and trimming. With fiction, there is no naturally occurring richness, like there is in reality; the story and structure have to come from somewhere, and it is best if that happens before the camera starts rolling. Again, quoting Jones, 'when there is practically blood dripping off the Steenbeck after editing a documentary, the film is likely to be very good; but a bloody Steenbeck is a bad omen for fiction film'. So yes, it was certainly Owen's idea to make an improvised feature, but he did not make the film in isolation; the massive resources of the NFB were there for him at every step. The more interesting version of events, Owen as rebel auteur, lived on in the press. For years, the popular conception was that *Nobody Waved Good-bye* was, in the words of the *Toronto Star*'s Martin Knelman, 'an embarrassing bit of evidence that the NFB is the sort of chaotic place where the creative staff makes fools of the executives' (4 November 1967).

This belief was so strong that the NFB was called to task in Parliament. Douglas Fisher, an MP for the left-leaning New Democratic Party, wanted to know 'what was going on inside the agency to give rise to Owen's remarks'. The National Film Board was an agency of the Canadian government, and had traditionally made films that served some public purpose. The idea that filmmakers were using public money to fund their artistic conceits, and that NFB executives were being duped in the process, was appalling. Gary Evans' history of the NFB, *In the National Interest*, states that 'Roberge [Guy Roberge, film commissioner] wrote to the minister and denied Owen's remarks categorically. This was the ebullient statement of a young director who did not operate with the complete independence his statement suggested, he claimed.'

Owen and the NFB continued to disagree about the exact nature of Owen's rebellion. On 24 July 1965 he told Sylvia Fraser of the *Toronto Star Weekly* that Grant McLean berated him after the shoot, and that it was not until Unit B 'assembled a three-hour version of the film to show him' that McLean 'became quite enthusiastic'. McLean thought Owen's account was overly simplified. 'Owen makes this sound like a wildcat operation', McLean said. 'It's impossible to make a feature here without our knowledge. We knew he was experimenting. When he returned we saw he had the makings of a full-length film and so we re-budgeted for it.'

From this distance, the argument is hard to follow. Everyone agrees that Owen was experimenting, and that a lot of the story was found during the editing process. The disagreement is about who knew what when: did the Film Board know what Owen was doing while he was shooting, or did they only find out once production was complete? At a deeper level, the argument is about responsibility and decision-making. Whose decision was it to make the film? Did Owen decide, or did the Film Board? The child, or the parent?

This disagreement, between Owen and the NFB, is a mirror of Peter's struggle throughout the film, which revolves around his desire to make decisions for himself. Whenever he demands the opportunity to make his own decisions, he bungles them. Peter's life consistently gets worse as a direct result of his own actions. Returning home late one night, he fights with his mother before she kicks him out:

Peter: When exactly will I become a big boy, Mother?

Mother: When you begin to act like one.

Peter: Well, I'm going to start to act like one right now, okay?

And he does, he acts; he pretends to be an adult by behaving as adults appear to behave, by choosing his own actions and making his own decisions. But his choices are not his own; they are rejections of the choices that others try to make for him. Peter Harcourt, in his essay 'The Years of Hope' (reprinted in Seth Feldman and Joyce Nelson's *Canadian Film Reader*) writes that the film 'records a series of rejections: rejections of school, of the established rules of society, of the values of his parents as Peter sees them … Finally, possibly (for the film is really ambiguous about this), the film records the rejection of the responsibilities of father-hood.' These blind, unthinking rejections are the behaviour of an adolescent, someone more concerned with making his own decisions than with making them well. Peter is the hero of *Nobody Waved Good-bye*, but his formless, inchoate worldview keeps him from gaining our sympathy. Although he tries to be an intelligent critic, his criticisms are scatter-shot and accusatory, as in this rant he directs at his sister's fiancé:

> Did you ever stop to take a look at the kind of life you were leading? Did you ever stop to sort of consider it and consider your values and the things you were living for? Did you ever really? No, I mean, did you? Or did you sort of live without any goal or any reason for it?

He does not wait for an answer, but takes his accusations as confirmed and rolls on, letting his contempt and criticism build; this is the Socratic method as practised by an angry teenager. Though he is attacking his sister's fiancé, Peter is describing himself; he seems blind to this, as he does to most of the implications of what he says. Peter has very little to say, but he says it loudly, bitterly and often. Seth Feldman, in his essay 'The Silent Subject in Canadian Film' (in his anthology *Take Two*), writes that 'what is true of Peter in *Nobody Waved Good-bye* is true of the entire line of losers in English-Canadian features … [they have] an exuberance of language equal to their erratic behaviour. The more they speak, the more certain we become that their words are divorcing them from their actual circumstances.'

Peter's speech distances him from reality in two main ways: his assertions are quickly disproved, and he describes his worldview through negation. Throughout the film, Peter makes confident statements with no basis in reality, such as 'There's nobody watching these intersections … all the cops are in the middle of the city.' Police lights become visible immediately, and Peter is arrested. He tries to appear certain, knowledgeable; but is instead revealed as foolish and uncertain.

Furthermore, Peter is unable to express himself except through negation, rejection; he can ridicule the values of others, but he is incapable of describing his own. This point is driven home most eloquently in his coffee-house scene with Julie and their Québécois friend. Peter catalogues what his values are not, and says that he has his own. 'What are they?' his friend asks, 'I'm not asking you what they are not; I'm asking you what they are.' Peter is incapable of answering.

The third version of the theme of adolescence is the film itself, which spans the divide between the old world of government documentaries, and the coming world of fiction features. For twenty-five years, the NFB had been a dominant force in Canadian film. By the late 1950s, filmmakers began to stray from the Griersonian tradition of self-analysis for the public good. Many of the early features retained some link to NFB traditions: they were made in a quasi-documentary style, or had moralistic themes, or were made by sometime NFB filmmakers.

There are three films that illustrate this transition better than the rest: the accidental features of 1963–64, three film board documentaries that grew into features, which include *Drylanders* (Don Haldane, 1963) and *Le Chat dans le sac* (Gilles Groulx, 1964) as well as *Nobody Waved Good-bye*. The Film Board did not expect any of them, and was not experienced with distributing features. Add to this the embarrassment that Don Owen was causing them in the press, and perhaps it is no surprise that when the NFB released the film theatrically, they did so with a minimum of fanfare. Famed Canadian journalist Robert Fulford reported in the *Toronto Star*, and was re-quoted in a *Cinema Canada* article by Natalie Edwards, that 'it seems too bad that the National Film Board is bringing its latest feature into town in such an apologetic way … [they are] bringing it here in something like secrecy. No publicity campaign that you can notice.'

The domestic response for *Nobody Waved Good-bye* was correspondingly poor. At the Montreal International Film Festival, the feature prize was given to *Le Chat dans le sac*, another NFB film about discontented youth. At that year's Canadian Film Awards, the jury decided that nothing was worthy of 'Film of the Year'.

Despite this, *Nobody Waved Good-bye* screened to wide acclaim internationally. It won the Flaherty Award for best feature-length documentary in London, and the CIDALC award in Mannheim, Germany. At the New York Film Festival, it caught the eye of Donald Rugoff of Cinema V. He put it into his New York theatres in April 1965, and, according to Natalie Edwards, spent $70,000 on promotion, almost as much as it cost to make the film.

Cinema V toured the film across the US, where it became the highest grossing Canadian film to date, and back into Canada, where it did vastly better than on first release. According to the *Regina Leader-Post* (10 March 1966), it broke attendance records in Saskatoon, and *Cinema Canada* reported that in Toronto it made $5,000 a week, almost three times as much as during its first run in December of 1964. The film's Canadian ad campaign continued to quote American reviews ('An exceptionally fine movie' according to *The New Yorker* on 24 April 1965)

and Gerald Prately wrote in the February 1967 issue of *Take One* that even the NFB's information sheet did not reference a single Canadian review.

Following its commercial tour, *Nobody Waved Good-bye* began its life as a non-commercial screener for the NFB, and according to Gary Evans' *In the National Interest*, it consistently ranked among their top ten films until the early 1970s. The Toronto *Telegram* reported that the film was used by schools and church groups to prompt discussion among teachers, teens and parents. The film was also published as a play, first as part of a collection in 1966 (published as *Nobody Waved Good-bye and Other Plays* by Macmillan of Canada), and again on its own in 1971 (also by Macmillan of Toronto). Both books were intended for the educational market, and included such topics for discussion as: 'Who is at fault in Peter's delinquency? ... Can we place the blame on Peter's parents, or does it rest largely on his shoulders? Then, in a deeper sense, is society to blame? Are our values in life wrong?'

The film occupies a strange middle ground, halfway between an educational government documentary and a commercially successful fiction film. In the way it was distributed, and the way it was made, it is the awkward teenager of Canadian film history. This transition is evidenced not just in the making of *Nobody Waved Good-bye*, but also in the fabric of the film itself. We can almost see the growing pains as the film struggles against its roots; early scenes, such as Peter's arrest, his meetings with the probation officer and his first job search, exhibit a bureaucratic morality; they show the systems of Canadian society attempting to deal with a juvenile delinquent.

These sequences seem to come from a different film than the scenes between Peter and Julie, and Peter and his parents, some of which are presented with an eloquent beauty. The idyll that Peter and Julie share in the subway station, during their first moments of independence; Peter's touching lunch with his mother, as they reach out for one another, fumble badly and fail to reconnect; and Peter's fight with his father, when he uses all his old tricks, bullying and cajoling his father – and is shocked when his father finally snaps, casting Peter out with fury and contempt. 'At such moments', said *Time Magazine* (30 April 1965), '*Nobody Waved Good-bye* conquers its simple ideas and tangled verbiage with cool cinematic assurance, turning a problem play into a poem.' That sentiment suggests as much about Peter and Owen as it does about the film. In those heady days in the early 1960s, all three shared the characteristics of any young firebrand. They were awkward, and filled with promise.

Marsh Murphy

REASON OVER PASSION

JOYCE WIELAND, 1968

I was in a panic; an ecological, spiritual panic about this country ... I photographed the whole length of southern Canada to preserve it in my own way, with my own vision.

– Joyce Wieland

It is striking how, for many years now, identity has been a pervasive theme manifested in the practice of thinking about and the historicising of Canadian domestic filmmaking as a 'national' cinema. However, embedded in the texts of Canada's experimental media art (film, video, and more recently, new media) are discourses of fragmented identities, whether individual, collective or 'national'. The fringes of cinema practice in Canada proffer numerous representations of 'our' marginal status as individuals, as peoples, and as such, merit serious analysis and criticism with respect to how these works shape, liberate and/or constrain interpretations of 'our' culture(s), from both inside and outside our geopolitical borders. In recent years, curators and critics of Canadian experimental media art have displayed a fascination not only with the concept of 'experimentalism' as it pertains to artistic production, but also with what is distinctively identifiable as 'Canadian' in such work. Canadian experimental works such as Joyce Wieland's landmark 1968 film *Reason Over Passion* (or, alternately, *La raison avant la passion*) evoke the idea that as Canadians, we are subjected to speak in a language that is not uniquely our own and, in so doing, further problematise the possibility of identity construction through the distinctive medium of cinema.

Historians and theorists of Canadian cinema have long cited that, given the dominant traditions of documentary and narrative filmmaking in this country, that nature (or realism) is a purveying influence in the construction and understanding of a binding Canadian cinematic aesthetic. This observation is not entirely surprising, given the similarities the medium of cinema shares with its predecessors in artistic expression, such as literature and visual art.

A number of thinkers have written about the impact of nature on the Canadian experience as it is observed in cultural ephemera. Chief among these thinkers is Northrop Frye who, in his first 'Conclusion' to the *Literary History of Canada* (1965), notes that the Canadian experience has been shaped by nineteenth-century sophisticated ideas being thought out in the setting of the vast emptiness of an often terrifying and primitive nature. Frye argues that the result has been that Canadians, as a people in search of their collective identity, have been obliged to ask not 'Who am I?' but 'Where is here?', and to develop technology in transportation and communication to provide a vocabulary and grammar in which to answer that question. The cinema, of course, is at its most basic, a technological medium of expression and communication.

Wieland's *Reason Over Passion* is an attempt to develop 'communication to provide a vocabulary and grammar' in which to pose Frye's iconic question, 'Where is here?' The film never answers this quandary conclusively, nor is this (exclusively) its goal. The film itself is about questioning, at it posits a re-thinking of the Canadian experience that engages structuralism so as to interrogate the tyranny of realism and authenticity when making cinematic representations of physical space and lived identity. The film asks 'Where is here?' from a vantage point that sees 'here' as a construct, a space in persistent flux which is shaped by language, symbolism and power. It is by no means an easy film for an audience to digest, as Wieland's self-professed 'panic' is evident in the work's structure and form. (The film must be endured, as a requisite part of experiencing it.) Equal parts visual chaos and aural order, *Reason Over Passion* challenges the norms of the travelogue documentary by using re-shot handheld footage to distort geographic and temporal unity; for example, the season of winter does not necessarily follow autumn, nor does Saskatchewan always follow Manitoba when traveling westward across Canada.

The film takes a statement from then-Prime Minister of Canada Pierre Trudeau ('Reason over passion, that is the theme of all of my writings') as its cohering element, as its caveat about devaluing assumptions and emotions in the search for (supposed) rationality and truth. Wieland uses rudimentary computer technology of the time to expose paradoxes implicit in Trudeau's quote, as throughout the film 537 computer permutations of his phrase 'Reason Over Passion' play out on screen and are superimposed on to the material image. In particular, the jumbled type is most visible in the recurring sequences Wieland filmed during her own trans-Canada car and train travel, as if to stamp the natural landscape with a foreign, technological presence. Trudeau's statement is rendered incoherent, literally, by the seemingly random scrambling of the letters of the alphabet that make up his original utterance and, metaphorically, in what (if anything) this statement says about Canada. In so doing, Wieland makes a powerful statement about what becomes of passion in the face of obsessive ordering and rationality; it loses meaning, it loses sense.

Experimental film, or what Canadian filmmaker and writer Mike Hoolboom prefers to call 'fringe film', is personal and produced independently; the practice exists in parallel to (or perpendicular to?) more mainstream modes of representation that mark for-profit productions. As well, it would appear that fringe Canadian artists actively attempt to speak outside the limitations of the apparatus of (North) American cinema, in favour of the positing of 'new', alternate filmic forms of speech that call attention to the fractured qualities of their meanings. That being said, audiences must give credence to the resistant quality of fringe works themselves, in that the artists who create them attempt to resist strict categorisation according to social, political or artistic movements of the day. Wieland's *Reason Over Passion* fits all of these descriptions of a fringe film (and more), as she enacts her own personalised approach to cinematic form and style to subvert the types of filmmaking practices that the work addresses, which is to say documentary, travelogue, narrative, first person/autobiographical, even avant-garde.

Conversely, Canada must be described as a nation in proximity. The multiple *I*s which form a discursively constructed Canadian *we* share, as 'our' common defining bond, the lingering awareness that our national consciousness is being surveyed from the outside-in. Hollywood narratives' very dominance and popularity as a formal, ideological engine for a naturalised film viewing experience has proven difficult to overcome with respect to critics' ongoing arguments towards a distinctive definition of Canadian cinema or, indeed, any 'national' cinema. Yet Canadian fringe media artists who make work on the margins of the margin – unlike Canadian feature filmmaking, which is just at the margin of (American) cinema – 'make use' of their social, cultural and political position of marginality, so as to enact their works as a means of re-configuring, or complicating dominant aesthetics and meanings. In the context of the fringe, Canadianness, as a plurality of identities, can be seen as valuable, in that its formlessness and fragmentary nature conditions a system of production and reception wherein an alternative cinema can exist without the burden of having to destabilise a centre.

Canadian experimental film artists like Wieland give voice to the conventionally voiceless, enacting a muted discourse that explores issues of filmic representation that have traditionally been brushed over by the consuming illusion (and end goal) of Hollywood-type 'wholeness'. Freed from the sort of burdens that condition Canadian feature filmmaking (in how these films share a more direct, albeit oppositional relationship with the centre that is the [American] mainstream), marginal works encompass numerous themes largely centered around notions of difference (of gender, identity, and so on) that rarely appear in the image-surfaces of mainstream representations; or, if they do, they appear more simplistically. Wieland approaches the issue of voiceless-ness and identity quite literally in *Reason Over Passion* when she places herself as a subject in the film who attempts to sing the Canadian national anthem. In a series of extreme-close-ups, Wieland's lips appear at times out-of-focus and distorted, though always silent. What the image 'says', in its denial of her voice, is striking; which is that Wieland, as woman, as artist, as Canadian, is denied access to asserting her own power and political agency.

Throughout the film, Wieland exposes the ideological limits of the cinema apparatus in using the tools of the apparatus against itself. She carries this notion to extremes in her deployment of audio, in the form of an incessant 'beeping' soundtrack that is heard through much of the piece's eighty-plus minutes, as well as visually, through her jagged cutting of handheld, whip-pan shots of soft-focus landscapes. In a 1998 essay entitled 'Appreciation of the Films of Joyce Wieland', Barbara Goslawski describes *Reason Over Passion*'s formal and aesthetic strategy this way:

> Our sense of time and place is uprooted as the images race across the country, giving us a strange sense of unity. Despite this speed, we feel the slow progress of the film, heightened by the soundtrack's relentless, repetitive beep. Wieland superimposes titles over these images, dozens of scrambled permutations on the phrase, "reason over passion", eventually rendering it meaningless.

The inherent power structure is de-stabilised and re-shaped by Wieland, who exists as a marginal aspect of North American society traditionally put under erasure by powers that (regrettably) be. The idea then is that Canadian fringe artists do exist as multiple dualities, subjected to a persistent self-conscious flux and flow that shifts between re-determining their identities on their own terms, and doing so under the shadow of a society which either deters artists from so doing, or force-feeds them mass cultural denotations of just who and what they should be.

Canadian experimental film interrogates the limits of the ideological framework imposed on narrative by the myth-makers and storytellers of commercial (North) American cinema. This is to say that these artists' 'anti-strategies' to narrative clarity (or broadly, the tyranny of cause and effect), inform a playful multi-layered position whereby the text and structure of the work self-consciously acknowledges presence as absence, and vice versa. Wieland interrogates the means by which contemporary society's acquired 'knowledge' has been informed by culturally codified means of storytelling, whose essential goal is to perpetuate the spectator's false sense of how knowledge is acquired by way of narrative. Indeed, the 'story' of *Reason Over*

Passion is undeniably obtuse and is constructed from various extra-textual elements (Trudeau, the Canadian Flag, and so on) that may be out of reach to viewers. In acknowledging the formative power of received ideas and the problematic ways in which ideas have historically been transferred and received, Wieland's film expounds the fragility of human memory as it confines pre-set notions of reality and truth. Her juxtaposition of particular cultural formats and loose genres (such as travelogue and first-person documentary) only serves to reveal the contradictions between several sets of received ideas and does not propose to speak to any authoritative truth claim.

The intent of this chapter is not (necessarily) to challenge more conventional readings of Wieland's *Reason Over Passion* and fringe film, but rather to attempt to move experimental works into a realm of critical thought that emphasises the importance of analysing and understanding how fringe film and video works are individually (and culturally, and historically) *experienced*, as well as produced. Thus, the fringe audio-visual work should be considered neither as an object that offers access upon its critical observation to finite knowledge or information, nor as a thing that is unique merely in its positioning as being 'different' from, or unlike, a conventional film. Again, the intent here is to enact this analysis of Wieland's film and Canadian experimental media art works generally as a necessary critical engagement with them at the *experiential* level. Broadly speaking, each experimental film artist appears to enact her/his audio-visual works in such a way as to invite the viewer's *participatory* experience. It can then be said of Canadian fringe media art that its images have to provide an experience which amounts to *more* than what is seen under usual circumstances; the practice has to develop processes for presenting images and for extending the manner to which they evolve sufficiently for the viewer to engage in a perceptual process not normally undertaken. It can be argued then that this process of engaging the viewer of Canadian experimental film in a 'perceptual process not normally undertaken' is accomplished formally and thematically in numerous ways in *Reason Over Passion*, such as playing with form and structure, challenging relationships between image and audio, or self-consciously complicating the texts' own ideological position. This process fosters a kind of symbiotic relationship between engaged, participatory subject and object/text of the film itself. Yet what makes this kind of experiencing by a viewing subject distinct from any other kind of cinematic experience? And furthermore, is there anything 'Canadian' about this cultural exchange between self-aware artist/author and experiencing audience?

The answer to both questions may lie in the 'non-sense', a concept that first emerges in the writings of philosopher and phenomenologist Maurice Merleau-Ponty. This is later developed by Gilles Deleuze in his book *The Logic of Sense* (1969), which equates 'non-sense' with anti-idealism. By extension, my reading of 'non-sense' is that it comprises feelings, ideas, that are themselves marginalised from conventional modes of understanding; it is the sentiments and thoughts outside of the route to determining 'useful', empirical knowledge. Earlier, in *Sense and Non-Sense* (1948), Merleau-Ponty describes the notion of 'non-sense' as prior to and always potentially disruptive of order and rationality. Thus, 'non-sense' does not imply the mere destruction of logic and sense, inasmuch as it invites a newness of approach by complicating the conventional associations we make between sensory observation and actions in or judgements about the world. Through the study of Canadian experimental films like *Reason Over Passion* as individualised experiences that may lead to alternate modes of thought, the perceiving critic may usefully rely on non-sense in order to make sense of such works, without abandoning the awareness of their status as marginal. Furthermore, this notion of non-sense seems in keeping with the idea that Canadianness involves engendering cultural meaning through a plurality of fringe artistic practices. The alternative that non-sense poses to making sense of cinematic texts only in order to confirm already-held 'logical' assumptions, leads to the beginnings of an affective approach to viewership. This methodology serves to emphasise the importance of the study of one's own *experience* of audio-visual objects, in tandem with the objects themselves. It is a process that seems to point out intersections as much as polarities between the works being seen, heard and felt. This methodology is thus a 'non-sensical' analysis/understanding of how experimental works impress upon the viewer as a perceiving participant, and it requires one to continually be aware of their role, as viewer and listener, in that symbiotic relationship.

To experience fringe works in the context of this notion of 'non-sense' maintains the phenomenological tension of what is seen and heard in an experimental production, and refuses to reduce the experience of the work to a strictly cognitive one. This approach supports the understanding of fringe films like Wieland's as meaningful theoretical and cultural phenomena, precisely because they resist being assimilated into conventional culture. This affective means of experiencing fringe film both coincides with and diverges from strictly cognitive approaches, and indeed, from other paradigms that dominated particular periods of experimental media art production. On the one hand, affect *is* deployed so as to enable its audience to make sense of what the work is trying to do, as Wieland herself does not embrace structuralism to the extent that no recognisable signifiers are present. Indeed, her film includes various sequences that concentrate on the image of, the symbol of, the Canadian flag; it is not mere abstraction. Affect occurs both in the expression of the work itself and in an audiences' reception of the work's expression. Moreover, the affective value of fringe films like *Reason Over Passion* lie in its subjective qualities, as if the work is relaying to its audience the message, 'I do not want you to ever fully *know* me'. Perhaps this, in turn, is where the 'pleasure' of experiencing marginal media is derived, in that a work can never be truly known, but only experienced multi-sensorially through affective engagement with its form, aesthetics and content.

Nevertheless, one's own embodied, social and political located-ness as a subject initiates a particular affective reception of the expressions of experimental media. This in turn provides a valuable interpretive tool as to how to understand fringe works as (cultural) theory. Perhaps the fringe moving image artist is best characterised as one who makes the relationship between her/his works and the viewer as 'open' as possible? Therefore, it is important to restate a critical emphasis on writing about fringe works like Wieland's in a way that continues them into the viewer's socially and politically located body, rather than simply 'containing' them as texts, to be analysed. Let us revisit then the affective means by which Canadian fringe media art works represent, challenge, or re-configure 'fixed' notions of how national or personal identity is constructed. Again, marginality is a defining aspect of Canadian cinema in general. Fringe films engage their marginality as works of audio-visual theory that can productively address cultural and social phenomena. In this regard, *Reason Over Passion* can be seen as an emphatically political film that addresses tensions about how the artist perceives her country and her place amongst its peoples, its land. A phenomenological approach, which emphasises bodily and sensorial response, in conjunction with strictly cognitive processes, allows the viewer to see experimental media as works of theory, because it allows the art work to be understood on its own terms, in such a way that the most richness – of affect, of experience, of 'knowledge' – can be gleaned from them.

Currently, there is a shift away from conventional understandings of the margins of film production as merely reactions to a centre, in order to examine the fringe in its own regard. Wieland's *Reason Over Passion* can be seen as embodying this tendency and as one of the earliest examples of a fringe film that is not strictly oppositional in its formal and aesthetic concerns. The fringe film artist has grown beyond functioning simply as an *opposite* to the dominant mode of producing images in the service of constructing firm understandings of socially produced identities. Any cursory survey of the body of fringe works produced in Canada observes notable formal and thematic changes in the ways the marginalised fringe artist, as cultural producer, approaches the organisation of images and sounds so as to construct open meanings that are not simply oppositional or reactive, but 'productive'. Wieland's film provides an interesting marker for this shifting tendency, as a good portion of her work concentrates on appropri-ated images of Trudeau shot off a television screen during the 1968 Canadian federal election. While Wieland's mass media images reveal their origins in that they are visually discernible as having been produced in order to stimulate profit and desire, their conceptual re-arrangement, in conjunction with Wieland's aesthetic concerns with manipulating their materiality, gener-ates the effect that their meaning is not just being critiqued or opposed, but *altered* somehow. This is significant, as Wieland appears simultaneously to fetishise, deplore, adore and mock the mass media's spectacular images, so as to not quite oppose (in a rigid sense) the conserva-tive politics at work therein, but in order to use film as a cultural intervention that exposes subversive meanings which lie dormant in the faces of cultural figures of varying notoriety, such as Trudeau, in this historically-specific instance. The film enacts form and aesthetics so as to reveal the Other in the normal. This activity, though informed by formalist and structuralist filmmaking concerns of her era, signals the beginning of a movement by artists away from making experimental works that are strictly oppositional, moving instead towards making works which are deceptively more complex and less easily cognisable.

Thus, within the histories of Canadian experimental film practice, there has emerged a renewed engagement with the prospect of developing an indigenous audio-visual expression that does not function primarily so as to critique mainstream culture and dominant ideol-ogy. Rather, these works are moving beyond identity construction in order to produce visual and audio cultural theory from the problems of identity. A film like *Reason Over Passion* is one of the precursors to this shift in how artists comment on and contribute to the Canadian experience, as it formally alludes to what is lacking in the normal (read: mainstream) as that which may have been present from the outset. But what seems 'new' is that it is not strictly the intention of Wieland to valorise her culturally marginalised position, to point out problems with the dominant language of power and 'go home', if you will. Instead, her film deserves to be read as a marker of a transition within the broader discourse of marginal, experimental cinema in Canada. It moves away from the mere critique of encoded, dominant cinematic ideologies and shift towards a newer understanding of the marginalised as not strictly opposite to the mainstream, but capable of theoretical work that is productive: in particular, the work of epistemology and history. The film provides viewers a difficultly learned vocabulary as to how Canadian-ness can be articulated in all of its multiplicities.

James Missen

THE WINDS OF FOGO

COLIN LOW, 1969

07

The development of *cinéma vérité*, sometimes known as direct cinema (a spontaneous, voice-over-free documentary style made possible by lightweight camera and sound gear), in English Canada differs from the form's development in French in significant ways (Marsh Murphy explains the anglophone forms in his chapter on *Nobody Waved Good-bye* (1964) in this volume; Gwenn Scheppler does similar work in his chapter on *Pour la suite du monde* (*Of Whales, the Moon, and Men*, 1962). Perhaps the most significant of these ways is the different kinds of relationships that anglophone and francophone filmmakers sought with their subjects. The signature work of francophone *vérité* is certainly Pierre Perrault's *Pour la suite du monde*, wherein Perrault sought a *cinéma vécu*, a 'lived cinema' that involved an intimate, semi-collaborative relationship with the subjects. The roughly contemporary and equally central English-Canadian documentary, *Lonely Boy* (1962), looks very different indeed. In that film, Wolf Koenig and Roman Kroiter followed teen idol Paul Anka on a road trip; although the camera is frequently acknowledged, as is the artificiality of the whole endeavour, *Lonely Boy* has nothing near the kind of intimacy that we see in a film like *Pour la suite du monde*.

This tendency towards detachment and away from participation reached something of a crisis point in 1966, with Tanya Ballantyne's film *The Things I Cannot Change*. That film chronicled the travails of the Baileys, a family in Montreal beset by poverty and frequent husbandly fecklessness. One particularly striking scene features Mr Bailey being beaten up by a man who owes him money; that violent debtor then calls the police *on Bailey*, who the police then try to find. It is a crucial moment of crisis for an emerging documentary practice; although new camera and sound technology provided a previously unheard of intimacy with subjects, anglophone filmmakers had not yet developed a new ethical or philosophical framework to deal with that intimacy.

As Farbod Honarpisheh discusses in this volume's chapter on *You Are on Indian Land* (1969), the Challenge for Change programme was meant to rectify that gap. Begun in 1967, the programme's impulses were twofold. One impulse was clearly to get filmmakers to think about their connection to their subjects, and to use film as a means of social change via increased communication. The other impulse was regionalisation; filmmakers were sent to the prairies, to the arctic, and to the Atlantic provinces, all regions that had long felt marginalised in a country whose power and influence is *highly* concentrated in the central-Canadian provinces of Ontario and Quebec.

It was appropriate, then, that the flagship programme of Challenge for Change was the Fogo Island series. Fogo Island is a small island off the northeastern coast of the island of Newfoundland; plagued by poverty and infrastructure problems, the Newfoundland government was considering evacuating it. The Fogo Island films were intended as a communicative effort, an attempt to improve communication between the two villages on the island, presumably leading to a stronger sense of shared destiny and so a more sustainable community. The films were directed by Colin Low, an Alberta-born mainstay of the English-language National Film Board of Canada (NFB) whose pre-Fogo work had oscillated between highly artificial films (such as 1957's *City of Gold*, which manipulated photographs of the Klondike gold rush on an animation stand, strongly influencing filmmakers such as Ken Burns) and intimate works of socially conscious vérité (such as 1960's *Circle of the Sun*, which documented the rituals of the Blood Indians of Southern Alberta). As I will try to explain, the Fogo Island series, and especially *The Winds of Fogo* (1969), combined these tendencies. Memorial University of Newfoundland, for whom closeness to the communities of Newfoundland has always been a *very* high institutional priority, was a collaborator on the series. There were 32 films in the series altogether; some of them were just a few minutes, and quite minimalist (*Discussion on Welfare*, 6m; *Jim Decker's Party*, 6m), some longer and a bit more rambling (*Citizen Discussions*, 28m; *Fisherman's Meeting*, 27m). The conclusion of the series was marked by a thirty-minute film (the only one in colour), *The Winds of Fogo*, the ostensible topic of this chapter. In 1972, the NFB produced a 42-minute follow-up film called *Memo From Fogo* (produced by Low, it was directed by Roger Hart).

One of the key components of the Fogo Island films was that the members of the Fogo communities were meant to be involved in the production of the series. What this meant in practice was that in addition to close consultation with community members before doing interviews, members of the community were also to be consulted *after* the interviews. This was mostly done in community halls, where rushes and rough cuts were shown and slight changes in editing decision were made as a result. This process of intense collaboration and discussion became informally known as the 'Fogo Process', which could broadly be seen as a slightly more socially engaged version of the sort of feedback that we see in a film like Jean Rouch's *Chronique d'un été* (1960). This process of film production, and its link to community development, is without question at the root of community television initiatives (which are far more common in the United States than in Canada, largely due to different regulation of cable television). Filmmakers associated with the project toured widely, preaching the gospel of community-oriented media practice. *The Advertiser*, a Newfoundland newspaper, reported proudly on 8 August 1968 that 'Colin Low of the National Film Board, and Donald Snowden, Director of Memorial's Extension Department, have been hired as consultants by the US government' as part of the Lyndon Johnson administration's War on Poverty.

Perhaps as a result of the combination of governmental approval and activist seriousness that circulates around the Fogo Island films, a consensus seems to have emerged that these are basically dull works with very little cinematic importance. D. B. Jones, in his seminal history of the NFB, *Movies and Memoranda*, writes that 'aesthetic criteria were no longer applicable'. He also believed:

> Traditionally, films have seemed to make economic sense when used as mass communications. Twenty-three films useful mainly to a small community of five thousand people constituted very expensive social change. It is true that the films were used widely, but they were interesting to national and international audiences mainly for their proto-typical value, as examples.

The NFB itself has encouraged this impression in an oddly aggressive way. In an anonymously written 1968 NFB booklet called *Fogo Process in Communication*, we read that 'It is crucially important to appreciate that the films are subsidiary to the purpose they serve and that the process deals with community action rather than filmmaking'. A 1972 report on a seminar held on 'Film, Video Tape and Social Change' (called *Cinema as Catalyst* and written by Sandra Gwynn) says of the Fogo films that 'Far more important than the films themselves, was the process of making them. More important still was the process of screening them, a month or so later, for the people of Fogo.' I take the point Gwynn is making here, that the Fogo film-makers wanted to move beyond traditional ideas about of documentary filmmaking towards something more locally rooted and responsive.

I also believe this is an example of how the NFB is often its own worst enemy. I reject the assumption that these films are unimportant *as films*, or that they must be read as purely functional tools whose aesthetic properties are entirely an afterthought. Some of vérité's loveliest moments can be found in the Fogo Island series. *Jim Decker's Party*, for example, is a very short, entirely self-contained film (truly the title says it all); but it is also a marvel of vérité aesthetics, intimate and kinetic and using the power of lightweight sync-sound cameras to capture resonant images that speak volumes about the rhythms of life on Fogo. Understanding these films in aesthetic terms is not merely some cinephile indulgence. Sensitivity to these sorts of considerations are, to my mind, a crucial part of understanding what these filmmakers had to offer to a process of social engagement. They were not there because they knew how to switch on a camera. They were there because they knew how to speak about complex, vibrant societies and knew how to do that through the language of images. Degree-zero-style community TV efforts (which are often based on the assumption that *anyone*, regardless of cinematic inclination, can make films and videos) that claim Fogo as an inheritance miss this essential point. The Fogo Island films are valuable as social work and as cinema, just as James Agee and Walker Evans' *Let Us Now Praise Famous Men* is valuable both as social documentation and modernist literary and photographic sensibilities. Anyone equating that landmark book with community newspapers would be almost universally understood to have missed something profoundly important; so it is with those who see the Fogo Island project purely in terms of its connection to community access media.

The summary film in the Fogo series, *The Winds of Fogo*, is a good example of the combination of aesthetic and social idealism. There is very little in this film that deals explicitly with economic issues (unlike other films in the Fogo series, such as *Some Problems of Fogo* or *Tom Best on Co-operatives* (both 1967)), but there is still a great deal that explains the distinctiveness of life on Fogo and the political complexities that define it.

Indeed, for all of the noise made about the need to make films from a local's perspective, Low is clearly taken by many distinctive aspects of life on Fogo that are meant to interpret this part of Canada to other Canadians (to paraphrase the NFB's official mandate to 'Interpret Canada to Canadians and other nations'). We see this in the way that Low lingers on the details of boat building, for example. On a soundtrack comprised *both* of sync-sound and a voice-over from one the Wells boys (who are helping their father William to build a boat), we hear about the desire of young people to have their own watercraft, and to build a life on the island. The camera is handheld and often mobile, and is placed very low, in a way that highlights the lines of a still-skeletal boat in a way that is graphically striking. This gives the viewer a detailed sense of a slightly anachronistic practice (building boats from scratch), but does so in a way that feels very intensely cinematic, emphasising both visual design and kinesis, both mimetic sound (still relatively cutting-edge in the late 1960s) and clear, semi-poetic narration. We get in this sequence a sense of complexity, of in-between-ness in terms of tradition and modernity. We are well outside the realm of the folklore documentary, but we are also well outside the realm of just-the-facts-ma'am, cinema-as-communication-only vision that the NFB literature presents the films as embodying. This is, in short, an example of socially informed cinematic art.

Something very similar is going on in a sequence just before this boat-building passage, where Wells and his boys take their small boat out to the Grand Funk islands. Just as the images of the boat-building are an example of part of the quotidian life of Fogo (and probably unimpressive to locals) rendered striking via Low's cinematic sensibilities (in a way that would make it seem even more impressive to outsiders), we have here an example of the everyday facts of life in an island community rendered cinematically striking, seemingly for the benefit of outsiders who would wish to understand the contours of life there more clearly. The scenes going out to the Grand Funk are shot mostly in close-ups; exceptions here are occasional cutaways to shots of the boat chugging along through a slightly choppy sea and very striking images of an iceberg that they pass by. This combination of the intimate and the enormous is certainly emotionally affecting, but the strategy shifts dramatically once the boat reaches the Grand Funk. After a sequence (shot with the camera well back) where the boys jump off of a smaller boat onto the island itself (they have to wait until the waves lift their boat high enough, and avoid being dashed against the rocks as they leap off; it is an insanely dangerous procedure), Low lingers on them sitting on the rocky island itself. Through a series of long shots and medium shots, we see the boys wander around a landscape that is literally thick with birds; there must be hundreds if not thousands of them there. The soundtrack, which is also comprised of both wild sound and voice-over, is comprised of shrieking birds (basically mimetic/diagetic sound, although not really synchronous) and the boys talking about how they had never been to the Funks before, and about how incredibly strong it smelled up on the rock. This shift from a extreme long shot/close-up combination to an emphasis on medium long shots and medium shots is a kind of visual reconciliation of the awe/immediacy dialectic that defined the but on the sea, but is also an attempt to capture striking images, distinctive to this region, in a way that is both immediate (to give some sense of emotional affect) and wide enough to be detailed (to give a sense of local detail by way of interpreting the island's life to outsiders).

The Winds of Fogo also contains important details of political life on the island, although it is most interesting when, again, the filmmakers interpret the political situation in a way that moved beyond purely local concerns. The Fogo Island series was nothing if not explicitly political; titles like *Brian Earle on Merchants and Welfare, Joe Kinsella on Education, Thoughts on Fogo and Norway* (all 1967) make that more than clear. And these were definitely important political interventions, helping to clarify and communicate complex positions about important aspects of life on Fogo. But this political discussion shifts gears significantly in *The Winds of Fogo.* The concluding sequence of the film, in particular, seems to be trying to place the island, and by extension the film project of which it is a part, in the context of a rapidly changing Canadian identity. This sequence features a kite being flown in a large field, a kite made from a Canadian maple leaf flag. The images where the kite shoots up through the air and then slowly rambles downward are graceful and kinetic, like so much in the film. But the fact that this kite is made of the maple leaf flag is quite significant. In 1967, when the project was being shot, this Canadian flag was just over two years old (having been approved by parliament in 1964, it was officially ratified by the Queen in February 1965). It replaced a flag that integrated the Union Jack on a red background, and that replacement spoke to an emerging post-British conscious-ness in English Canada. An equally important aspect of this new Canadian identity, though, was a slowly emerging awareness that the experiences of white, anglophone central-Canadians had been disproportionally conflated with Canadian identity as a whole. Growing engagement with francophone, Aboriginal, or immigrant experiences sought to rectify this in part. But a slightly less threatening – although no less de-centring, so to speak – experience could be found in the highly distinctive culture of Newfoundland. The fact that the province had only joined Canada in 1949, and after a *very* narrowly-won referendum, made it a particularly vivid example of the ways in which Canadian identity was changing, and becoming more diverse. So the fact that this film, and for all practical purposes this series, closes with an image of the Canadian flag unpretentiously soaring (it has been made into a kite after all) over Newfoundland, points to its inseparable connection with a revitalised, and modernising, Canadian nationalism. That it makes this link through the language of images is entirely consistent with the way that the film emphasises *both* the political and the visual, *both* the communication and aesthetics, and refuses to sacrifice one for the other.

It is not entirely unreasonable that the Fogo Island series is mostly remembered for utili-tarian reasons. Its link to media-based projects of community development is indeed easy to see, both via the collaborative process by which it was made and the economic and cultural marginalisation that it seeks to rectify. But it is a mistake to assume that such projects must inevitably be the dry, didactic snooze-fests that we do indeed see on so many community tele-vision stations throughout North America. Instead, the real value of the Fogo Island series is for the way that it seemed to offer a project that never fully materialised. These films suggest, like James Agee and Walker Evans' magnum opus, that the details of daily life can be given a deeply felt aesthetic realisation, a realisation that speaks both to the mostly formal concerns of the day (modernism for Agee/Evans, *cinéma vérité* for Colin Low) and to the political realities (the Great Depression for Agee/Evans, the modernisation of Canadian identity in the 1960s for Low). This is a highly optimistic view of what documentary can do, one that sidesteps both the John Grierson-influenced drabness that many feel has held Canadian cinema back, and the probably futile hope for a sustainable narrative cinema that could compete with Hollywood. The Fogo Island series offered an aesthetically open-minded, socially engaged vision for Canadian cinema at a crucial time in Canadian history. That Canadian cinema as a whole basically decided not to follow its path does not make it any less important.

Jerry White

YOU ARE ON INDIAN LAND

08

MIKE MITCHELL/MORT RANSEN, 1969

The working title of the project that eventually became *You Are on Indian Land* in 1969 was 'International Bridge'. The 36-minute documentary was produced by Challenge for Change (CFC), the acclaimed National Film Board of Cananda (NFB) programme that 'brought together' a number of individuals and institutions varied in their aesthetic approaches, social weight and political leanings. Launched in 1967, the year of Canada's centenary and Expo Montreal, CFC was soon joined by its Québécois counterpart Société Nouvelle. Under the auspices of the Liberal administration of Pierre Trudeau, the initiative was financially sustained, for over a decade, through subsidies from six government agencies. From the outset, the stated goal of CFC was to further democratise Canada by providing the means of media production to the marginalised communities of the nation. More specifically, it was to give a voice to those who were perceived as under-represented, particularly the poor, by making it possible for them to make use of film, video and cable television. The underpinning assumption, inspired partly as a result of the debates initiated by Colin Low's Fogo Island Series (see Jerry White's chapter on *The Winds of Fogo* (1969) in this volume), was that through engaging the targeted communities in the process of filmmaking it was possible to make films *with* rather than *about* them. Equally important to those who initiated and supported the CFC was the hope that it would, according to its mandate statement, 'encourage dialogue and promote social change'. Accordingly, as an attempt to integrate the margins into the mainstream, it was to bring about progressive change through dialogue, in time reducing the possibilities of social conflict. If initially the margin was mainly identified as the poor, leading to the making of films that dealt with issues of poverty, before long the definition was expanded to include others like single mothers, blacks and the First Nations.

In 1968, it was decided at the NFB to engage Canada's First Nations in the Board's activities by providing training in different aspects of filmmaking to a small group of young volunteers. Influenced to a large extent by the model of participatory representation (initially put forward by Colin Low), this initiative was fully in line with the general perspective of the CFC. Consequently, the Company of Young Canadians (a newly-founded volunteer organisation funded by the federal government and involved in different community-based projects aimed at social change) was assigned the task of recommending a number of would-be trainees. Candidates deemed qualified were to be selected from different indigenous communities across the nation. The first group of seven, six male and one female, started their training by the spring of the same year. While the NFB supported the project by providing training, supervision and production material, the CYC covered minimal living expenses in Montreal and on filming locations. From the beginning, the approved plan was that the trainees would be volunteers for the CYC, and *not* NFB employees (an arrangement that later on led to complications for the trainees). As part of their training, they filmed their first project at the Akwesasne Mohawk Nation, each member of the team in turn serving as cinematographer, director, editor, interviewer, and so on. Later, two edited versions of this collaborative 'exercise' were produced. One edited by Noel StarBlanket (a Cree from the Starblanket Reserve), a short documentary on the past as well as contemporary relevance of the Longhouse religion, was released with the title *These Are My People* (1969). Eventually from the original group, that came to be known as the Indian Film Crew, Willie Dunn (Mi'kmaq) and Michael Mitchell (Mohawk) emerged as film directors. The first major work completed by the crew was *Ballad of Crowfoot* (1968). Directed by Dunn (who also wrote and performed the song for the soundtrack.), *Ballad of Crowfoot* was essentially a short found-footage film, composed almost entirely of archival material (mostly still photographs, but also some old film footage and contemporary newspaper clippings) related to the 'conquest of the West'. *You Are on Indian Land* was the next project in which the native crew was extensively involved, with Mike Mitchell playing a notably major part from the start. Yet many sources, particularly the more contemporary ones (NFB's website for instance), simply name Mort Ransen (staff member of the NFB since 1962 and later director of numerous titles, including *Margaret's Museum* (1995)) as the film's director. A more detailed account of the film's production is bound to be more complicated though, pointing, above all, to Mitchell's crucial input. The film's original titles are somewhat ambiguous, as they credit Ransen for 'location direction', while acknowledging Mitchell (along with Noel StarBlanket and the people of Akwesasne) for 'collaboration'. However, Ransen himself, on several occasions, including in one unpublished 1974 interview, has maintained that he considers the Indian Film Unit in general, and Mitchell in particular, as the main creative forces behind *You Are on Indian Land*. Furthermore, Ransen commends Kathleen Shannon (filmmaker, founder and Executive Producer of the 'women's studio' Studio D) and Mitchell for the film's final editing, insisting, 'I didn't have anything to do with that at all.'

Now, to shed light on this issue, recounting a history, however brief, of the events that took place before and during the film's production is in order here. As we will see, the extraordinary circumstances surrounding the production of the film not only led to its peculiar 'question of authorship' but also informed the final results, the very 'texture' of the film itself. What is more, as one of the earliest manifestations of First Nations involvement in the medium of filmmaking in Canada (and beyond in fact) *You Are on Indian Land* should find its deserving place in the history of this exceptionally hard-to-create corpus.

With *You Are on Indian Land*, the somewhat 'elusive author' of our documentary simultaneously played the twofold role of the activist documentarian, crossing those lines perceived to separate the agitator from the filmmaker. Being from the Akwesasne Mohawk Nation (the St Regis Reserve, about an hour drive from Montreal), Mitchell had remained in touch with his community during the training period at the NFB. This proximity to home, combined with an interest in grass roots politics, allowed him to emerge as a vocal figure in the Mohawk protests against the policies of the federal government of the time. Divided between two sovereign states (the US and Canada) and two Canadian provinces (Ontario and Quebec), the issues related to border-crossing were at the heart of Mohawk grievances. Notwithstanding the implications of the borders that split their land on larger questions of sovereignty, citizenship and (national) identity, these boundaries also left their mark on the community's everyday life. More recently, as customs agents required the residents of the reserve to pay taxes on the personal purchases brought across the border, local complaints had galvanised around the issue of duty rights. This form of border taxation, Mohawks argued, was contrary to the Jay Treaty of 1794.

Back at the NFB, Mitchell informed George Stoney (Executive Producer of the CFC at the time and a strong supporter of the Native Unit), of the protest actions that were being planned after the breakdown of talks with the government. Mitchell asked for a film crew to be present on location to film what was expected to be the next phase of the campaign – blocking the international bridge between Canada and the United States. Expecting Mitchell's extensive involvement with the protest itself, Stoney asked Ransen to direct the film instead. Ransen, however, agreed only when assured that no other member of the native crew was available, and even then he saw his part more as 'an assistant director or adviser to Mike' (this was sourced from an unpublished NFB manuscript of the interview mentioned above). A film crew was put together in less than twenty-four hours, again largely thanks to Stoney, who helped them slip by the bureaucratic hurdles of the NFB. The team, which now included Mitchell, Ransen, and the skilful cinematographer Tony Ianzelo (who filmed Bonnie Sherr Klein's *A Continuing*

Responsibility (1968)), reached the reserve before the protest began. A few hours later, on a cold December morning, a small group of Mohawk activists began the blockade by stopping the surprised motorists: 'Sorry. You are on Indian land.'

You Are on Indian Land, however, does not begin with the protest, instead starting out with a segment that functions as a prologue to the rest of the film. The opening shot is that of a largely native assembly gathered at the Cornwall Island Community Hall. Standing somewhere in front and facing the camera, Mitchell – who is wearing an Iroquois choker necklace – is addressing the audience: 'We don't want to be a Canadian citizen, we don't want to be an American citizen. They told us a long time ago that we were North American Indians, and today we feel this way too.' What follows is a map of the St Lawrence River at the juncture where Akwesasne and its neighbouring territories are located. Animated lines signifying the border between Canada and the US, as well as the one between Ontario and Quebec, are drawn on the map. Meanwhile, the voice-over (Glen Lazore, a Mohawk from Akwesasne) declares:

> The people of Akwesasne, which the white man calls the St Regis Reservation, lived on this land long before the two countries decided to draw a line between themselves. That line was not meant for Indians, and our right to cross it with our belongings, paying no duty, was confirmed in the Jay Treaty of 1794. The Canadian Government never got around to making this treaty into law.

As the shot lingers, the voice-over continues with a brief history of the dispute over the bridge and the new Customs House, built on the reserve without the consent of the Mohawk community. Cut to a tilted shot of a building marked Canada Customs, and the words 'YOU ARE ON INDIAN LAND' are inscribed, one by one, in bold.

Of course, the imagery of maps and diagrams abound in the cinema, especially in documentary films and newsreels. Not long ago, at the height of European colonialism, these images evoked, among other things, the very idea of empire itself. Endowed also with an aura of the scientific, they made it easier for the colonial spectator/subject to imagine and identify with the far-away, if often unruly, regions of 'his' realm. Later, with the emergence of the sovereign nation-state, maps came to intimate a sense of familiarity with the nation and the territory it inhabits, from one borderline to another. With their symbolic weight aimed at glossing over ever-present internal tensions, maps thus have come to occupy a central place in most modern national (Western or not) iconographies. One example, among many, of such representations can be found in the celebrated *This Is Our Canada* (Stanley Jackson, 1945) a postwar NFB documentary that begins and ends with a map-image of what the voice-over repeatedly speaks of as 'our home'. But, with *You Are on Indian Land*, something uncanny takes place: the imagery of the map does not uphold notions of a unified nation living harmoniously within its rational borders. To the contrary, it is the very naturalness of these boundaries that are thrown open and into question. As the voice-over reminds the viewer, the border is a 'line' that was never 'meant for Indians'. The map, a familiar trope of documentary filmmaking then, is here appropriated for articulating a Mohawk account of history. And if, at least potentially, this version is waiting on any nation-building project, it is not of the kind Canadians are used to.

In fact, with *You Are on Indian Land* one can decipher a series of 'appropriation tactics' at work. Above all, they point towards a conscious desire for the reconstitution of certain conventions, whether legal or cultural, in support of native empowerment. What is more, these tactics can be posited both within the discursive space of the film, as well as in the historical experience of the protest itself. Thus, we see the Mohawk activists from the very beginning adopt the authority of a Canadian government decree to make a case for their blockade. (Conscious of the irony, this stance is at times treated with a touch of humour by the protestors themselves, for example, when one playfully suggests that they should arrest the police officers on the scene.) Immediately after the title shot, a printed copy of the ruling fills the screen: 'NOTICE – THIS IS AN INDIAN RESERVE.' Mitchell's voice continues to read the pamphlet, which warns the would-be trespassers of a fine and/or a prison term. Mitchell pointedly adds '…that's what we are gonna use – their own medicine'. With a copy of the notice posted on the flagship car (and joking about the forgotten scotch tape), the protestors drive into the middle of the road that joins Canada and the United States, bringing the traffic to a halt. The blockade is on.

Similarly, placed in its historical context, the issue of the voice-over in *You Are on Indian Land* can be seen as another manifestation of the film's reworking of already established modes of representation. Here appropriation involves stylistic practices, but as is often the case, with political ramifications in the end. As a narrative device, the 'voice of god' commentary is typically associated with that category of documentary filmmaking that Bill Nichols, in his book *Representing Reality*, has referred to as expository. In the more specific framework of Canadian cinemas, a considerable number of NFB productions, particularly those within the Griersonian tradition, can be characterised (retrospectively) as classic expository films (for example, Stuart Legg's *Churchill's Island* (1941); see Michael Brendan Baker's chapter on that film in this volume). However, this mode of filmmaking has often been linked to aesthetic and political conservatism (Brian Winston's book *Claiming the Real* critiques the Griersonian legacy along these lines). More recently, with the coming out of that diverse body of critical-theoretical literature generally termed as post-colonial, it is the ethnocentric and authoritative impulses of this category, especially in its conventional ethnographic variant, that have come under critical examination. As for *You Are on Indian Land*, its straightforward instructive commentary might for some observers imply a 'throw-back' to an aesthetic device associated with an earlier period in the history of cinema; even at the time of its making in 1969, it might be argued, the NFB had already experienced – largely as a result of the availability of new technologies such as sync-sound recording – nearly a decade of producing 'more innovative' documentaries, most notably in the style of *cinéma vérité* (sometimes known as direct cinema). But the rather extensive usage of voice-over in *You Are on Indian Land* can be more productively understood by moving away from such unidirectional historiographies of cinema that ultimately see the medium in evolutionary and hierarchical terms. In other words, the specificities of the historical context, the particularities of native filmmaking, need to be recognised here. The key question, hence, should be, who is using the voice-over, and to what end? And it should be remembered that, by all accounts, the spoken narration in *You Are on Indian Land* provides us with an early, if not the first, moment in the Canadian cinemas, when the noun 'we' can genuinely be claimed by a Native collectivity. Maybe sometimes it is not a bad idea to relinquish more authority to a film's voice, however 'omnipotent' it might seem.

Overall, on the formal level, *You Are on Indian Land* renders a style that might most accurately be described as eclectic and hybrid. It assembles an array of aesthetic strategies that are often associated with different traditions of documentary. In *You Are on Indian Land*, to use Nichols' seminal typology and terms, one can note an overlapping and coextensive use of elements from 'expository', 'observational' and 'interactive' (and mostly because of the latter, maybe even 'reflexive') modes of documentary filmmaking. Therefore, juxtaposed to post-synchronised narration, there are long passages of indirect address (typical of the observational mode). At the same time, such arrangements like the use of the intermittent interview (interactive), an acknowledged presence of the crew and camera(s), as well as the filming of the printed word (newspaper excerpts and subtitles) call attention to the cinematic artifice in *You Are on Indian Land*. This mixed-mode quality becomes more apparent as the film proceeds with the sequence that records the protest itself.

With this 'middle segment' of the film, the voice-over rhetoric gradually becomes less central and the focus shifts to the unfolding events. Consequently, appearing at increasing intervals, through the blockade sequence the commentary mostly functions as a means to provide background information for what is taking place in front of the camera. It should also be noted here that for the duration of the blockade, Ransen assumed a major part in the task of directing the film crew, while Mitchell became increasingly involved in organising the protest. Ransen later described the experience of filming the uncontrolled and hurried events as being more 'like riding on a horse rather than riding a horse'. Ransen further recalls Ianzelo's method of shooting with appreciation, especially his ability to follow the action as it was quickly developing in front of the camera. And the film certainly gives the viewer an idea how matters turned increasingly restless. Soon after the start of the blockade, the first contingent of the white police officers (from the neighbouring town of Cornwall) arrives on the scene. Still a bit disoriented by what is happening, they make their first attempt to convince the demonstrators to end their blockade and open the 'road between the two countries'. In response, the Mohawks point to their right to have jurisdiction over their reserve, insisting, 'this is our land, we are just standing on it'. Framed in medium shots, the negotiation between the police and the locals – the first of many in the film – are shot with a handheld camera that often moves from one participant to another, producing a semblance of a shot/reverse-shot effect. Increasingly, as the action unfolds, the film's style exposes qualities and elements often associated with direct cinema: linear time, synchronous (sometimes muddy) sound, indirect address, shaky handheld cinematography, and a fondness for 'smaller' acts and encounters.

Before long, having failed to convince, the officers start arresting the demonstrators. For the most part, the remainder of this segment of *You Are on Indian Land* revolves around the Mohawks' struggle to keep the blockade together. Images and sounds are recorded vigilantly: the cameras follow a number of arrests, as each protestor is led, or forced, into a police car; there is plenty of pushing and shoving; a car is towed, then pushed back into the barricade; in the intermittent moments of calm, youngsters sing and tease the officers. Soon, as Mitchell himself is taken into custody, the soft-spoken Ernest Benedict (founder of the Native North American Travelling College) emerges as a spokesperson for the group. Despite this focus on the image of Ernie Benedict, *You Are on Indian Land* depicts a Mohawk community that is not homogenous but rather multi-voiced and even tension-ridden. This foregrounding of the heterogeneity in Mohawk politics, however, does not mean that the film abandons its subjective and critical stand: on the one hand, for instance, there is the outspoken Kahn-Tineta Horn who fervently warns of 'blood shed in this country'; on the other, the conflict with the band council Chief, likened to a 'puppet of Ottawa' by a female protestor, is clearly displayed; and still further, there is criticism of those band council members who, according to the voice-over, offered their support but 'were not there' when the time for action came. Amid the scuffles and arrests though, talks between the police and civilian officials on one side, and the demonstrators on the other, continue sporadically. Both parties meanwhile seem to be highly conscious of the presence of the camera(s), aimed at them by the NFB crew and other media reporters. Throughout the negotiations, while demanding an immediate end to the blockade, the officers repeatedly insist, 'You made your point, now leave', and when asked what that really means, they answer, 'You got recognition'. The film's 'social actors' indeed receive and interact with the camera in different ways; positively, when communal grievances are expressed in an interview, and disapprovingly, as for instance when the chief tells the cinematographer, 'I'll break that thing on your head.' What is more, cameras, microphones, sound recording booms and the people who carry them (and/or their shadows) are frequently caught in the frame, most likely, thanks to the unruly state of affairs.

Following cycles of growing tension and random moments of dialogue, *You Are on Indian Land* depicts a rather anticlimactic and inconclusive ending to the blockade. Near the end of the segment on the protest, we see Ernie Benedict stand on the back of a truck and talk to the assembled crowd. He tells them that passions are rising and tempers shortening, that it is better to recede to the community hall before things go wrong, before 'anybody gets hurt'. Most of all, he calls for future meetings and debates to decide on 'what should be done'. Framed in a low-angle medium shot, his address is mainly in the Mohawk language, with the English translation left to the subtitles. In response, a young man in the crowd calls out in Mohawk, 'Hey Ernie, let us arrest all these officers and put them in jail'. After a moment of laughter, the protestors turn their backs and move away, the image fades to black.

Functioning like an epilogue, the next and final segment of *You Are on Indian Land* echoes many of the formal qualities of the film's opening. What is at issue this time, however, is the aftermath of the protest – its impact, consequences and ultimately its future. Highly non-linear and slotted in a tight arrangement, the imagery from now on consists of a series of shots forming constellations that can be described as subsections: close-ups of newspaper clippings reporting the dispute, the blockade and/or the subsequent court-related issues; more of the footage of Mike Mitchell giving a defiant speech at the Cornwall Community Hall; and another protest march, this time in front of the contentious customs house. Simultaneously, the voice-over, stronger and more forthcoming than ever, narrates what has taken place since the blockade, retelling some of the community's grievances. We learn, among other things, that the Mohawks 'received support as far away as Peru' and that the detainees were eventually acquitted by the court. More significantly, we find out about the ongoing struggles, staging of more protests, meetings with government representatives, making links with other communities. *You Are on Indian Land* ends at the same location where it began, at the Community Hall gathering of the film's opening. In the last scene of the film, while addressing a somewhat aloof official, Mitchell reiterates native treaty rights and demands mutual accountability, 'We are still at peace, we didn't break our side, we didn't go to war … yet'. A freeze-frame captures his last word. Cut to the film's final shot, a silent view of the 'International Bridge'.

The open-ended quality of *You Are on Indian Land*, already a feature of many Canadian documentaries (both English and Québécois) since the late 1950s, was also in keeping with the CFC-expressed objective of using film as a 'catalyst for social change'. Avoiding closure was seen as a natural way of inspiring dialogue between conflicting groups and so reducing the possibility of social strife. Soon after the day of the protest, with Mitchell's insistence and Stoney's backing, the film's rushes were developed and roughly edited. This unfinished version (more than two hours long) was projected in several communities in and around Akwesasne. To foster discussion and understanding, on at least one occasion it was shown to a mixed audience that included Mitchell, other activists, police officers and civic officials. Discussions did follow. These screenings, however, roused the objection of some, as many of those detained on the day of the blockade were still awaiting trial hearings. In time, *You Are on Indian Land* won awards and was sent to screenings across Canada and abroad. As for Mitchell, he continued to work with the NFB for a few more years, collaborating on a number of CFC documentaries (such as *God Help the Man Who Would Part with His Land* (George Stoney, 1971)), and directing a short film called *Who Were the Ones* in 1972. But like other members of the first Native unit before him, Mitchell left the NFB and returned to his home community to become more fully involved in the First Nations cultural and political life. He was elected to the Mohawk Council of Akwesasne in 1982 and served as the Grand Chief from 1984 until 2002. Today he is still part of the Mohawk Council where he sits as district Chief for Cornwall Island.

Farbod Honarpisheh

ON EST AU COTON COTTON MILL, TREADMILL

09

DENYS ARCAND, 1970

On est au coton (*Cotton Mill, Treadmill*; aka *We're Spun Out*; aka *We're Fed Up*, 1970), a three-hour documentary on textile workers produced for the National Film Board of Canada (NFB), represents a uniquely important moment both in the history of Quebec cinema and in the development of Denys Arcand as a filmmaker. Filmed over two years during a period of intense nationalist ferment in Quebec which saw the founding of the Parti Québécois in 1968 and the October Crisis of 1970, *On est au coton* was famously cut, shelved and left unreleased by the NFB until 1976, the year the Parti Québécois came to power on an openly separatist platform. But if the production and distribution history of the film could be said to reflect, in a minor key, the evolution of Quebec nationalism from suppressed radicalism to electoral respectability, the film's real importance goes beyond its status as a political *cause célèbre* in the paradoxical history of nationalist filmmaking within the federally-funded NFB. In addition to remaining an exceedingly powerful document on the nature of industrial exploitation, *On est au coton* also marks a turning point in Arcand's understanding of the relationship between cinema and politics – never an easy relationship at the best of times, but especially fraught in Quebec during the 1960s, 1970s and 1980s.

Largely Marxist in its analysis of capitalist exploitation (for which it was effectively censored by the NFB at the behest of an outraged textile industry), but singularly unrevolutionary in its focus on the resigned satisfaction of the workers (for which it was roundly condemned by leftist intellectuals), *On est au coton* was simultaneously criticised for being both too radical and not radical enough. A paradoxical situation perhaps, but appropriately indicative of an abiding fascination with unresolved contradiction that would characterise Arcand's film style. Those familiar with *Le Déclin de l'empire américain* (*The Decline of the American Empire*, 1986; see Peter Harcourt's chapter on the film in this volume) will recognise a filmmaker with a marked preference for exteriority over engagement, analysis over action, and cinematic confrontation over narrative (or ideological) resolution. It is a vision many critics have called cynical, pessimistic or sarcastic. But it also reflects the aesthetic of a filmmaker who, at an early stage in his career, preferred the questioning of the camera – and of the editing bench – to the pat

09

answers of political parties and ideology. As a young intellectual writing for the Marxist review *Parti-Pris* in the early 1960s, Arcand, like many others at the time, envisaged the coming of a truly national cinema ('a cinema of conquest, not of failure', as he wrote in a 1964 polemical article called 'Des evidences') accompanying the social liberation brought by an independent Quebec. But after his encounter with the textile workers of *On est au coton* and his subsequent analysis of Quebec politics in his documentary on the provincial election campaign of 1970 (*Québec: Duplessis et après/Quebec: Duplessis and After*, 1972), he came to realise that neither the workers' revolution nor national independence was likely or even desirable under present circumstances. The theoretical certainties of nationalism and Marxism thus belied by Arcand's own experience, he suddenly found himself, as he said in a 1971 interview with Michel Houle *et al.*, at an 'ideological impasse', judging the articles he had so earnestly written eight years before as nothing but 'tissues of stupidities'.

But it was an ideological impasse that led to a cinematic solution, a turn to fiction from which Arcand would not look back. In that same year, 1971, Arcand left the NFB to begin shooting a Godard-influenced crime film provisionally entitled *Calibre 45* (released as *La Maudite Galette/The Damned Dough*; aka *Dirty Money*, 1971). He would go on to shoot two more fictions in quick succession: *Réjeanne Padovani* (1973), a satire on political corruption in Montreal, and *Gina* (aka *Stone Cold Revenge*, 1975), which tells the twin stories of a team of filmmakers from the *Office National du Cinéma* [*sic*] and a stripper from Montreal who both travel to a dying textile town in northern Quebec. With *On est au coton* still sitting on the shelves of the NFB, the fiction of *Gina*, with its direct quotation of Arcand's own (as yet unreleased) documentary material and its narrative addition of exploited strippers and disaffected snowmobile gangs, allowed Arcand to produce a mordant response to the institutional and industrial contradictions which arose from that earlier work. That his next (and last) major documentary, after five years of cinematic silence from 1976 to 1981, should be his cynical but archly lucid commentary on the 1980 referendum, *Le confort et l'indifférence* (*Comfort and Indifference*, 1981), is telling on this score. As he would later say to Michel Coulombe in response to both the nationalist and federalist critics of that film, 'I took no sides in the debate, save for the side of cinema'.

Like almost all who came out of the fertile crucible of Quebec cinema in the 1960s, Arcand began his career at the offices of the National Film Board in Montreal. Although he had participated in two films when he was a student, Arcand would claim that he came to direct his first films at the NFB by accident. Hired first as a researcher and then as a scriptwriter for a series of historical films commissioned in preparation for the Canadian Centennial celebrations of 1967, he was asked to direct the film he wrote on Samuel de Champlain (*Champlain*, 1964) when the executive producer, Fernand Dansereau, could find no one else at the NFB willing to do it. It was on that film, and the two following (*La Route de l'ouest/The Westward Road* and *Les Montréalistes/Ville-Marie*, both 1965), that Arcand learned the fundamentals of film-making at an institution which, since the late 1950s, had become internationally famous for its documentaries, and especially renowned for working at the vanguard of a documentary style known as direct cinema (often known in the anglophone world as *cinéma vérité*). Even with such notionally dry and potentially formulaic subjects as those provided by textbook Canadian history, Arcand soon showed himself to be a provocative filmmaker, and his films came in for criticism from those higher up in the administration. Pierre Juneau, the then-director of the French-language section of the NFB, decided to cancel the project, and the last two scripts Arcand had written for the series were never shot. Although a permanent employee of the Board by that time, there were no more commissions forthcoming. The problem, as he said in that same 1971 interview with Houle *et al.*, was that whenever he made films, 'it cost money and it made trouble. For the NFB, a filmmaker is at his best when he makes no films and attends the maximum number of meetings. There is nothing quite so easy to administrate nor less politically offensive than a filmmaker in a meeting.' He then spent almost a year being paid for doing nothing. But the idea of an unproductive sinecure did not please Arcand, and in 1966 he decided to give up his regular paycheque in order to work in the private sector. Unfortunately, almost all of the money available for making films in those days came from public sources – the Canadian Broadcasting Corporation (CBC) or the NFB – and Arcand found himself forced to return to the NFB, though this time as a freelancer.

Arcand directed two short films on contract (*Volley-ball*, 1966; *Parcs atlantiques/Atlantic Parks*, 1967) – once again because no one at the NFB had any interest in doing them – before submitting an idea of his own for a feature-length documentary. It was Arcand's first original film proposal, and it was made possible by Guy Roberge's departure as Commissioner of the NFB and his replacement by the more audacious Hugo McPherson. Filmmakers were now increasingly brought in for contractual work and allowed to propose subjects themselves to production committees which included, for the first time, filmmakers and not only administrators. Originally, Arcand's aim was to make a film on the rise of computer-assisted technocracy in Quebec. He wanted to show, by contrasting the seemingly intractable contradictions of a concrete political and social situation with the impersonal solutions provided by technocratic 'management systems', how technocracy can lead people even further into social catastrophe. By choosing the textile workers of Quebec, some of the worst-off and least protected workers in North America, he envisaged scenes with a certain amount of tragic irony, such as 'an engineer from IBM trying to help a weaver from Granby'. His proposal, provisionally entitled *Les Informateurs*, was quickly approved and a team was assembled which included Alain Dostie and Serge Beauchemin, technicians who had worked with Pierre Perrault and already had a solid experience in filming direct cinema. The crew went to Coaticook in the industrial heartland of Quebec and shooting began in February 1969.

His initial plan, however, had to be modified for two reasons. The first was that it became rapidly clear to the filmmakers that the work and money required to bring management technology to film would exceed their limited budget (computers, remember, were at that time cumbersome and expensive things). The second, more fundamental reason for change, however, was that within a few months of filming in and around the Penman's Factory in Coaticook, Arcand discovered that the human story of the factory workers had taken on such depth and drama that the contrasting analysis of technocracy ought to be relegated to the background. But without the focus on technocracy, how then would the film be structured? Arcand, faithful to his credo that a good documentary is an adventure whose outcome is only revealed to the filmmaker in the cutting room, suspended filming and began editing the material he had already shot. To his surprise, he found that despite the atrocious conditions of the textile factories (constant exposure to 90 decibel noise, airborne cotton fibre, stifling heat and humidity, mindlessly repetitive tasks, low wages, impending factory closures, layoffs with no compensation, and so on), most of the workers he filmed did not express the utter revolt that orthodox Marxist theory told him to expect. Rather, they seemed content to accept their lot. Instead of a chorus of 'we're fed up!', the workers he interviewed would say 'things aren't too bad'. It was at that point that Arcand realised that *On est au coton* would not be about rebellion (and still less about revolution), but about resignation. Indeed the title, which is usually translated as 'We're fed up', actually means something more akin to 'We're exhausted' in Quebec French (whilst also of course punning on the cotton of textile mills).

In one sense, *On est au coton* documents a simple story: the resignation of poor French-Canadian workers faced with sub-standard wages, terrible working conditions and finally the closure of their factories. But such a description barely does justice to the visual, sonorous and narrative threads that Arcand weaves together over the course of two and a half hours (the film was cut from 173 minutes to 162 minutes in 1970, and then to 159 minutes in 1971). Watching the film today, one of the things that immediately strikes the viewer is its dramatic structure, a structure not obviously 'scripted' (there is, for example, no directorial voice-over), but rigorously constructed through film montage. As in the classic films of Sergei Eisenstein or D. W. Griffith, much of the film's power comes through the juxtaposition of scenes and images in order to supplement meaning or to visually accentuate contradiction. Of course, *On est au coton* is not a silent film. Workers, managers, politicians and union activists all speak on screen. But the voice that comes across most forcefully throughout the film is the inarticulate, monstrous expression of the factory itself. Carding machines, spinning frames, automatic looms, cutting tools and sewing machines all combine to create a deafening background to the workers' daily existence and a cacophonous leitmotif to the film itself. Arcand would say much later that he wished that he wished he had been able to use THX sound during the filming to properly convey the unbearable reality of working in such a constant din; this is mentioned in passing in Réal La Rochelle's 1995 essay on the film. Given the limited means of sound reproduction he then had at his disposal, however, the only way he could emphasise the on-screen noise was through montage, alternating loud images with quiet ones, thereby in effect providing something like a musical counterpoint which would throw the clamour of the factory into sharp relief. What could easily have become a straightforward investigation into working conditions or mill closures, is here, as La Rochelle argued, given the depth and form of operatic tragedy.

The beginning of the film is telling in this regard. It opens with a close-up of the deputy mayor of Coaticook looking suspiciously through a haze of cigarette smoke, trying to get a sense of who the filmmakers on the other side of the camera represent ('so you're with the federal government … [pause] … The National Film Board … [long pause]'). Cut to an electric typewriter, where the credits are typed onto a sheet of paper headed 'L'OFFICE NATIONAL DU FILM, CANADA'. We then cut to the inside of a factory, the camera following Arcand and another man, presumably a factory manager, as they walk through rows of clattering spinning frames, the noise almost entirely drowning out their conversation. A long tracking shot of the machines takes over the frame. The shot then cuts to a slow wide-angle pan of a similar room, but empty, the same machines now still, the soundtrack silent but for a creaking door. This movement is repeated again: a long scene of mechanical tasks ending with a worker cutting sheets of cotton followed by a quick cut to a dust-covered cutting machine sitting silent on an abandoned factory floor. The next shot follows on from the first: the deputy mayor, still smoking, tells us of the company's decision to shut down the Penman's factory in Coaticook and his own reaction to the news – shock, but also impotence before a decision taken elsewhere, magically justified with impersonal and apolitical 'figures' ('I asked them to prove that they had to close. They presented me with figures showing a loss … I said, "what can you do, you know your own business…"). Cut to a long (almost two-minute) close-up of an elderly woman with a fixed expression performing rapid, efficient, mechanically repetitive gestures. She is sewing, one after another, elastic waistbands into men's briefs. Finally, the camera pulls back to reveal dozens of other women performing similar tasks before focusing on one very young woman. Cut to a reflection of the factory floor in the pendulum of the time-clock: it is four o'clock, the end of the shift, and the women queue to punch their time-cards and leave.

Thus do the opening ten minutes introduce, almost in the manner of a musical overture, the central themes which will run throughout the film: implication of the filmmakers in the film they are shooting, their own ambiguous relation to political power, the relation of politics to the factory, and the relentless turning of the factory's machinery, with its terrifying noise, its potential silence (also terrifying, but for other reasons), and its direct effect on the workers, many of whom are women, its mechanical rhythms imprinted on their own movements. The young woman we glimpse at the sewing machine, initially presented as a contrast (but also, of course, as an identity – 'What I am, you will be') with the older woman in the previous shot, will return later on in the film. She is Carmen Bertrand, a worker who leaves Coaticook for Montreal. Her story, however, is not one of escape, or redemption from the drudge of the factory town, but of continued alienation. More precisely, she is the figure of 'happy consciousness' that Arcand discovered after his first edit, and which became a central thread in the finished film.

Happy consciousness is a term borrowed from the philosopher Herbert Marcuse's post-marxist analysis of modern society, *One-Dimensional Man*. He argues that the wholesale technological reorganisation of modern society, from its labour practices to its leisure activities, has produced a generalised conformism which has deprived man of his freedom. Even the classical Marxist concept of alienation, originally a state which could be overcome through revolution (by seizing control of the means of production), has, for Marcuse, become questionable by virtue of the extent to which people now 'recognise themselves in their commodities; they find their soul in their automobile, hi-fi set, split-level home, kitchen equipment … The result is the atrophy of the mental organs for grasping the contradictions and the alternatives and, in the one remaining dimension of technological rationality, the Happy Consciousness comes to prevail.' Indeed, the dryly ironic and at the same time extraordinarily poignant montage near the middle of the film seems to have been constructed with Marcuse in mind. The first scene juxtaposes a factory floor of women at their sewing machines with a soundtrack of two radio broadcasts, the first of which is a pompous editorial lambasting intellectuals for propagating the empty and seditious 'cult of alienation', and the second an advertisement which has Che Guevera promoting a certain brand of trousers as the only way to be a 'real revolutionary leader'. This is followed by an interview with Carmen in her Montreal studio apartment, eating alone in front of the television, recounting her aspirations to the camera. Needless to say, her dreams are in no way revolutionary, but rather a striking illustration of Marcuse's thesis: a new coat, a sports car ('silver outside, black inside') and an apartment decorated 'in the Spanish style'.

Although he would later call it a 'sort of post-script' – Arcand claimed to have come across *One-Dimensional Man* by chance as he was finishing the editing of *On est au coton* – he nevertheless decided to make his affinity with Marcuse explicit in the final version of the film through the use of intertitles. This allowed Arcand once again to borrow from the grammar of the silent film, but to modify it in two fundamental respects. First, the extracts he chose are almost always less than a full sentence, and never actually flagged as quotations. Thus wrenched from their original context, Marcuse's words no longer function as narrative bridges for the construction of a coherent story, as intertitles tended to do in classical cinema; instead, they almost take on the character of maxims, self-contained gnomic truths, offering at regular intervals a sort of pithy distillate of the images, sounds and stories brought together on the screen. Unlike narrative, it is the nature of the maxim – or rather the collection of maxims, with its essentially fragmentary form – to place the burden of coherence on the reader. And so it is in *On est au coton*: in the absence of a single narrative voice, it is largely left to the viewer to make sense of the relationship between image, sound, maxim, story and history. As Arcand himself said in that 1971 interview with Houle *et al.*, directly responding to the criticism that his film offered no solution to the workers' plight, 'all I can offer as a filmmaker is distanciation'.

The second difference to note from silent film is that Arcand's intertitles are not simply projected onto a blank screen. Rather, they are hammered out in capital letters on an electric typewriter, its percussive *ratatatat* intentionally foregrounding mechanical noise as a signifier in the same way as the images shot on the factory floor. Indeed, it is through the amplified noise of the typewriter that a clear analogy is established between the machinery of the filmmakers and the machinery of the textile mills: in both cases, political circumstances force the operator and the machine into an ambiguous and not altogether happy relation. The last title, typed before the film's closing image of a working loom growing ever louder, will moreover lend this analogy a devastating performative irony: 'THE MACHINE IS THE MOST EFFECTIVE POLITICAL TOOL'.

09

ON EST AU COTON

In the event, both machines were reduced to silence: the Penman's factory closed in 1969 and the following year *On est au coton* would be shelved and ultimately declared 'dead' by the new (and unilingual anglophone) Commissioner of the NFB, Sydney Newman. Nevertheless, despite having spent the better part of two years on a film which was suppressed by the very organisation that commissioned it, Arcand remained at the NFB and continued to kick against the pricks. The editing of his next film, *Québec: Duplessis et après*, was not yet begun before Arcand had submitted a new project to the NFB. It was to be called *Les Terroristes*. His working thesis, arrived at after the experience of his two last films, was that Quebec would see an increasing number of people choosing terrorism as 'the only alternative to a sort of collective suicide'. The project went before the committee on the 5 October 1970. On that very morning, four armed members of the Front de Libération du Québec (FLQ) broke into the Montreal residence of the British Trade Commissioner, James Cross, and kidnapped him, plunging Quebec (and Canada) into a terrorist crisis which would culminate a week later in the kidnap and assassination of Quebec minister Pierre Laporte and Canadian Prime Minister Pierre Trudeau's declaration of Martial Law. Not surprisingly, Arcand's proposal was refused. It was at that point that Arcand turned to the private sector, and to fiction, taking his team of Dostie and Beauchemin with him. After the pessimistic conclusion to shooting *On est au coton*, a pessimism stemming both from the workers' relation with the textile industry and, perhaps more profoundly, from Arcand's own relation with his bosses at the NFB, Arcand found that the violent universe of the commercial crime film – 'a world of barely articulate sub-humans, living on guns and hold-ups' – suited that pessimism perfectly. He shot *La Maudite Galette* in a month and described it to Houle *et al.* as an 'act of revolt, like the terrorism of the day, but from the comfortable position of the artist'.

In *One-Dimensional Man*, Marcuse wrote that the happy consciousness of technological society tends to assimilate everything it touches, playing with contradiction, absorbing opposition. Despite the pessimism which infuses *On est au coton* and its chequered distribution history, Arcand gives us a film which holds fast to contradiction, which maintains its opposition, which steadfastly refuses to be assimilated. From the comfortable position of the artist, Arcand makes the position of the spectator somewhat less so, and for that we should be grateful.

Craig Moyes

ASIVAQTIIN THE HUNTERS

MOSHA MICHAEL, 1977

10

The international success of Zacharias Kunuk's 2001 film *Atanarjuat: The Fast Runner* brought Inuit media-making to wider attention than it had ever enjoyed. This attention, however, brought only part of the story to light. For while there was much important discussion of how Kunuk got his start in television and video art, there was no discussion of other early Arctic media initiatives, such as the attempts by the National Film Board of Canada (NFB) to train residents of Arctic communities in filmmaking. According to a promotional flier produced by the NFB:

> In the early 1970s, television was slowly being introduced into communities in the far north. Peter Raymont, a director/producer who was then working for the NFB, was sent to Iqaluit [then called Frobisher Bay] to set up a workshop, co-sponsored by the NWT [Northwest Territories] government and the NFB, to train young Inuit in filmmaking. It was there that he met an extraordinary talent, a teenager named Mosha Michael.

There are a number of important political and historical questions spilling off the edges of that seeming innocuous statement. Explaining them will help explain why Michael's films play such an interesting role in the development of Aboriginal media in Canada.

From 1949, when Newfoundland joined the Confederation, until 1999, Canada had ten provinces and two territories. The Constitution grants provincial governments significant power over environmental, economic and cultural affairs, but the territorial governments are, in essence, subject to the decisions of the federal government. The old versions of the two territories, the Yukon and the Northwest Territories, took up the full northern half of the country, from west to east. The Yukon is large and sparsely populated, and has a significant Aboriginal population. This is true in a much bigger way of the Northwest Territories, in both its pre- and post-1999 formations. Until 1999, the Northwest Territories covered nearly a third of Canada, sharing a southwestern border with Alberta, and a northeastern border with Greenland. And it has always had a significant Aboriginal population, particular in the eastern Arctic, which was inhabited mostly by Inuit. Due to its sheer size and relative paucity of natural resources, the old Northwest Territories became known as an ungovernable tract of poverty.

This reputation is partially what led to the creation of the new territory of Nunavut, which came into existence on 1 April 1999. The immediate policy context of the creation of the territory was an ongoing land-claim dispute between Inuit groups and the Canadian government. According to a 1999 factsheet produced by the government of the old Northwest Territories in 1976,

> the Inuit Tapirisat [Brotherhood] of Canada (the main political Inuit organisation of the day) proposed the creation of Nunavut as part of the comprehensive Inuit land claim settlement, including the Inuvialuit area of the Beaufort Sea ... Two years later the Inuit Tapirisat of Canada released a paper calling for division of the Northwest Territories within ten years and provincial status for Nunavut to follow in five years.

The general idea of the new territory (comprised essentially of the eastern half of the old Northwest Territories) eventually became the creation of a self-governing territorial entity for Canada's Inuit people, who comprise roughly 85 per cent of its population. Its creation was in many ways influenced by the experience of 'Home-Rule' devolution between Greenland and Denmark (the quest for provincial status for Nunavut has been abandoned for the time being).

The official language of Nunavut's Legislative Assembly is Inuktitut, the assembly has no political parties, and the Nunavut government has much more control over natural resources, culture and education than the other territories. The territory sends only one MP to Ottawa, and apart from providing subsidy aimed at making it financially solvent, Ottawa strives to take a 'hands off' approach to Nunavut's governance. The territory's population is still sparse: on the date of creation, Nunavut had a population of approximately 27,000 and covered almost 2 million square kilometres (Nunavut is now Canada's largest territory). The details of its exact financial profile are widely disputed, but poverty remains widespread and infrastructure remains a major problem.

One of the earliest lightning rods both in terms of broad questions of Arctic sovereignty and specifically in terms of media control was the launch of the Anik communication satellite, which made radio and television available in the Arctic when the satellite became fully operational in 1973; both Laura U. Marks and Gail Valaskakis have written extensively and eloquently on these topics. As they document, television signals had been receivable in the Arctic as early as 1967, partially through the Canadian Broadcasting Corporation's (CBC) Northern Service. Anik and the increased visibility it brought to Canadian television were widely seen as part of a project of cultural defence against the encroachment of mass media from the United States. But those kinds of concerns cut both ways. Indeed, Michael Robert Evans points out that 'as Canadian programming invaded the North, communities in the Arctic developed the same concerns that their southern counterparts had developed in response to the American invasion'. Arctic communities had not been part of any consultation process; their status as willing receptors of southern broadcast signals was taken for granted.

Televisual-communications experiments, enabled by Inuit communities gaining some access to various communications satellites, defined the earliest experiences of locally-generated Arctic broadcasts. The most famous of these experiments was the Inukshuk project, which linked several remote villages via communication satellite uplinks (an Inukshuk is a traditional Inuit marker, a statue made out of flat stones and in the shape of a person; it has become an icon of Inuit cultural belonging, and is on the new flag of Nunavut). 'Via Anik B', Laura Marks notes in her 1994 article on the Inuit Broadcasting Corporation, 'teleconferences were set up among organisations such as the Hunters and Trappers Association, local education committees, and firefighters from different communities'. But most crucial to the understanding of filmmakers like Mosha Michael is the explicitly non-commercial framework that gave birth to indigenous Arctic media. Indeed, Marks also writes that 'it is interesting to note that a non-commercial, experimental use of the medium was so technologically ahead of its time'. Inukshuk enunciated a distinct, geographically rooted idea of electronic communication, and in addition to being technologically ahead of its time, it would prove prophetic in terms of its insistence that broadcast in the Arctic had an essentially non-commercial mandate.

The creation of the Inuit Broadcasting Corporation (IBC) moved Arctic media closer to the models of conventional broadcasters, although a connection to the cultural politics of the region remained central. According to Marks' article, the Canadian Radio and Television Commission (CRTC) licensed the IBC in 1981, and it went on the air in 1982, transmitting four hours of programming a week. The IBC has since become an important part of the Arctic broadcast environment and has been at the centre of some of the key controversies in the region. Less discussed by scholars, however, are the films produced as a result of the presence of the National Film Board of Canada (NFB) in the Arctic, discussed earlier. Placing the Arctic in the context of early Canadian Aboriginal media projects, Gail Valaskakis, in an essay in the 1992 book *Ethnic Minority Media*, recalls:

> In 1971, a community video project was mounted in La Ronge, Saskatchewan. This project reinforced the National Film Board's interest in the relationship between film and video and social change. Applied on a small-scale basis, these media could provide regional communication to increase Inuit participation in northern communities. At the same time, Inuit films could be televised, allowing Inuit the first opportunity to see themselves on broadcast media. In 1972, the National Film Board began the Cape Dorset film workshop in Baffin Island. This lead to the Iqualuit film workshop that, begun in 1974, became Nunatsiakmuit a year later.

But judging from the relative lack of specific information about or analysis of this initiative, there seems to be something of a consensus among media scholars that nothing significant came of this experience, at least not in comparison to later manifestations such as the IBC or independent Inuit producers such as Kunuk and his group Igloolik Isuma Productions.

Mosha Michael's work, however, predates both the IBC and Kunuk. His first film, *Natsik Hunting* (1975), documents a seal hunt; his next two films, *Asivaqtiin* (*The Hunters*) and *Qilaluganiatut* (*Whale Hunting*) (both 1977) also document hunting activities (all three films are between 7 and 13 minutes in length). They were, according to the text that opens *Natsik Hunting*, the product of a 1975 workshop in Frobisher Bay, in the eastern Arctic (Frobisher Bay is now called Iqaluit, and Iqaluit is now the capital of Nunavut). This workshop was launched in conjunction with the Ikayuktowick Correctional Centre, a penitentiary that encouraged rehabilitation of inmates (who were there called 'members') through participation in important parts of traditional Inuit life. These included hunting trips on the open sea. Michael says in the voice-over in *Asivaqtiin* that he spent three weeks as a member at Ikayuktowick, although it is not clear if that is meant to be taken that he was incarcerated there or merely observing a hunting expedition. According to the 1998 NFB flier quoted earlier, all three films were shot and edited on colour Super 8 (splices are occasionally visible); they were then blown up to 16mm at the NFB's labs in Montreal, where sound editing was also done. Michael also co-performed the music for *Natsik Hunting* (with Etulu Etioluie) and *Asivaqtiin* (with Kowmagaek Arngnakolak).

Natsik Hunting is the most lyrical and non-didactic of the three films. Like *Asivaqtiin* and *Qilaluganiatut*, *Natsik Hunting* is both clearly engaged with the documentation of traditional cultural practices and possessed of a non-narrative, photographic sensibility. The film opens with images of snowmobiles and canoes on the sea-ice, and then cuts to a medium shot of three Inuit men in a small boat heading out to the sea; Michael (with the camera) is on the other end of the boat, facing them. This is followed by a shot of the tip of the boat, another medium shot of the men shot from the same angle, and then a heavily shadowed long shot of the three men as they take aim at a seal. We see the boat approach the dead seal, red trail of blood quite visible in the water.

This sequence is quite typical of Michael's aesthetic. He is clearly taken by the landscape of the seaside Arctic, but he is visualising that landscape in a kinetic way. There are no simple still images of fjords or seascapes; both the camera and often several planes of the images are in motion. This sense of a landscape in movement speaks to a genuinely cinematic conscious- ness on Michael's part. The camera is not simply there to fade into the background and record the hunting, *cinéma-degré-zéro*-style. That said, we do see images of seals being sliced up, blood spilling onto the ice, and so on. The film's connection to a project of keeping traditional hunting, including the blood, in the realm of the visible, is clear, and it is not difficult to see how such a project connects to ongoing attempts to recover and make sustainable the cultures of indigenous peoples.

Asivaqtiin and *Qilaluganiatut* both look and move similarly; the key difference is the pres- ence of a voice-over in both. Like in *Natsik Hunting*, the camera is in almost constant motion in both films. The first images of *Asivaqtiin* are shot off of a small steamer boat as it heads out to sea; Michael zooms in and out, and the boat is moving up and down on the waves. The voice-over explains the protocol of hunting with the Ikayuktowick facility, and makes mention of the modernisation of hunting via the use of motorised transport and rifles. There is also, early on, a shot of a dead seal bleeding into the ocean, off the side of the boat, with folk singing on the soundtrack. Michael had already shown men shooting at the seal both in close-up and in long-shot (gunshot sounds are dubbed in). *Qilaluganiatut* opens with a pan across sea ice as men are loading a canoe onto the ice; the voice-over states that in springtime, 'groups of hunters pack their canoes full of supplies and head out across the bay, to hunt for whale'. The process of pushing the motorised canoes beyond the sea ice and into open water is shown in some detail, and the voice-over specifies that the canoes must be pushed because spring ice is too thin for snowmobiles and that the process takes two days. The voice-over also talks of melting ice to make tea, the use of kayaks by an earlier generation of Inuit, and so on; this is explained over an image of men loading canoes and finally over images shot off the side of the canoe as it heads out to the sea. Midway through the film is another series of carefully composed shots of men on one end of the canoe as it trundles out; it strongly recalls the composition of *Natsik Huting*. *Qilaluganiatut* features many patient long takes, both of the seascape and of men running along a frozen landscape once they return to the land to hunt for seals. Once a beluga whale is shot on the sea ice, there is an image of it bleeding in the water, followed by a series of close-ups of the whale among chucks of loose ice and a hunter tying a knot into its fins, with the voice-over explaining the Inuit's historic handiness with knot-tying.

While it would be easy to see these films simply as Super 8 diaries of someone involved in traditional hunting practices, it is important to take note of the photographic sensibility at work because it helps place the film in the context of critical ethnography, a context that will become important to Arctic media. The way in which these films are kinetic, their occasional forays into the realm of the *very* carefully composed, and their favouring of visually-packed close-ups all distinguish them from simple point-and-shoot approaches to scientific or cultural documentation. We are invited to see these films not as simple reflections of reality but as the mediated presentation of someone with a vested interest in the proceedings documented (hence the close-ups and the stoic-looking composition). Bill Nichols, in his book *Blurred Boundaries*, has talked about the difference 'between seeing through a film to the data beyond and seeing film as a cultural representation', insisting on careful attention to the formal qualities of ethnography. This is in direct contradiction to arguments that Aboriginal media tends to dispense with European understandings of aesthetic in favour of more utilitarian cultural work. Faye Ginsburg has made this argument in relation to both Arctic and indigenous media from Oceania (see especially her essay 'Mediating Culture' in the book *Fields of Vision*). Such arguments are far from unreasonable; a great deal of Aboriginal media is possessed of an aesthetic that does not conform to the formal patterns or technical standards of mainstream fiction or documentary, and is all-too-easily dismissed as amateur-ish or somehow naïve. Such dismissal would be a grievous error resulting from a narrow sense of formalism. And no doubt much Aboriginal media has a tremendously important function as a cultural mediator, precisely because such cultures have been so badly misrepresented by mainstream media.

Still, it is important to be aware of how Michael is asking his viewer to *see film* here, not simply to see a hunt. The formal self-consciousness of the work speaks to the sophistication of these films' relationship to ethnographic representation. A similarly sophisticated approach has become *de rigeur* in Inuit media, particularly in the work produced in Igloolik (a small settlement well north of the Arctic Circle) in the 1990s. It is important, then, to notice that this formal reflexivity is visible at the earliest stages of media production in the Arctic; this kind of sophistication has become a signature aspect of much work from the region.

One of the reasons, then, that it is worth considering the context Michael's work as well as the work itself is that it helps us see important part of Canadian cinema more clearly. There has, for instance, been very little discussion of the visual aspect of Kunuk's *Atanarjuat: The Fast Runner*, just as there is not much discussion of the visual aspects of indigenous cinema generally. This tendency to emphasise the narrative of *Atanarjuat* is not so surprising, since that film is so self-consciously cast in the mould of an epic oral tale. But that is the exception, not the rule, for both Kunuk's work and Inuit cinema generally. Indeed, it would be difficult to overly-emphasise the narrative of Michael's films; there just is not much story there. His films are, like Kunuk's early videos *Qaggiq* (*Gathering Place*, 1989) or *Saputi* (*Fish Traps*, 1993), narratively minimalist portraits of aspects of the Inuit everyday. They do not repay a simple, content-oriented analysis; on that level, they are about hunting and little more. Instead, they demand a cinematic analysis, as they speak eloquently about the complex relationship that Inuit have with landscape, modernity and memory. These films are influenced by contemporary representations of the northern landscape, but they are clearly trying to move beyond that set of representations, trying to find something culturally nourishing and emotionally satisfying. That quandary certainly tells us a great deal about the Inuit worldview circa 1975; that is where the meat of these films lies, so to speak. The literal meat – the fact that these men are hunting and then cutting up and eating whales – is relevant, but it is not of primary importance. In this way, then, Michael's work belongs not only alongside other Aboriginal films dealt with in this volume like *You Are on Indian Land* (1969) or *The Learning Path* (1991), but also 'handmade' films like *Reason Over Passion* (1968), or, I suggest cautiously, *En pays neufs* (1937). This is all work where content is important, but it is only the beginning; it is also work that is distinctively subjective, and with filmmakers acting essentially as artisans (a single filmmaker working or a filmmaker working in a *very* small group). This is, as Atom Egoyan notes in the preface to this volume, a fairly important tradition in Canadian film-making, English, Quebec and Aboriginal. This is distinct from, say, the American situation, which tends towards extreme situations such as Stan Brakhage working alone and in an utterly visual and non-narrative mode (or Frederick Wiseman working basically alone and making sprawling mega-documentaries), versus studio and 'independent' films (the latter of which almost always has crews whose size renders them basically indistinguishable from modest studio productions). *Asivaqtiin* is as far from Stan Brakhage/Frederick Wiseman as it is from Steven Spielberg/Steven Soderbergh. The way in which filmmakers like Michael come up the middle, so to speak, between conventional and avant-garde strategies, is actually a characterising feature of a lot of important cinema in Canada.

I freely admit that *Natsik Hunting*, *Asivaqtiin* and *Qilaluganiatut* are, on the surface, fairly innocuous films. None are longer than 15 minutes, and none moves beyond very specific local concerns. But these films offer a preview of the Inuit media that is to come. They are both important documents of cultural preservation *and* works of art that understand the way that only cinema can play in this kind of preservation. Neither naïve nor avant-garde, they helped cut a new path for non-fiction filmmaking, a path that would be followed by filmmakers like Zacharias Kunuk a decade later.

Jerry White

MOURIR À TUE-TÊTE SCREAM FROM SILENCE

ANNE-CLAIRE POIRIER, 1979

Regrettably, the feminism of the 1970s has not aged well. Subjected to derision, dismissal and mockery, this era of the feminist movement (and much of its legacy) has been unfairly diminished to, at best, a rigid and humourless stance, and, at worst, a corner from which hysterical women, in an attempt to be righteous, hypercritically denounce and disapprove. Women, in this so-called post-feminist age, may passionately embrace girlpower, rock 'n' roll and porn, and do it for gender-specific reasons, but it is hard for them to call themselves feminist – at least not without a string of apologetic mitigations. Perhaps it is not surprising that contemporary women would want to disown – or distance themselves – from a 1970s brand of feminism that tended (and certainly not without good reason) to characterise issues of politics, lifestyle and representation in bipolar terms. What often gets lost, however, is that feminism has never been a homogenous discourse, and that the peevish, frumpy, closed-minded feminist from which most of us are careful to distinguish ourselves is such a stock figure because of mainstream representation – reductive, unsympathetic, reactionary representation. This media version of the tiresome feminist is so unfriendly that one is reminded just how relevant feminist critiques of representation still are. Thus, a touchstone film such as *Mourir à tue-tête* (*Scream from Silence*, 1979) is best viewed not as a naïve artefact of an over-earnest age, but as a rigorous, politically based, theoretically informed text which aims to cut through theory's abstractions into a visceral, emotionally compelling account of lived experience.

A pioneering manifestation of the 'docudrama', Anne Claire Poirier's *Mourir à tue-tête* combines several modes now recognisable as devices of polemical documentary: segments of dramatic re-enactment (a fictionalised account – an aggregate based on the stories of interview subjects – of a young nurse, Suzanne, abducted on the street, dragged into a van, and humiliated and raped in a prolonged sequence), self-reflexive examination (provided by two of the filmmakers – actually actors, although the editor is played by Quebec actor and director of *Sonatine* (1983), Micheline Lanctôt (see Damien Detcheberry's chapter on that film in this volume) – conferring over representational choices while working on the final cut of the film), voice-over narration both poetic and statistical, and stagy testimonial sequences. The latter, in which smock-wearing, blindfolded women plead their respective cases to an off-camera authoritarian voice-of-Law, is probably the most token 1970s feminist stylistic (not because it actually dominated feminist film form, but because the jumble of Brechtian stylistics with soft-psychoanalytical confessional monologue was so ripe for parody; indeed, the popular comedy show SCTV did just such a parody, featuring a flaky and hyper-earnest Andrea Martin in fine form). Admittedly, this segment of *Mourir à tue-tête* feels the most dated, and in its climactic gathering of schoolgirls to gaze at the camera (demonstrating to the uncaring tribunal the many victims of familial sexual violence) the poignant force it likely once had is somewhat undone by what now reads as awkward cliché. And yet, the narrative trajectory of this soliloquy-driven mini-drama, in which the women – having to defend their cases in a classic 'victim put on trial' scenario – move from pained justifications to an emboldened rejection of the system as, for women's purposes, inherently inimical, is much more sophisticated than the apparent stylistic contrivances might lead one to believe.

Thus, some inevitable instances of outmoded aesthetic sensibility are hardly regrettable when considered apiece with the quest for stylistic innovation, not just to counter objectionable representational modes, but as a tool of reclamation and revitalisation. Poirier has said, in an interview in *Cineaste* in summer 1980, that her use of self-referential modes in *Mourir à tue-tête* was not for the sake of reflexivity itself but to set up a dialogue outside the emotions of the fictional narrative. This is precisely the strength of committed feminist filmmaking: experimentation is not played out, in emblematic postmodern fashion, on some abstracted plane with signifiers and signified unmoored; rather, here, since representation is at stake, everything is at stake.

Québécois film may proudly assert its claim to pioneering feminist filmmaking with an impressive concentration of classic contributions such as Mireille Dansereau's *La vie rêvée* (1972) or Paule Baillargeon and Frédérique Collin's *La cuisine rouge* (1980), not to mention the always-challenging *oeuvre* of Poirier herself. Indeed, Poirier's work is still an important part of feminist cinema, undiminished in its formal and political vigour: some standouts are *Les Filles du Roy* (1974) and *Tu as crié LET ME GO* (1998). Québécois feminist films are of particular interest in a consideration of the intersection of diverse politically-charged resistance strategies, and the manner in which issues of gender and sexuality will inevitably emerge alongside matters of political unrest and cultural marginalisation. Dansereau, director and co-writer of *La vie rêvée*, the first feature to be directed by a woman in Quebec, commented in Brenda Longfellow's 1984 essay that her film met resistance among fellow activists:

The men thought that if I made a film on women, it should be militant ... a very political film. But you see, that is a *man's* idea of what is revolutionary about women. They think we should get together and form a political party and fight, and give intellectual ideas about the problem of women as related to our society and to Quebec. Men thought that what would bring a change in the status of women is a clear analysis of women: socio-logically, politically and financially. They couldn't accept my intuitive, very emotional and personal approach.

This tension between a masculinist formation of 'legitimate' theory or political action and women's perhaps more personal, body-oriented (feelings, senses, intuitions, common and singular experiences) approach to these issues has been directly addressed by feminist theory and praxis. Without having to claim any essential gendered characteristics about art and repre-sentation produced by women (thereby avoiding claims that such texts are necessarily more personal because, say, women are more 'sensitive', or more 'in touch with their emotions'), we can see much feminist film as insisting on a revalorisation of the quotidian and lived experi-ence as a politically and theoretically valid referent. Thus, the feminist articulation of (the well-known and well-worn slogan) 'the personal is political' enables a through-line for an array of feminist-identified expressions. Whether or not explicitly political, or theoretical, a common ground may be found in the importance of lived experience as a strategy for maintaining a sense of self based on salutary body and community interaction, rather than on the inadequate and fragmented non-self reflected by a patriarchal system of commercial capitalism. Such a strategy does not come naturally, but requires an *act* of resistance. The existence of feminism is a testament to *active* intervention, to a critical, self-aware and self-reflexive relationship with the dominant culture and its representations.

A feminist critique, inclusive of overlapping counter-hegemonic modes of address, may be said to act both outside of and in opposition to dominant cultural forms which presume a seamless relationship between the spectator and the most evident ideological identifications encouraged by the text. I say 'most evident' because, of course, reading a text for ideology should not be a reductive process (just as feminist criticism has come to embrace against-the-grain readings and, from there, theories of reception and active spectatorship that take into account the singular relationship – pleasure-and-critique-finding modes of engagement – that are not strictly dependent on the text itself, but on everything from hard-to-account-for personal quirks to venue and viewing context). Nevertheless, even taking into consideration that commercial film is a heterogeneous group, one is still hard-pressed to deny that main-stream and even 'alternative' media culture is predictably limited in its address (that is, directed at a heterosexual, white, middle-to-upper-class conservative male). In contradistinction to just this kind of naturalisation of address, feminist/counter-hegemonic discourses highlight a struggle to come to terms with the limitations and the possibilities inherent in speaking within but outside of a dominant language.

The problem of self-consciously *speaking a language* (including a formal/representational language, as with cinema and other media) makes clear the need to struggle for self-actualisation, the need to consciously counter the still pervasive representation of woman – and her body – as expendable. This action of struggle and confrontation – directed towards the dominant culture *and* towards oneself as a culturally-coded body – is of course still of particular interest to women: how does one operate within an often antagonistic system and yet express opposition? Must one inevitably make a point of illustrating the brutality, or might one find a way to set forth terms of celebration?

The reality of the lived/living body insistently comes through in this kind of feminist articulation, and the immediacy of experience rends away any purely abstract or theoretical concerns with language and representation. Rather than suggesting a hopeful but vague programme of exchange and mutual influence between differing viewpoints, resistance is viscerally reinforced. The communication of a general experience of violence and rupture is crucial, for the concept of 'exchange and mutual influence' suggests some kind of participation from the dominant culture. Instead, the experience is much more one-sided, with the burden on the marginalised group to bridge the gap between themselves and the unaware, unconcerned or downright hostile. The most relevant works of resistance evince a radical discontent with this paradigm. Such work is not interested in making it easy for the dominant culture to palatably appreciate and then incorporate (that is, neutralise) the predicament of the marginal. Sympathy and reasoning – bidding for the attention of the dominant culture – may be part of the strategy; Poirier's films are made through public funding and therefore with a nod toward public awareness and bridging social gaps. But any such act of resistance must come from an acute awareness that the hard work involved in building – or acting as – a bridge will not likely be reciprocated in kind, an unfortunate reality characterising the condition of any liminal figure whose plight receives the kind of issue-of-the-week attention of a culture eager for sympathetic/sensational causes but hardly a radical shift.

Counter-hegemonic resistance proceeds from the lived experience of this condition, a present condition that is added to the accretion of acts and discourse that can make the reality of living in a female body anguish. Rage, fear and pain do not function simply as fissures in the text, they *are* the text. Such works fight to speak on their own terms, for their own sake. If these texts are speaking to the dominant culture it is not to demurely plead 'Please let me explain my point of view'; rather, the text rages: 'Look what you have done, what you are continuing to do, to me!' This is conveyed through the raw effort of a marginalised voice/body to cope with and transform constant dehumanisation.

Poirier's unflinching *Mourir à tue-tête* takes up the issue of women shamed within unjustly degraded bodies. The film evinces a grisly insistence on foregrounding the necessity of confrontation: not just, at the most immediately gripping level, confronting the dominant culture with the horrors of the systemic perpetration of exploitation and oppression, but also confronting the very terms laid out by hegemonic discourse in the hopes of exposing and transmutating such exploitative, oppressive norms. We are shown women struggling with violence not only at the literal level (a long, painfully drawn out, decidedly un-erotic rape sequence) but at the theoretical level (the filmmakers debating the nuances of representation; a panel of initially blindfolded women arguing their respective claims before the off-camera, authoritarian voice of the Law). The film presents women fighting to come to terms with a cultural complex of representation, discourse, violence and law, none of which offers justice or solace.

The cruel irony that *Mourir à tue-tête* hinges upon is the pervasive regularity of rape concomitant with the silencing shame the act engenders in the victim. Rape is not an isolated thing, not a rare thing, not a crime far removed from 'good' homes, but a quotidian event, quotidian not only as in daily, but also as in common, or as in *systemic*. Yet the act of rape, no matter how widespread, is devastating for the victim. Just how inevitably devastating is a question taken up during one of the film's reflexive sequences in which 'the filmmakers' debate the representational ethics of having the Suzanne character commit suicide. In order to argue the intensity of the damage rape instils, should a portrayal resort to despair? Is it more effective – as well as better serving the subject in ethical terms – to render rape as ultimately and utterly devastating (thus negating arguments about the strength of any individual woman's character: women are destroyed by the system not because they are too weak but because the system is inherently destructive for women)? Or is a better approach to offer hope for women's recovery and agency even within a brutalising system (a tactic which threatens to lessen the charges against a rape culture by downplaying its overwhelming harm)? One collaborator (the 'editor') wonders if the 'real' case study for Suzanne did in fact kill herself; the other (the 'director/writer') responds by solemnly acknowledging that she did, and replies regretfully that she could not help her. The argument being presented here is a kind of reality-based approach to representation, or 'representativeness', in which the real-life facts determine the course of action taken within the text, with the representations within the latter justified by the former.

Of course, the film recognises the limits of this approach, expanding upon any one-to-one relationship between 'facts' and representation. The 'filmmakers'' on-screen conversation brings up a dilemma that cannot be articulated through any declared agreement. We do not hear them decide which fate is most politically efficacious for the Suzanne character. In part, a decision cannot be reached between the two women because in terms of the issue they are debating no answer exists: rape *does* damage irrevocably, but women *do* survive it and achieve a measure of healing. In addition, the conclusion of Suzanne's narrative cannot be resolved simply on the basis of that particular women's 'real story'. In the film, 'Suzanne' is meant to exemplify the singular *and* the communal. In order to create a main character with whom the viewer can identify and sympathise, as well as to present the life of a real, particular woman who cannot be abstracted, Suzanne embodies an individual, unique, personal, irreducible experience. But for a truly forceful treatise on systemic rape the representation cannot stop at the individual level. Suzanne must resonate as more than a fictional character, even more than a fictionalised account of a real woman.

That said, the filmmakers seem to think that women will not have trouble identifying with a specific rape story; at least, their fictional counterparts are not shown debating the issue. Instead, concentrating on a close-up freeze frame of the actor's contorted face, these characters wonder pointedly whether men will be able to identify with the rapist, or whether they will simply feel distanced from what they perceive as an unappealing character quite unlike themselves. Men, the filmmakers imply, are not likely to engage in the affective experience created by the film. Instead, they are inclined to watch with critical distance, staying uninvolved.

This seeming simplification of gender response is better served by symbolic terms, in which 'men' represent an abstracted, totalising culture which denies women access. Rage over this denial of access – as with the cold, unmovable Law, insensitive to the pleas of the female defendants – is a key point addressed by the content and form of the film. The film recognises a fluidity in storytelling that is markedly different from the restrictions of a factual, linear 'statement'. The women in the film participate in the act of 'making statements' or 'confessing'. Both of these terms, however, apply to the law, to the kind of institutional mindset that excludes women. And so, *Mourir à tue-tête* reconstitutes such verbal acts as more intimate, more personally resistant, and personally curative.

Mourir à tue-tête stages what could be called a trauma narrative: the particular, acute trauma of rape, but also, more generally, the trauma of living as a woman in a misogynist dominant culture. The foregrounding of trauma – making a controversial and bold declaration meant to stir feelings of unrest in the dominant culture and, hopefully, to facilitate catharsis in the oppressed group – can be viewed as a therapeutic strategy, one intent on having art perform a salutary function, meant to open channels of expression leading, optimally, to healing. In keeping with a thematic of insistent, resistant expression as cultural practice, this therapeutic approach functions as a 'talking cure'. Instrumental to a talking cure is the particular presence and self-definition of the speaking person. The singularity of experience is called upon, but within an affective framework that recognises commonality. The talking cure is about getting in touch with deeply-felt personal content, but it is also dependent upon an intentional performance – the presence of an articulative and gestural body performing for an audience, actual or assumed. The performance is for the sake of identifying and demonstrating the trauma, in order ultimately to integrate the wisdom of experience. This catharsis performs a therapeutic function not just for the individual but for the community, which gains from the declarations and insights of the individual.

Regarding *Mourir à tue-tête*, the filmmakers apparently reach an answer to the dilemma of Suzanne's fate. Suzanne herself gives in to despair: she appears lifeless upon her bed, surrounded by glowing white light. But this is not the limit of the representation provided by the film. The cinematic form allows for a multiplicity of realities to be portrayed, not just by telling us of various outcomes, but, much more viscerally, by showing us bodies as a testament to lived experience. So, while Suzanne's story has an end, life goes on, as it were, through the film's refusal of a linear narrative. We move forward into multiple perspectives: the particular voices of the testifying women spreading outward into the implied, future voices of the chorus of girls to, finally, in a stirring finale, the eerie dissonance of whistles, adamantly piercing the silence in their announcement of female 'distress' over 'the great abuse of our bodies'. This last articulating performance in the film is hardly a sign of a positive reality; certainly the implication that arming ourselves with whistles as a practical countermeasure to abuse and inadequate societal protection is a bitter irony. Nonetheless, as filmic representation it offers possibilities of the kind excluded from the Suzanne narrative. If Suzanne's story is the tragic tale of a women crushed by a dominant culture, the other strands of the film allow for a feminist cultural inter-vention. By foregrounding the female body/voice as site of articulation and resistance, and giving us multiple bodies expressing multiple subjectivities, all towards a unified truth (the brutality of misogyny), *Mourir à tue-tête* creates both singular affective identification and a sense of community. And, as such, it performs a talking cure.

Jodi Ramer

SONATINE

MICHELINE LANCTÔT, 1983

The only people with happy memories of being a teenager are adults who can't remember properly.

> – François Truffaut

A film about the inner malaise of two teenage girls on the verge of becoming women, *Sonatine* (1983) conveys with rare sensitivity the ambiguity of the chaotic transition from puberty to adulthood. Like filmmakers such as Maurice Pialat (*L'enfance nue* (1970); *A nos amours* (1983)) or Agnès Varda (*Sans toit ni loi* (1985)), Micheline Lanctôt uses a spare *mise-en-scène* that, through restrained treatment and telling detail, takes us to the heart of the matter: the existential confusion of a generation whose ideals and desire for tenderness run up against the brutality of the world around them. The dreadful conclusion of the film, which ends with the suicide of Chantal and Louisette in the midst of overwhelming indifference, might account for an entirely tragic sensibility were it not for the director's undeniable talent in capturing the sincerity and humanity in moments of life, using a raw quasi-documentary narrative style. From a dark, desperate act, she creates a timeless film on adolescence that avoids the many clichés around that subject and stands as a work of passion and beauty.

The following analysis is a study of the narrative development of Micheline Lanctôt's film, which is modeled on the sonata. The film is made up of three movements just as in the musical form: exposition, development of two themes, then re-exposition. The two themes developed here are the respective love stories of the female characters, Chantal (Pascale Bussières) and Louisette (Marcia Pilote). Each of these two separate adventures responds to and resembles the other, particularly in their structure (meeting – disappointment – break-up) and they lead the two teenagers to a bitter realisation about the indifference and cruelty of the adult world. Developing alone in the first part of the film, the two girls meet in the second part, which is concise and tender, and puts in place the elements that foreshadow their suicidal act. Throughout *Sonatine*, Lanctôt assembles scraps of ruined existences, examining fragments of the lives of two teenagers in an attempt to grasp their desperation and their reasons for giving up on life.

The opening, scene-setting sequence, which barely lasts as long as the opening credits, introduces a key element for understanding the personalities of Chantal and Louisette. In steady close-up, a Walkman tape recorder is in the foreground from the very first shot. While a tape rolls, the two teenagers comment on an almost inaudible monologue while remaining off-screen themselves. This Walkman is the leitmotif of the film: it moves the viewer from the world of one heroine to the other and links the two friends in their adventures. Our attention is repeatedly drawn to it (each girl has one and uses it constantly), and it serves as a confidant, or diary. The girls record poems and anecdotes, and a list of the important dates in their short lives. Just as Lanctôt does with her camera, they capture on their tape recorders bits of everyday life that they save, appropriate and reinterpret in their own way. Their inner voices are revealed through the Walkman, voices made of doubts, questions and a poetic vision of the exterior world.

The story of Chantal begins immediately after this opening scene. It unfolds within a weekly ritual that has probably been occurring for some time when the viewer witnesses it. Every Friday night, Chantal takes the bus home from a physiotherapy session and meets the bus driver she has fallen in love with. By the time the viewer is invited to watch, the relationship has already developed its codes and habits: Chantal sits behind the driver's seat, her earphones around her neck, and talks to him. Yet except when she is on the bus, Chantal is portrayed as a timid, introverted teenager. Pascale Bussières, in her first film role, makes the character of Chantal pouty but smooth-featured, wearing an impenetrable expression while also lending her a special aura of madness and mystery. Later, when the two girls are brought together, a carefully composed shot is particularly revealing. It shows Chantal and Louisette slumped on a sofa, while in the foreground the water in a transparent pot bubbles wildly. The light filtering through the pot reflects onto Chantal's face, transferring to her its furious activity. We can guess at the intense inner turmoil hidden behind the impassive face of the young girl, who suffers from her inability to break through the shell of timidity that keeps her silent. To Chantal, the world to explore is first of all the world of everyday life. Through habit, the bus has become a reassuring place in which she feels at ease, particularly with the driver. He adds a human presence to this temporary space, which Chantal converts into a space of social exchange. The bus trip is thus the setting for privileged, timeless moments in which the outside world no longer exists.

Lanctôt adopts a very sober style for these sequences, with numerous ellipses, retaining only a few diffuse fragments, snapshots that illustrate the story of their relationship. There are powerful moments at first, then a gradual let-down leading to the inevitable break-up. The tenderness is reciprocated: the bus driver, flattered by the girl's interest in him, flirts openly with her, bringing her hot chocolate and whistling 'Happy Birthday' to her when she mentions it in a note slipped onto the dashboard. Chantal, for her part, lets him listen to her Walkman, thus allowing him to share her privacy. She records their conversations, and this lends the Walkman its poetic function. When the driver tells Chantal that he thinks she is pretty, she plays these words back ('You look pretty') repeatedly, but after she has listened to them a few times, they change slightly ('You look really pretty!'). Not only does the Walkman let Chantal keep the driver's words, but it also allows her to internalise them. By possessing them in this way, she can change them at will, fantasise about them, and finally control them.

Apart from these moments of intimacy, Chantal's love story remains for the most part a fantasy. And because it is largely internal, this infatuation inevitably clashes with the life of the driver, which is beyond the teenager's control. The driver already has a social life, including a love life that is quickly becoming impossible to reconcile with his desire to show Chantal some tenderness. In order to avoid breaking off the ritual that ties him to the girl, he at first refuses to leave his job to join the planned public transport strike in the city. Finally, some fellow workers get on the bus one evening to argue with him. Noticing Chantal, they begin to use increasingly obscene language and the driver has to endure their humiliating taunts before he can get them off the bus. With his pride wounded, he becomes aware of the dilemma he faces. If he decides to carry through in his relationship with Chantal, he will have to give up part of his social life and the respect of other people. In another significant sequence, Chantal in turn realises that their relationship is impossible. The driver is having a lover's quarrel with his wife, who is sitting on the bus across from the girl. Chantal stares jealously at the beautiful, mature woman before suddenly asking to get off the bus. Faced with a reality beyond her control, she prefers to flee, if only momentarily, rather than adjust to it. Still, she stays true to her fantasy and cannot bring herself to end the relationship, seeing these incidents as mere temporary obstacles. It is the driver who instigates the break-up, shortly after this sequence. One evening, Chantal is shocked to see a new bus driver. *Her* driver must finally have chosen between his two lives and has taken the coward's way out by deciding not to see the teenager again. His indifference is the worst kind of cruelty because he ends their innocent romance by dropping Chantal without even giving her an explanation.

Chantal is so shocked that she completely forgets about getting on the bus: in one last shot, the doors close on her stricken face.

A sonatina in F major, background music for the ending of Chantal's story, provides the rhythm for a dance of empty buses leaving the depot to drive off into the night. For the space of one shot, we see the lights on a ship leaving port in the distance. An empty bus travels along the docks, nearly hitting a young girl who is walking alone down the road. This is Louisette. The link between the two girls is violent and ephemeral, as if the sad ending of Chantal's story, symbolised by the bus now empty of passengers, had just warned Louisette about the heartache that lies ahead. But Louisette is more of a tomboy, more rebellious, more adventurous. Feeling the same desire for tenderness as her friend, she has chosen headlong flight towards it. It is a senseless flight, an escape into the unknown guided by a fantasy of exoticism and secrecy. For that reason, her brief love story does not emerge from everyday life as it does for Chantal, but is part of the dark, cold world of a shipboard; her Prince Charming is a Bulgarian sailor who does not speak French. The sailor, surprised at first by the girl's intrusion, gradually softens before finally entering into a chaste game of seduction. Louisette, rather more skittish, lets him get close to her but ducks questions about why she has run away. When the sailor asks her in approximate Franglais, '*Why partir?*' she replies simply, '*I don't know*'. Her final, categorical answer is '*Because*'. But words do not matter – Louisette and the sailor soon have no use for them in their relationship. Both take pleasure in their incomprehensible dialogue. When he tries to seduce her and caresses her face, she pulls back at first and says *no*. In refusing, she shakes her head, but the sailor lets her know with a smile that in his language, the sign for *no* means *yes*. He repeats his request and Louisette cheekily replies *no* while nodding her head *yes*. Yes, no, maybe… The connection between them is beyond language, and lies instead in actions. The two of them begin a game of hide-and-seek when other sailors appear, during which they dance a strange *ronde* around the ship. As they do so, they become even more attentive to one another, exchanging looks and caresses.

In Louisette's hands, the Walkman becomes a device through which to express the strange new feelings she is experiencing. When she suddenly begins to cry in the arms of the sailor, the Walkman turns on, and her voice says: 'He didn't have to say a word to console me. He only had to be there.' The sailor does not need to hear these words to understand her, but he also knows that their relationship is doomed to fail. In an attempt to get her to understand the absurdity of the situation and to console her, he gives Louisette his cap and jacket, turning her into the sailor that she wanted to be when she came to stow away on the ship. He borrows her raincoat and Walkman and imitates her words: 'please, mister sailor, I want to stay. Partir, on the boat.' Louisette does not belong on the ship. The sailor tells her: 'Maybe I'll come back one day' but the change in his tone of voice betrays his lack of conviction. Louisette, a prisoner of her naïveté, still does not understand him. Again, the Walkman speaks for her: 'I had lots of plans for him. I wanted us to travel together, for us to love each other. Not saying anything, watching the sea.' Covering his eyes so as not to see her, he asks her to leave, and she does so after giving him a furtive farewell kiss. There is no missing the bitter irony of the situation: the sailor, who does not speak Louisette's language, still manages to make her understand the reasons for what he is doing, whereas the bus driver had fled from Chantal like a coward. If the break-up here seems gentle, however, this somber, melancholy moment nevertheless marks a cruel end to Louisette's hopes for tenderness and the beginning of a period of withdrawal. She had looked for this tenderness in someone who could have taken her away, taken her under his wing to lead her toward adulthood. But the sailor has chosen to leave alone. Symbolically, the shot of a bus catching fire in the bus garage reminds us that Chantal has suffered a similar fate, and ends the second movement on a sad and desperate note.

Next comes the re-exposition, and the meeting of the two teenagers. In a few sequences, Lanctôt shows their boredom with daily life, which unfolds in a sterile suburban world. Chantal and Louisette stroll through arid scenery, go roller-skating past tidy buildings in deserted suburbs, and spend their afternoons in metro stations where no one arrives. Their favourite spaces remain deserted and anonymous. Later, in Louisette's bedroom, they lie on her bed waiting in vain for someone to lift them out of their existential ennui. These sequences may show why these two girls went in search of love in the first place. Is it not likely that Chantal and Louisette went looking for tenderness to escape this world? Similarly, is it not likely that they created a separate, more poetic world – with the Walkman as both its symbol and tool – in order to escape this ennui? Together, they whisper things that no one else can hear, exchanging cassettes and experiences. These scenes, which remove the girls from the outside world, obviously refer to their failed adventures, particularly Louisette's. For here, once again, words seem unimportant. The two friends understand each other, while the world around them does not. In two short sequences, Lanctôt demonstrates their isolation from their parents, who are incapable of seeing that the girls are going through emotional turmoil. In the first shot-sequence, Louisette sits through an argument between her parents. While she eats breakfast, the camera keeps her in the centre of the shot while her parents move in and out of view, gesturing and screaming without registering her presence. We know nothing about how the argument began or what it is about, and it is drowned out by the sounds of the teenager chewing, which gradually take over the soundtrack. These internal sounds cut the girl off from her parents, just as they have left her out of their quarrel. Chantal reacts in the same way a few sequences later: the principal of the school has confiscated her Walkman and is playing the cassette for her parents. Stripped of her intimacy, violated by her parents' intrusion into her private world, Chantal defends herself from this act of aggression by covering her ears to block out the principal's lecturing.

While these scenes are palpable indicators of existential malaise, it is nevertheless difficult to understand why a senseless act such as suicide might have seemed the only possible means of escape. Here, Lanctôt is careful not to give a simplistic explanation of teen suicide. Through these sequences, she shows above all that Chantal and Louisette do not really see suicide as a choice, but rather as an absence of choice. Their isolation is neither sudden nor deliberate. It develops slowly, as if, having considered every solution for overcoming their malaise, they had finally resigned themselves to it, seeing suicide as the only way out. In their search for a solution, they even go to the school counselling office and provocatively ask a psychologist how many pills it would take to commit suicide. The psychologist, who responds unemotionally to this disturbing question, simply signals them to have a seat and wait. Suicide becomes a last act of provocation aimed at adults who have been unable to show the girls any tenderness or understanding, and who have failed to listen to them. That is why they choose to carry it out in a public place – the metro. Turning their suicide threat into a public act is a way of making one final appeal for help. Sitting in the metro, they set a sign out in plain view that reads: 'Oh indifferent world, we are going to die, you must stop us, do something!' It would suffice for a single person to take this threat seriously and strike up a discussion with the teenagers to stop them from going through with it.

What is shocking in this last sequence is not the act of suicide in itself, but the indifference in the midst of which it is carried out. Although the sign is positioned in such a way as to draw the attention of the people in the metro station, they show nothing but disdain. No one in the metro steps in, not even the policeman on the train, who faces the teenagers like a passive observer, just like everyone else. Through these passengers, these anonymous strangers, the director seems to be challenging the viewer directly: is suicide not the result of our indifference, our egoism, our failure to understand a clumsily-expressed need for love? That being the case, the act itself is carried out with troubling gentleness and apathy. There is no abrupt action, no violence in the girls' decision to end their lives. Chantal and Louisette, resigned to the idea of dying, still hold onto childish things to the very end. They eat the pills as though they were candies, washing them down with chocolate milk. Death comes calmly in an atmosphere of general indifference, as Chantal and Louisette fall asleep side by side. The steady shots and long silences, broken only by the sound of the automatic doors, poignantly convey the sense of abandonment that weighs on this final sequence. Chantal and Louisette are forgotten even in death: the conductor whose job it is to check that no one is left in the station at the end of the day stands a few feet away from them without seeing them. Startled by an announcement over the loudspeakers that the general strike has begun, he leaves without finding the two bodies, abandoning them in the deserted metro station. Lingering one last time over the bodies, Lanctôt ends her sonatina like a requiem: her two anti-heroines have left the world as discreetly as they lived in it. They have left through the back door, the door for the world's rejected who, like Albert Camus' 'Outsider', have gained nothing from their earthly existence save the bitter realisation that they have not lived for anything or anyone. At the end of Camus' novel, the condemned man signs on behalf of all these lost souls an epitaph that we might have heard on Chantal and Louisette's Walkman: 'And I, too, felt ready to start life all over again. It was as if that great rush of anger had washed me clean, emptied me of hope, and, gazing up at the dark sky spangled with its signs and stars, for the first time, the first, I laid my heart open to the benign indifference of the universe.'

Damien Detchberry
Translated from French by Kathy Durnin

FOSTER CHILD

GIL CARDINAL, 1987

From modest beginnings as a student taking courses in filmmaking at the Northern Alberta Institute of Technology (NAIT) and as a cameraman at Access Network (both in Edmonton), Gil Cardinal has moved on to become a critically acclaimed director with more than thirty documentaries and dramas to his credit.

Cardinal's productivity has likewise been matched by numerous honours from his peers. Since receiving a Gemini Award for *Foster Child* in 1988, he has gone on to win Best of the Festival at the 1994 Alberta Film Awards for *Our Home and Native Land,* Best of Festival for *David with F.A.S.* at the 1997 Dreamspeakers Festival, and Best Story/Script at the American Indian Film Festival in 1998 for *Big Bear.* His most recent production, *Totem: The Return of the G'psgolox Pole*, won acclaim at the ImagineNative Film Festival in Toronto in 2003 (winning the Alanis Obomsawin Best Documentary Award) as well as at the Environment Film Festival in Washington, DC in 2004. A National Aboriginal Achievement Award, received in the midst of all of these accolades, recognises not only his accomplishments as an aboriginal filmmaker but also establishes his role as both model and mentor to the next generation of aspiring film-makers.

While it is beyond the scope of this chapter to do justice to the history of the National Film Board of Canada (NFB), I do want to note that they invited Cardinal to join their Aboriginal Filmmaking Program (AFP) in 2004, thereby further confirming his mentoring role. The NFB, according to their website, allocates over $1 million a year to support Canadian Aboriginal film-makers, a sum that represents approximately one-quarter of their operating budget. To date, the AFP has sponsored twenty-four documentaries. Some of these productions are by well-established filmmakers like Alanis Obomsawin and Gil Cardinal, but others, such as Nancy Trites Botkin and Daniel Prouty's *For Angela* (1995), Loretta Todd's *Forgotten Warriors* (1996) and Doug Cuthand's *Patrick's Story* (1999) highlight a growing cadre of talented Aboriginal directors. Whether dealing with foster care, army veterans, or the repatriation of tribal arte-facts, an emerging tradition of Aboriginal documentary filmmaking continues to explore and address issues related to individual and community healing.

In this chapter, I will focus on one of the award-winning director's many films, *Foster Child*, made for the National Film Board in 1987. His autobiographical strategies, or his creative use of film for self-representation, merit close examination because Cardinal's Aboriginal identity, as well as his subsequent reputation as one of Canada's foremost Aboriginal filmmakers, is firmly grounded in this documentary. It marks an important transition point between such early films as *Children of Alcohol* (1984) and *Discussions in Bioethics: The Courage of One's Convictions* (1985), which tackle contentious issues, and the majority of his later films that emphasise Native themes.

In interview, Cardinal has said that he did not set out in search of Native identity; what began primarily as a search for self-worth led to its reclamation. For him, the two matters are inseparable. Negative self-worth is posited in relation to the primary issue of abandonment. His view of self as an unwanted child co-exists with being ashamed of being Indian, due to his limited exposure to Native people: 'When you don't know, you distance yourself from everything', he says in *Foster Child*. 'I had a safe and secure life. I didn't see brown skin around me. I gradually became self-conscious.' Less prominent but still present and unresolved in the film is the prospect of uncovering a secondary issue of trauma that may have occurred prior to his placement with the Wilson family.

Foster Child, like Obomsawin's *Richard Cardinal: Cry from a Diary of a Métis Child* (1986) and Cuthand's *Patrick's Story*, fits within the contours of a larger historical trauma that Ojibway writer Drew Hayden Taylor, in his book *Funny, You Don't Look Like One*, refers to as 'the scoop up'. Alienation is posited as the normative condition for the many Indian and Metis children who have been taken from their birth families and extended kin groups by government-sanctioned policies and agencies to spend their formative years in foster care, residential, mission and convent schools, or adopted out into non-Native families. Gil Cardinal, Richard Cardinal and Patrick Bird are similarly caught in the autobiographical paradox of self-representation that, consistent with Leigh Gilmore's schema for trauma-based autobiography, makes the individual unique and yet representative of many. Cardinal's awareness of this autobiographical paradox is fully evident in his expressed understanding of the political importance of the film – it fits comfortably into both the classroom and the counselling group where it may be used to help others.

Foster Child differs from these other NFB productions, however, in that it is autobiograph-ical and it foregrounds the challenge of resisting neatly-packaged resolutions; his assertion that 'life is a lot messier than art' easily serves as the thesis for a life narrative that must be constructed from fragments. This in itself might provide a basis for adopting a victim stance, yet *Foster Child* is not an exposé on victimisation, vis-à-vis Obomsawin's portrayal of the tragic 17-year-old Richard Cardinal who commits suicide after being shunted through 28 foster situations. Rather, Cardinal avoids such an approach by strategically framing his search for his biological family with scenes that display his foster family's affection for him and their approval of his project. The Wilson family is an ongoing source of inclusiveness and security from the opening scene at their kitchen table to his being welcomed at a Wilson-family wedding at the end. He may make a self-referential claim to difference – brown skin and a name that is 'not-Wilson' – but it is uttered within the context of displaying photos that show he is part of their family. Belonging encloses his search for his mother, Lucy, and informs his final assessment of his situation: he concludes in *Foster Child* that 'I belong to two realities: I have two mothers, two families, and two cultures.'

The autobiographical subject who admits to being 'ashamed of Indian drunks', who thinks it important 'to look Indian, to be Metis' and not like a 'little brown white man' when he visits Uncle Simon, and who sees Lucy as a 'hard Indian' clearly exposes his, and likewise other foster children's, vulnerability to the 'dialectical magic' of essentialist definitions of 'Indianness' that contribute to low self-worth. He decides to retain his negative reaction to his Mother's photo as evidence of self-honesty, yet in a 2002 interview with Jerry White and William Beard (collected in their volume *North of Everything*), he admits that the comment about Lucy distressed and embarrassed him when viewed after the fact. From this we can conclude that the subject position is a learned position; a positive self-image grows out of learning to recognise internalised stereotypes and resist perpetuating them. His newly emergent bicultural Metis identity acknowledges a diverse range of possible Aboriginal experiences and is, therefore, a rejection of victim-models.

Cardinal occupies an urban 'boundary zone' in a strategic refusal of the 'homecoming' trope. The imagined 'homecoming' that symbolises healing and reclamation of Native identity in such fictional works as Scott Momaday's *House Made of Dawn* (1966) and Leslie Silko's *Ceremony* (1977) is too simplistic to account for Indian heritages that have been so severely altered by historical contingencies as to make 'homecoming' virtually impossible. 'To be home', as suggested by Cree writer Neal McLeod in his essay 'Coming Home Through Stories' (part of Armand Ruffo's anthology *(Ad)Dressing Our Words: Aboriginal Perspective on Aboriginal Literatures*), means 'to dwell within the landscape of the familiar, a landscape of collective memories'. Since Cardinal neither dwells in his mother's Colling Lake landscape nor shares any experiences or memories with his blood relations, he exhibits what McLeod calls a contemporary Native experience of spatial and ideological diaspora, or exile, from 'home'. *Foster Child* thus tacitly suggests that those who have been dislocated from their origins cannot lay claim, as does Neal McLeod, to a more 'traditional' focus on landscape, language and collective experience as the basis for identity. Rather, the dislocated exile must explore alternative modes of connection.

Foster Child, consistent with Phillipe Lejeune's formula for autobiography, is autobiography in the first-person in that the multiple roles of the subject (the enunciating self who tells the story, the narrating 'I' and the protagonist) merge with the proper name of a real individual. The real individual, Gil Cardinal, co-ordinates and stars in the search, but his own memory cannot provide the glue that gives coherence to self-representation. The autobiographical subject neither knows his family nor is known by them; he has no memory and must rely on others to fill in the gaps. Autobiography is here created from third-person testimony. Positioning himself as the generic 'foster child' is an important strategy that forces the viewer to rethink the role of memory in autobiography.

At the same time, however, the orality of film readily lends itself to the creation of what Arnold Krupat, in *The Voice in the Margin,* defines as a 'dialogic model of the self'; the Native self 'most typically is not constituted by the achievement of a distinctive, special voice that separates it from others', according to Krupat, 'but, rather, by the achievement of a particular placement in relation to the many voices without which it could not exist'. David Brumble, in his *American Indian Autobiography*, confirms the fluidity of the 'dialogic model' and notes that oral conventions have previously been adapted to fit written as-told-to life narratives, making it impossible, for example, for John Neihardt to record Black Elk's story without the corroborating testimony of other Oglalas. Historically, Aboriginal oral life narratives upheld high standards of corroboration, according to Brumble, and witnesses were 'privileged to make corrections'. While oral cultures rely on the mediating role of witnesses to provide an important system of checks and balances against fraudulent claims, they strategically serve *Foster Child* as mediators who reinterpret Lucy's life and therefore challenge the official Family Services narrative.

Cardinal's reclamation of the present through a process of reinterpreting a history that can never be relived closely parallels Mary Evans' view of autobiography, put forward in her book *Missing Persons: The Impossibility of Auto/biography*. The task of reinterpreting history through a 'dialogic model' is accomplished through a series of interviews and personal encounters that lead the generic 'foster child' to re-evaluate the issue of abandonment and subsequently to revalue self as a worthy subject. Ultimately, Cardinal demonstrates a relativist perspective that autobiography is a genre whose conventions and readers are subject to historical change and open to diverse forms of self-expression, a position Philippe Lejeune puts forward in his essay 'The Autobiographical Pact', in the book *On Autobiography*. When viewed from this relativist perspective, Cardinal does not so much strain Western autobiographical conventions to the limits, as Leigh Gilmore suggests in *The Limits of Autobiography*, her analysis of trauma-dominated autobiography, as modify the indigenous oral life narrative to suit the needs of a twentieth-century aboriginal filmmaker.

In *Foster Child,* the camera bears witness to multiple 'truths': a thick case-file, a Ward of the Court document, three photos, and his mother's obituary verify one truth – a life defined by Social Services. Witnesses on the other hand, interact with the subject to verify connections, contradictions and alternative points of view. I would also include here the possibility that the camera and the viewers are enlisted as *ad hoc* witnesses in the accretion of conflicting evidence that supports reinterpretation. Film documents both material evidence and dialogic performance between the subject who has no memories and those who contribute their memories and speculations to the construction of his narrative. In the end, we, the audience, corroborate the competing truths that surface in *Foster Child* and constitute him as a Native subject.

One of the advantages of film, Cardinal has said, is that it is 'more visceral and its impact more immediate'. In this respect, performance makes every rupture transparent and every effort to establish a connection across those ruptures a joint experience of the subject's hopes and disappointments. The viewer can empathise with Cardinal's frustration in the face of institutional policy. The camera records and the viewers see Clara the Welfare worker perform the official narrative. Dialogic interaction is present here but censored by institutional policy. Clara is visibly distressed by the prospect of disclosing confidential information and selectively extracts tidbits from his case-file. Viewers see her avert her gaze and hear the hesitancy in her voice when she tells him that his mother never came back for him … that she was in jail on an alcohol-related offence … that he was encoded 'neglected'.

Oral testimony creates connections with family members and places that were previously outside of his experience. The viewer is a witness, for example, to Uncle Simon's observation that Cardinal is 'a big man, just like my Dad, I guess'. Uncle Simon's memory of his father, like the photo of Lucy that Cardinal receives at this time, corroborates a connection between the past and the present and the subject latches onto both in the search for correspondences. Louis Owens, writing in his book *I Hear the Train*, acknowledges the poignancy of one's longing to find signs of self in old photos, especially when other evidence is in short supply; 'to gaze upon a photograph', he says, 'is to appropriate into our own originary history the object of the photography. I cannot deny that I am attempting to appropriate a kind of "Indianness" into my life'.

Lucy's photo connects the subject to his mother, to the unfamiliar landscape of Colling Lake, and has ongoing importance here in relation to a second photo that Cardinal's sister-in-law Linda (married to his brother Donnie) introduces during a later conversation. Cardinal identifies with the young Lucy of the first photo but not, as previously mentioned, with the older, more embittered Lucy of the second photo: 'She looks like a hard Indian. I'm not prepared for that', he says. Prepared or not, however, the strongest connection made between the two brothers and their mother occurs here where all are historically fixed in photographs and film as two generations scarred by 'the scoop up', the defining point of alienation. Lucy's images, caught between two points in time, create a striking before-and-after contrast. In one, she is a naïve young woman whose mission school experience left her unprepared for the demands of motherhood or the harsh realities of urban living. In the other image she is an older woman, sick and living on welfare, who might logically seek to escape the conditions of extreme poverty by drinking. Linda also alludes to Donnie's life in terms of before-and-after: she situates the mission school experience as the transitional point between the innocent child and the moody, heavy drinking artist that she remembers. Cardinal's identification here with Donnie's alienation has to be inferred from an earlier comment that 'I'm still the kid who hid under the table at the Wilsons" and a later admission to being guarded and unable to accept love.

The importance of a 'dialogic model of self' to this documentary is particularly evident when the now adult 'foster child' interacts with four women who serve as Lucy's defence; they are sources of memory, wisdom and experience. The process of reinterpreting an official history of abandonment and neglect gains momentum through their memories and speculations. One individual known only as 'my Mother's niece' remembers Lucy as 'very lonely' and alludes to Lucy keeping tabs on Cardinal's growth. Another woman, identified as 'my last social worker' further develops the idea that Lucy continued to care about her son. She recalls in the film that Lucy 'had to give [Cardinal] up for adoption' but not for 'cruelty or neglect or anything'. She further verifies that Lucy had written a letter explaining her attempt to provide her son with an education and a way out of poverty.

Maria Campbell continues the process of reinterpretation by going so far as to posit abandonment as an act of love. The *kokum* (the Cree word meaning 'your Grandmother') of Canadian Native writing is the bridge between texts, generations and gender experiences.

Campbell, as the author of the classic Metis memoir *Halfbreed* (1973), is positioned here as a woman eminently qualified to function as an advocate for the now-silenced Lucy and as a surrogate mother for the abandoned adult-child who 'can't fathom why a mother would give up her baby willingly'. Campbell responds by telling him in *Foster Child*, 'You've never been sick or poor or without a job. I could understand.' Donnie's wife Linda completes the process of reinterpretation when she recollects that Lucy 'sort of gave you away so someone else could take good care of you, that's the impression I got'.

Ultimately, the worthy subject comes into being as a result of the dialogic relationship between self and many others. The dialogic process exposes the competing truths that stand between the subject and Lucy and so is foundational to the notion of reinterpreting history. Multiple voices represent a consensus of opinion formed at the level of community, which has a cumulative effect of challenging both a personal truth of being an unwanted child ('I always assumed I was a one night stand or something') and an official truth of being 'neglected'. This alternate truth of abandonment as an act of love defuses the indictment against Lucy's perceived lack of care and shifts the responsibility outward as a critique against the society that sanctioned 'the scoop up'.

In conclusion, Cardinal creates a particularly poignant view of the foster child's dislocation and search for a connection to origins; it is a daunting obstacle course strewn with fragments, red herrings and dead ends. His documentary opens up many questions about the role of memory in autobiographical practices, particularly with respect to the generic figure of the foster child who neither knows nor is known. Oral testimony forms the basis for a 'dialogic model of self'; it conveys the importance of third-person memories in corroborating origins and reinterpreting history and so is key to constituting identity. We see at the end of the film that acceptance is a mixed bag of contradictory feelings about what was lost and what was gained as a result of Lucy's sacrifice. The acceptance of a Native heritage and Metis identity is a beginning point for an exploration of self that is, by his own admission, unfinished. *Foster Child* successfully combines Western and indigenous autobiographical forms to create a bicultural life narrative. The bringing together of the contemporary view of autobiography as a means of reinterpreting history with an indigenous view of a dialogically-created self whose identity is constituted by an ongoing relationship between the one and the many effectively demonstrates that autobiography is always an experimental genre.

Colleen Irwin

I'VE HEARD THE MERMAIDS SINGING

PATRICIA ROZEMA, 1987

The reality of the 'two solitudes' is all too glaringly obvious in the mutual ignorance displayed towards each others' films by Quebec filmmakers and all other Canadian filmmakers respectively. On the one hand, most francophones refuse to acknowledge the strong Canadian roots of a filmmaker like David Cronenberg, whereas in English Canada, the names of Léa Pool, André Forcier or Jean Pierre Lefebvre, all prolific directors, arouse a certain mild interest, but rarely provoke serious discussion. And what does it mean to talk about a made-in-Canada star system? The major stars of Quebec television can walk the streets of Toronto in total anonymity. And according to mischievous gossip in Montreal, Halifax or Vancouver even the majority of English-speaking Canadian actors have exactly the same problem.

Any discussion of Canadian cinema as a whole has to come to grips with this indifference and with its unsettling effects. We cannot go on ignoring our geographic, cultural and linguistic situation when we peer down on the work of a filmmaker from the Prairies or the Maritimes through a Quebec-centered lens. Quebec film critics, myself among them, have focused their attention on Europe, the United States, and more recently Asia, and show little interest in the technical evolution of directors like Anne Wheeler, Bruce MacDonald or Michael Jones. Unless they receive the accolade of prestigious festivals – abroad, if possible – English-Canadian films cause scarcely a ripple on the screens of Montreal, Quebec's largest city and a solid bastion of film buffs. But even this bastion has its limits and its likes and dislikes, and is ever more gravely endangered by the skittishness of distributors, the tyranny of multiplex cinemas and the financial precariousness of an institution as well-known and universally respected as the Cinemathèque québécoise.

This context of persistent indifference – albeit punctuated by the odd burst of enthusiasm – makes it hard to catch the attention of the cinema-going public, which at the best of times tends to be a bit fickle, and set in its often deeply entrenched prejudices. And this is why any movie that manages to break through the barrier of cultural resistance is an honourable exception. Patricia Rozema's first feature film, *I've Heard the Mermaids Singing* (1987) is surely one of the rare made-in-Canada films that have made an impression on the Quebec scene. (The title of the film is taken from Rozema's favorite poem, T. S. Eliot's *The Love Song of J. Alfred Prufrock*; for a long time the working title of the film was *Oh, The Things I've Seen*.)

Quebec movie-goers are no different from other Canadians in responding to international approval; the triumphant success of Rozema's film abroad did a lot to arouse interest at home. Even the characters in the film refer to Canadian artists' obsession with gaining recognition elsewhere. The work of the artist on display in the art gallery which is the main setting of the film has value only insofar as 'New York is crazy about him'.

Polly Vandersma (Sheila McCarthy) is an incompetent Girl Friday who gets a job as secretary in the art gallery, The Church Gallery, run by Gabrielle St Peres (Paule Baillargeon). Moody, shy, awkward and more or less sexless, Polly is captivated by her sophisticated boss, whom she calls 'The Curator'. Naturally curious, not to say nosey, with or without her camera, Polly uncovers other facets of Gabrielle's personality: her past relationships with various men; another relationship, more or less over, with Marie Joseph, an artist (Ann-Marie MacDonald); her disappointed creative aspirations; and finally her intransigence and her duplicity. For Polly thinks that the paintings in Gabrielle's chic apartment – vast canvases of white light like great television screens – are her boss's work. The night after Gabrielle's birthday party, she steals one and hangs it in the gallery where it receives a rave review from an art critic – to Gabrielle's discomfort, since Polly acted without consulting her. The paintings are actually by Marie Joseph.

It is at this point that the suggestion of contempt creeps into the love story, when Polly, using a pseudonym, sends to the gallery a random selection of the photos she has taken in her wanderings. Gabrielle, who naturally does not know the true identity of the artist, pronounces them 'trite'. This blow is soon followed by another, more difficult for Polly to take, when she discovers that the paintings are by Marie Joseph. Since Gabrielle has the greater cachet in the art world, the fraud nets them a tidy sum. Hidden in the dim light under a bench in the gallery, and revealed by the luminosity of the canvases that are being unpacked by Gabrielle and Marie Joseph, Polly hurls herself in fury at her boss, and flees from the scene with her video-camera containing the record of this decisive encounter. Until Gabrielle and Marie Joseph turn up at her door, a moment when reality finally catches up with Polly after a ninety-minute escapade in her life, moving between memories (the representation of her meeting with Gabrielle), dreams (her fantasies which recur four times throughout the film when she imagines she is wealthy, elegant, learned, and so on) and confession (the video segment).

Characters dressed in period costume, special effects (Sheila McCarthy flying across the Toronto sky or hanging on to skyscrapers), colour (Polly's recent past) alternating with black and white (her dreams, with the exception of the one when, after taking her vengeance on Gabrielle, she pictures herself as an orchestral conductor – in Technicolor) and with video tape (the depressing reality of being yet again an out-of-work secretary), all kinds of small but engaging and even outrageous details give a certain flair to the film which was shot in 23 days on a budget of $350,000. There are no big names connected with the production – unless you count (for French-speaking audiences) the presence of Paule Baillargeon. Patricia Rozema had to struggle to get funding for her first feature and to overcome the nervousness of distributors, so she could hardly have imagined that her film would be selected for the prestigious directors' fortnight at Cannes. Not only did her career get a boost from this showcase presentation and from the Prix de la Jeunesse, but the international exposure was the starting point for what some have called the 'Ontario New Wave' and the 'Renaissance of English-Canadian cinema'. Together with other directors like Peter Mettler (*The Top of His Head* (1989)), Bruce MacDonald (*Roadkill* (1989), *Highway 61* (1991)), and above all Atom Egoyan (*Family Viewing* (1987), *The Adjuster* (1991), and so on) whose common influences are obvious (mix of film and video; repressed sexuality; dubious identities; problems of communicating), Patricia Rozema pushed a breath of fresh air into a film industry that was succumbing to general indifference and was being swallowed up into generic North American, as if the main feature of Canadian specificity was to be imperceptible.

How is it possible to recognise a film as Canadian, even when it is coasting on a wave dubbed 'new'? What gives *I've Heard the Mermaids Singing* a particularly 'Canadian' identity and label when its poetry, its rhythms and its humour, as they are revealed through the character of Polly, have their origins well beyond the Canada's three coasts? Even Quebec movie-goers who tend to look towards the south rather than towards the east or west set aside their prejudices to join the ranks of the fans of this lonely orphan, whose employers see her as 'organisationally impaired' and seem to give her a job merely out of charity. Some people have compared Polly to the character played by Melanie Griffith in *Working Girl* (Mike Nichols, 1988); one has her head in the clouds (quite literally) and has no particular ambitions for her future, while the other has her feet firmly planted on the ground, all the while making a rapid ascent up the ladder of the firm she is working for.

The English-Canadian 'New Wave' mentioned above was by no means made up of the kinds of former film critics and sons of well-heeled families that gave such a dramatic jolt to the cinematic world in Paris in the 1950s. Their Canadian counterparts were the offspring of immigrants – Rozema comes from a Dutch family who settled in Canada after World War

Two – and came from a background in television; they all belong to the same generation, a generation influenced by technological innovation in image production, and often working on each others' movies. Peter Mettler, for instance, was director of photography and cameraman for the early films of Bruce McDonald (*Knock! Knock!* (1985)), Rozema (*Passion: A Letter in 16mm* (1985)) and Atom Egoyan (*Next of Kin* (1984) and *Family Viewing*); Bruce McDonald did the editing for two films of Atom Egoyan (*Family Viewing* and *Speaking Parts* (1989)); in the collective film *Montréal... vu par*, the two English-Canadian directors invited to turn their gaze on the Quebec metropolis were Atom Egoyan and Patricia Rozema. They all displayed the preoccupations of their generation, namely a profound distrust of politics as well as a propensity towards all forms of instability (in matters of love, finance and jobs), outlining the concerns of their time at a moment when non-communication, urban rootlessness and isolation were becoming the distinctive marks of the cinema of the 1980s. Directors as far apart as Wim Wenders, Jim Jarmusch, Léos Carax, Jean-Jacques Beinex and in Quebec Léa Pool explored these themes. Through hyper-exaggeration, they are often reminiscent of advertising strategies, and also of music videos blown up for the big screen during these years like advertising tools for a run-down music industry. The aesthetic codes used by these directors (gigantic lofts, abandoned industrial parks, highways stretching into infinity, and the use of the video as a means of communication – the postmodern version of the confession-box) would soon become stereotypes, not to say clichés, rather than genuine signature marks of the filmmaker.

Rozema escapes neither the fads of her time nor the influences of her peer group, nor the desire, quite clearly stated – though not to the point of absurdity – of presenting the typically Canadian, not to say Ontarian, aspects of her film. A desire that is becoming less and less evident in her filmography if *White Room* (1990) and *When Night is Falling* (1995) are anything to go by, which are equally ethereal but more serious in tone. She has even ventured into the realm of the English novelist Jane Austen with *Mansfield Park* (1999). This is a far cry from Toronto, the city where Polly is anchored. In *I've Heard the Mermaids Singing,* the capital of the most populous and most wealthy province in the country is considerably more than a 'zone of absence' (which is what Geoff Pevere calls it in his essay 'La nouvelle vague ontarienne'). Often disguised as an anonymous North American, not to say typically American, city Toronto is still a place cherished by Hollywood, especially for economic reasons, but rarely shows off its cinematographic specificity. Some filmmakers are at pains to camouflage the CN Tower, the city's distinguishing landmark, which Rozema refuses to do. And just in case a foreign audience missed the reference to the setting of the film at the beginning, the director rammed home her point by sticking a Canadian flag on to Polly's touque (another useful object in these parts!) during her aerial – and imaginary – wanderings through the Toronto sky.

Beyond these few 'made in Canada' inscriptions (none of which is underwritten by politicians sadly lacking in patriotic pride), *I've Heard the Mermaids Singing* stands out as a 'Canadian' film in several ways: in the modesty of its production costs, the ambiguity of the characters' identity, and the non-resolution of the dramatic stakes, in a typically Canadian finale, avoiding confrontation to lose itself in the immensity of the landscape.

The whole of Canadian cinema occupies what is often merely a symbolic presence on a world scale and it is often the same back home. This marginality is not just a posture, it is, first and foremost, an incontrovertible reality of Rozema's film, as it was for so many of her fellow directors' films, whether they belonged to the 'Ontario New Wave' or not. The increased presence of video imagery in Canadian cinema of that time, for instance, was a response to an aesthetic concern, creating a deceptively realist image and a sense of closeness to the characters, but at the same time allowing – with very little effort – the insertion of images captured in another take with bigger resources. In addition to the films of Egoyan and Rozema, several other filmmakers, among them some from Quebec, have gradually incorporated videos and their falsely interpreted 'realist' aesthetic into their films. François Bouvier and Jean Baudry's *Jacques et Novembre* (1984) is one of the most striking examples of this technique. This grainy, impoverished appearance, with no depth of field, underlined the poverty and sense of urgency of the person who had made it, namely Polly, who, by placing herself off-centre showed both her amateurism and her spontaneity. Yet the character is conscious of communicating with an audience, looking straight at the camera to show she is in earnest, even though the whole film represents only her – highly subjective – point of view. The other two characters really only exist in the very last scene of the film, and not through the filter of the narrator's memory, when Gabrielle and Marie Joseph discover Polly's secret hiding place and interrupt her video confession.

The deliberately imprecise identity of this strange trio (this holy trinity?) depends on various devices, beginning with the names of the protagonists, who, in the case of Gabrielle and Marie Joseph, share in the frequent religious references in the film, but also evoke a certain sexual ambivalence. Gabrielle St Peres obviously puts us in mind of an angel, who, as we all know, has no sex at all. And Marie Joseph evokes a famous man/woman couple, the only one in the history of mankind, to have conceived a child solely through divine intervention. Rozema dares, not without a certain derision, to attach this name to the character whose homosexuality is the most clearly indicated, refusing both social hypocrisy (like Gabrielle's) and the erotic sublimation of her desires, which Polly achieves through videos and photography.

Gabrielle may speak in a weird accent that is meant to be Swiss – though its idiosyncratic intonation patterns would not fool anyone who knows anything about Quebec French – and Marie Joseph may be more concerned with trumpeting her lesbianism than in revealing her partner's artistic-cum-financial swindles, but it is Polly who is the most complex and ambivalent character in the film. Twenty years earlier, she would probably have taken up her pen to tell her story, but since she belonged to the generation director Denys Arcand termed 'visually challenged' in his movie *Le Declin de l'empire américain* (*The Decline of the American Empire*, 1986; see Peter Harcourt's chapter on the film in this volume), Polly plunked herself in front of a video camera, punctuating her speech with frequent hesitations, cowering glances, malapropisms ('pseudo name' for 'pseudonym', 'bachelorette' for 'bachelor girl') and bathetic philosophical considerations ('Isn't life the strangest thing you've ever seen?'). And contrary to what the viewer may have been thinking throughout the film, Polly's confession, in addition to its spontaneous and highly subjective side – since the other characters exist only through her eyes – ends up as extremely fragile, for no trace of it will remain. Whereas the audio tape, unlike a video film, can be reused, Polly's image and voice can only be transmitted via her camera screen, which contributes to the volatile, fleeting nature of her communication. What is more, she wields the dual power of being able to turn off her video camera *and* Rozema's; the final shot where she turns round to face the 'other' camera, and hence the viewer, illustrates the ephemeral, crazy and almost unreal side to this story.

Described by the director as 'someone you wouldn't talk to at a dinner party', Polly is in no way a social being, belonging rather, in Geoff Prevere's words, to the class of 'confused and stunned witnesses to the story'. She is constantly putting her foot in it (the scene in the Japanese restaurant is one of the funniest in the film), or, paralysed by the fear of the unknown (in this case the contemporary art world) she turns up at Gabrielle's birthday party after all the other guests have left. Polly's feeling of alienation, her problems in communicating, and expressing clearly her ideas and in asserting herself in surroundings where she has mastered neither the code nor the language make her an eternal loser, an emblematic figure of a whole sector of Canadian cinema, past and present. Unlike popular Hollywood films in which modest folk manage to break though class barriers, mainly through their own efforts, Polly, like some of Egoyan's characters – though without their cynicism and despair – uses aids to communication (videos, photography) to counter her evident difficulties in communicating, and in expressing her sexuality. Rozema refuses categorically to give a label to Polly's sexual orientation, itself an act of courage since it flies in the face of the comfortably obvious formulas used by various American filmmakers. In Gabrielle, is Polly seeking the reassuring power of a mother, the soothing authority of a mentor or the enveloping warmth of a lover? Polly takes her secret away with her, along with Marie Joseph, who has been included in the grand finale of reconciliation where the landscape is reminiscent of Group of Seven paintings: a typically Canadian image if ever there was one.

The international success of *I've Heard the Mermaids Singing* naturally gave a boost to Rozema's career for a while, as well as to the reputation abroad of English-Canadian cinema, which is all too often assimilated into American independent cinema, with which it shares the same language, and the same propensity for a lugubrious, schizophrenic universe. Like all waves, they lose their intensity. Rozema's other feature films explore sexual ambiguity and diffi-cult love relationships, but with the exception of her delightful short, *Montréal… vu par,* which also stars Sheila McCarthy, what we do not find again is the lightness of touch, the wry sense of mockery, the constant desire to defuse melodramatic scenarios by flights of imaginative fantasy. This is what gave *I've Heard the Mermaids Singing* its uniqueness, poetry and charm.

And if Polly is indeed a Canadian heroine, constantly apologetic, seeking the approval of others for her right to exist, she is proof that there is no lack of imagination or curiosity or creativity among English-Canadians. High up in the sky, hidden in a tree watching lovers embracing, or transformed into an orchestra conductor, or into an intellectual, the attractive character created by Patricia Rozema is in no way inferior, in terms of neuroses, to Atom Egoyan's, but Rozema treats it all as a joke. Which is a courageous thing to do in a cinema that is not, unfortunately, given to easy laughter.

André Lavoie
Translated from French by Vivian Bosley

LE DÉCLIN DE L'EMPIRE AMÉRICAIN THE DECLINE OF THE AMERICAN EMPIRE

15

DENYS ARCAND, 1986

> The only performing art my father enjoyed was opera … Like him, I have a passion for opera and it shows in some of my films … which are very operatic.
>
> – Denys Arcand

Whether consciously or not, the form of *Le Déclin de l'empire américain* (*The Decline of the American Empire*, 1986), Denys Arcand's mischievous presentation of the privileged lives of a group of academics, is demonstrably operatic. Indeed, in an essay called 'Sound Design and music as *tragédie en musique*', Réal La Rochelle claims that all of Arcand's films are operatic, even the documentaries. Each film, he maintains, is a *tragédie en musique*, with references back to the operas of Jean-Baptiste Lully and to the dramas of Molière and Racine. Certainly, *Le Déclin de l'empire américain* reveals a classical operatic structure: it has a prologue, two acts, and an epilogue – a distinctly non-Hollywood manner of organising a film.

The two initial scenes constitute the Prologue. The opening image reveals the beautiful face of a Vietnamese girl. The camera cuts back to pick up Rémy (Rémy Girard), her professor at the Université de Montréal, as we hear him articulate the three most important things in history: numbers, numbers and numbers. 'That's why', he explains, 'black South Africans are bound to win out some day and black North Americans will probably never make it. History isn't a moral science', he continues, 'legality, compassion and justice are ideas foreign to history.'

As the head credits roll, to the accompaniment of a stately overture by Handel we cut to an extended tracking shot down a lavish arcade, a roller-blader skating past us while the camera continues its onward journey towards two women sitting at the far end of this elongated space. Diane (Louise Portal), a contract instructor in the history department, is interviewing Dominique (Dominique Michel), the Chair of the department. Dominique has just published a book called *Changing Concepts of Happiness*. As the two women stroll back along the arcade, up an escalator and along a university corridor, Dominique explains the thesis of her book. She believes that when the sense of personal happiness takes precedence over the well-being of society, that particular society is in decline.

THE CINEMA OF CANADA 145

These two scenes are, simultaneously, dyadic in organisation and didactic in implication. First of all, in this increasingly globalised world, the only cultures that will survive are those demographically large enough to sustain their sovereignty. Rémy's pessimism about North American blacks parallels the situation of the Québécois, if not of all Canadians; while the face of the Vietnamese student hints at the abundance of non-Europeans who will inevitably soon invade the international marketplace – a hint reinforced by the brief appearance of an African historian, Mustapha. Secondly, because in their different ways all the characters are given over to the immediate gratification of their sensual pleasures, *ipso facto* (according to Dominique) their society is in decline. With the detached eye of cultural anthropologists, we are invited to examine this process at work – with all its pleasures, self-deceptions and, ultimately, its pain.

Unlike many of his colleagues in the 1960s and 1970s – unlike Pierre Perrault, Gilles Groulx, Jaques Leduc and Jean Pierre Lefebvre – Arcand was never caught up in the celebration of Quebec's pastoral tradition. Nor did he ever adopt the approved cinematic style of the day – direct cinema or *cinéma vérité*. Trained as a historian at the Université de Montréal, he was influenced by the pessimistic teachings of Maurice Séguin who believed that the Québécois were, as Arcand himself wrote in a 1987 book called *Maurice Séguin, historien du pays québécois* (edited by Robert Comeau), 'a people condemned to a fate of perpetual mediocrity, until the demographic weight and the pressure of the American empire would finally relegate it to historical oblivion'. (Describing himself, Arcand has said, 'I am a politically oriented person who is a filmmaker, therefore my end product is a politically oriented. If I wasn't a filmmaker, I would be a political newspaperman or a political plumber.')

Arcand's first documentary on Samuel de Champlain (*Champlain*, 1964) was, therefore, more analytical than presentational, more didactic than dialogic. Arcand was interested in power – in the power that, as a Frenchman, de Champlain brought to the establishment of the first French-Canadian colonies in North America and in how he used and abused this power.

Arcand's inquisitive eye has never blinked in the pursuit of this enquiry, whether it be the power of the bosses over the workers in *On est au coton* (*Cotton Mill, Treadmill*, 1970) or the power of money over everything in *Les Invasions Barbares* (*The Barbarian Invasions*, 2003). This concern gives even his least political films their political dimension. But Arcand has never wanted to change the world. Like Luis Buñuel, he wants to perceive it in all its contradictions and to understand why so few people choose to recognise it as it is.

Act One of *Le Déclin de l'empire américain* examines the different modes of power exercised by women and men but with ironic inversion. Utilising the lavish athletic facilities of the university, the women are working out while talking about sex; at the same time as the men, ensconced in a luxurious chalet in the Eastern Townships (a pastoral area just outside Montreal), are preparing an elaborate fish pie while talking about sex. Unless one is aware of the overall structure of the film, this talk might seem offensive, especially by the men. Rémy and Pierre (Pierre Curzi) objectify the women they have been to bed with. 'If I get an erection, I'm in love; if I don't, I'm not', as Pierre proudly declares. Claude (Yves Jacques), the gay character, has another way of describing the thrill of the hunt for sexual intimacy; while Alain (Daniel Brière), a student, hopes that his personal life will not become so promiscuously opportunistic. Although the talk of the women is gentler, more concerned with ridiculing the sexual vanities of their men than with objectifying them, they behave in much the same way – very much in the tradition of a classic French farce or an opera like *Così Fan Tutte*.

As the film cuts back and forth between the scenes with the women and those with the men, Arcand jump-cuts within the scenes as well, establishing a modernist disjunction between image and sound. Although the ubiquity of music videos has nowadays made this stylistic strategy seem all too familiar, in *Le Déclin de l'empire américain*, it might suggest that the talk of this charmingly indiscreet bourgeoisie is always the same, wherever they happen to be.

Fundamentally, however, this editing strategy highlights the dimension of performance, both of the actors and of the filmmaker. Rarely are there group shots. We see two-shots and three-shots – duets and trios, dyads and triads, if you will – which further highlight the performances of the cast. *Le Déclin de l'empire américain* is throughout a performance piece, the delight of which resides less in the referential dimension of the characters than, as with opera, in our appreciation of the virtuosity of the structure as a whole.

An emblem for this film is suggested by a scene that takes place between Rémy and Alain. Mounted on the wall in Rémy's study is the dual existence of the Borneo heteropterix, the male evidently an insect and the female a reptile. They have nothing in common except they mate. Like the arguably different species of women and men, this scene implies, they are bound together solely by sex – by *le cul*.

Act Two begins with the arrival of the women – the women entering screen left; the men, screen right. After they embrace one another, we cut to inside the chalet and the elaborate dinner of fish pie begins.

The talk now is about food but also about teaching – the point at which Diane can protest her lowly position on the academic totem pole while working as a single mom and a contract instructor. Louise (Dorothée Berryman) and Rémy also have children, references to which occur in a number of scenes; but except for a glimpse of Diane's daughter in a flashback, children are absent from the film. Only the gay character Claude wistfully declares that he would like to have had a child. 'Children', he explains, 'are an affirmation of life.'

The dinner conversation is interrupted by the arrival of Mario (Gabriel Arcand), Diane's sexual partner and the disrupter of middle-class *politesse*. Heinz Weinmann, in his book *Cinéma de l'imaginaire québécois*, has suggested that Mario is a caricature of the Québécois of the past – speaking *joual* (a rough, urban dialect of French, heard mostly in Montreal), refusing to eat fish and, preferring, no doubt, a local Molson to an imported pilsner. In his assertive brutality, he is heir to the thugs of *La maudite galette* (1971), Arcand's first feature, an existentialist and very violent heist film. At the same time, even if implausibly, Mario also represents some faith in the future. When leaving Diane after their rough night together, he gives her Michel Brunet's 1976 book *Notre passé, le présent et nous* (the title is shortened in the film – by error? – to *Notre passé présent et nous*), a historical account of the Québécois which is far more affirmative than that of Maurice Séguin, whose theories have had a lasting effect not only upon Arcand but also upon the lubricious historians of the film.

I think of Act Two as having two scenes, continuing the dyadic structure of the film; except that the change occurs more like a dissolve than a cut. *Le Déclin de l'empire américain* has been punctuated throughout by the music of Handel, reworked by François Dompierre. Indeed, if Arcand's script rigorously historicises his characters and incidents, the music of Handel universalises them.

After the dinner party, however, the mood begins to shift. Evening is settling in while the friends take a walk along the shore of the beautiful lac Memphrémagog, the mountains darkling in the background. The tone shifts from that of a French farce by Alfred de Musset to a tragedy by Ingmar Bergman. The autumnal light accompanied by the strains of a solo cello might now make us think less of Jean Renoir's *La Règle du jeu* (1939) than of Bergman's *Through a Glass Darkly* (1961). Pierre delivers his harangue on the tedium of monogamy and when they return inside and have listened to Dominique's recorded interview about our contemporary decline, the ever-trusting Louise suggests that an equally clever person could probably argue exactly the reverse.

Some critics have taken this remark as proof of her essential stupidity. I should like to disagree. Alone amongst the participants, she is not an academic. She is a music teacher – an activity which encourages a different orientation to life than one so dependent on the tyranny of language. Furthermore, as a musician, she must be aware of the transformative potentialities of art. Her intellectual naïveté, her vulnerability, her social blindness (*l'inconscience*) annoys Dominique who is, after all, supremely the intellectual but who also in her private life has been as promiscuous as Pierre. And as if to prove her thesis that the decline in social values is accompanied by the need for instant gratification, Dominique ends by seducing young Alain who, at this stage of his life, is as idealistic as Louise. After Dominique has revealed the extent of Rémy's philandering and the friends have gone to bed anticipating various degrees of pleasure or despair, the Epilogue to this film begins. A new day dawns. Mist is rising from the lake and the characters are recovering from the night before – especially Rémy, who is begging Louise to believe that she is the only woman he really loves and would ever want to live with.

Earlier on, Pierre had cited Wittgenstein, that relentless interrogator of the authority of language, who once claimed that the only certainty in life is the ability to act with the body. While he may not have intended this truth to reside solely within the body's sexual functions, his assertion does help to rationalise existentially the promiscuous behaviour of this declining bourgeoisie. At the end of the film as Alain and Dominique are negotiating a possible future for themselves, she declares, in English, 'Words are cheap, baby', and then adds, 'Touch-moi. Touch-moi, bébé.' As if touch were more reliable.

The word most thrown about when discussing Denys Arcand is cynicism. This word requires scrutiny. Feeling themselves failures as historians, Rémy and Pierre may well appear cynical about their work; and Dominique, to escape the inner rage she feels as a woman, might also behave as opportunistically as the men. Nevertheless, Arcand brings to all his characters an enormous compassion. Self-serving swivers though many of them may be, they are full of the love of life, of other people, and of the world. For Pierre, these people are his family. In some sense of the word, they all do love one another, whatever form that love may take.

A lot more could be said about the characters – about their individual psychologies, their isolated hopes and fears. Arcand throws out hints, such as the very different resentments felt by Diane and Dominique; but because he does not anchor them within a conventional narrative of cause and effect, they get backgrounded by the stylistic authority of the totality of the film.

The least anchored of all is the scuba diver who hangs out in the university pool. Initially, he frightens Louise and then returns to her in a nightmare after the evening of revelations, this time terrifying her by pulling her into the depths. Although the film does not psychologise its characters in this way, these scenes might suggest her sexual timidity. On the other hand, we had previously seen Danielle talking openly with him, his mask removed, along with any sense of threat. If we felt so inclined, we could analyse other characters at other moments in similar ways.

The ending of the film is gentle in the extreme. The light from outside is soft and beautiful. Alain and Dominique are abuzz for one another and, as the group gathers to prepare breakfast, they argue about the supposed affair of yet another colleague, although none of them can agree on the details. Danielle starts playing a simple waltz by François Dompierre on the piano, persuading the wounded Louise, now wearing sun-glasses as opaque as Mario's, to join her. While Rémy has grown silent within his circle of friends, the others are still talking about sex, although with less jubilation. 'I guess we'll never know the whole truth of this story', shrugs Pierre, as Diane and Claude, who have become confidants throughout the morning, share a little hug. She asks if he is okay: '*Ça va?*' she enquires. '*Ça va*' he replies. After this dyadic exchange, both Rémy and Pierre glance outside at the gentle morning light. The camera cuts to an exterior shot of clouds as the tail credits roll.

The piano duet continues (another dyad!), sometimes haltingly – less eternalising the situation now than humanising it, the young Danielle and the shattered Harriet brought together through the wordlessness of music. The scene has changed from fall to winter with snow washing away those uncertain smiles of that autumn night.

Although Arcand was never part of the pastoral tradition of Québécois filmmaking, which celebrated the vastness of the land, he is aware of its existence. Indeed, in interviews, he has frequently mentioned the landscape as one of the pleasures of living in Canada. In any case, in this as in his later films, he gives a special photographic credit to Jacques Leduc for his *images de la nature*.

Leduc has shot for directors as diverse as Jean Pierre Lefebvre and Anne-Claire Poirier and has also directed *the* most pastoral fictional feature of all time – *Tendresse ordinaire* (1973). Knowledge of these associations, I would suggest, intensifies the emotions we may experience from these closing moments of *Le Déclin de l'empire américain*. Not only do they evoke a tradition within Québécois cinema but they help to eternalise the human situation. Whatever happens to the characters or whatever the political future of Canada and Quebec, like the music of Handel, the beauty of the landscape will remain.

Partly inspired by Louis Malle's *My Dinner with André* (1981), *Le Déclin de l'empire américain* began as a low-budget film about people talking. Provisionally entitled *Conversations scabreuses* (*Indecent Conversations*), the film grew into something far more challenging. It became a celebration of human language with its ability in equal parts to animate and deceive. As in the conversational films of Eric Rohmer, language conceals as much as it reveals. That is why music is so important in the film. Music never conceals or reveals: it simply is what it is, moving us or failing to, depending on our cultural conditioning. So too with the spaces – and so too with the extraordinarily graceful choreography of Denys Arcand's *mise-en-scène*.

All his spaces signify – from the prolonged tracking shot at the opening down that monumental arcade which may intimidate us to the presence of snow at the end which might console us, cleanse us, even Canadianise us; but most of all, assisted by that piano duet, this closing sequence restores us to our own feelings, setting us free from language, with all its wit and many self-deceptions.

Attempting recently, in the Canadian film journal *CineAction*, to rescue *Stardom* (2000) from the black hole into which it fell after its festival presentations, I suggested that there was more to that film than met the eye. With *Le Déclin de l'empire américain*, we might say that there is more to this film than meets the ear. A film about language that destabilises language; a film about spaces that opposes different spaces; and a film that refuses the pastoral but which ends with the pastoral, *Le Déclin de l'empire américain* is an extraordinary achievement – a thoroughly modernist film set in these postmodern times.

Peter Harcourt

THE LEARNING PATH

LORETTA TODD, 1991

The past intrudes upon the present in Loretta Todd's 1991 documentary *The Learning Path*, as three Aboriginal women come to terms with their own experience of residential schools while forging a new educational future for First Nations people. Todd combines archival and observational footage, personal memories and dramatisation to document the transition from a painful history of assimilation in church and state-run boarding schools to emerging forms of Aboriginal-controlled education for children, youth and adults. The film expresses a strong sense of the imperatives for First Nations' self-determination in education, but also conveys a visceral experience of how pain and anger have become a persuasive force for change in these women's lives. *The Learning Path* is significant film in the history of Aboriginal cinema and Canadian documentary because it speaks broadly to the decolonisation of Aboriginal peoples, just as the text deconstructs our conventional expectations of the documentary form. Todd's focus on her three subjects as women, as teachers and as members of First Nations, expands the viewer's knowledge of the effects of assimilation policies. This is accomplished not by a litany of facts and events, but through the emotional range of memories, fears and aspirations that drive the filmmaker and her subjects' enduring stories of cultural transformation.

As the final film of a five-part series, *As Long as the Rivers Flow*, co-produced by Tamarack Productions and the National Film Board of Canada (NFB), *The Learning Path* focuses on a specific area of contemporary Native self-determination, as do each of the others in the series. Released in 1991, the film coincided with a watershed in First Nations politics and in the development of Aboriginal media in Canada. Within a few years on either side of the film's production, Canadians and Aboriginal people experienced several important political and cultural events including the confrontation between the Mohawk community of Kanehsatake, the police and the military over land rights in the town of Oka (see Brian McIlroy's chapter on *Kahnasatake: 270 Years of Resistance* (1993) in this volume); a five-year multimillion dollar federal Royal Commission on Aboriginal Peoples; the creation of Studio 1, a First Nations production unit at the NFB, and the launch of Television Northern Canada, a dedicated satellite network for distributing Aboriginal language and cultural programming across northern

Canada. *The Learning Path* must be situated within this environment of shifting relations between First Nations and the Canadian state. Todd's first film for the NFB, it reflected many of the underlying issues and encounters being articulated across the country in the early 1990s. To understand why *The Learning Path* is central to the emergence of Canada's Aboriginal cinema and why it is itself a significant and powerful film we need to consider the contexts of indigenous media which shaped it, the evolution of documentary genres to which it belongs, the narrative core of the film as a story of healing and renewal, and the formal structures and visual techniques Todd uses to present her subjects' past struggles and present achievements.

Aboriginal media in general, and Native documentary in particular, cannot be critically evaluated without some reference to their political content and contexts. Beginning in the late 1960s with NFB initiatives like Challenge for Change and films like Willie Dunn's *The Ballad of Crowfoot* (1968), Native filmmakers viewed documentary as an educational tool, a means of political critique, and a venue for cultural expression. Aboriginal people's growing demand for access to the means of cultural production in Canada is part of a global movement toward decolonisation and self-determination in which media played a key role. Similar trajectories can be traced in Australia, New Zealand, Central and South America, and in developing countries. Indigenous peoples used media technologies to break the silence of mainstream press, radio, film and television about the impact of colonialism on their lives. Indigenous and Aboriginal media worked to counteract the mass media in settler societies like Canada's by resisting negative and often racist stereotypes, and generating more accurate and meaningful representations of the cultural and social conditions in indigenous communities. The long-term effect of Aboriginal media has been to rewrite the colonial record, to undermine and ultimately reject the master narratives of Euro-Canadian history. Whether providing new interpretations of archival images, re-scripting documentary footage from the postwar period, or recording contemporary lives and stories, First Nations filmmakers are often implicitly or explicitly engaged in a form of cultural politics. *The Learning Path* clearly fulfils the educational, political and critical role common to other examples of Aboriginal media in the last part of the twentieth century.

A combination of factors in the emergence of Aboriginal media made documentary the most accessible genre for First Nations filmmakers. If Canada's documentary production is vastly overdeveloped in relation to its feature film industry, this is even more characteristic of Aboriginal cinema. Historically, the higher level of government funding for documentary through the NFB and its relatively low production cost reduced the barriers to entry to

Aboriginal filmmakers. This is in direct contrast to the almost complete exclusion of Aboriginal producers from feature film funding in Canada until recently (Zacharias Kunuk's internationally acclaimed 2001 film *Atanarjuat: The Fast Runner* was only completed after a sustained struggle by its producers at Igloolik Isuma to challenge the limited level of federal financing for Aboriginal-language films; see Darrell Varga's chapter on the film in this volume). But First Nations filmmakers have willingly and successfully embraced the documentary and have used its communicative strategies to explore key issues of racism, colonialism and social justice. In *The Learning Path* Loretta Todd uses documentary to examine these issues, but moves beyond its observational constraints to discover the emotional and spiritual impact of assimilation and non-Native education in the residential schools. Todd's incorporation of poetic and dramatic elements in the film marks a clear departure from conventional documentary form.

The Learning Path can be situated within three genres: Native documentary, experimental ethnography and performative documentary. Clearly, Todd hopes to affirm the unique attributes of the First Nations individuals, communities and cultures she represents in the film and calls for a return to the knowledge of the elders in recreating educational institutions. Yet the film strives to engage a non-Native viewer as well, as its subjects actively criticise the educational models and policies that were imposed upon Native people by the Canadian state.

Because Todd departs from the sole reliance on interviews and observational footage and tells a much more intimate and evocative story of abuse, isolation and recovery from the residential school experience, *The Learning Path* can also be seen as an instance of what Catherine Russell has called experimental ethnography. Todd has consciously worked to subvert the objective and empirical modes of classical documentary and ethnographic representation of Aboriginal people. The narrative content of the film challenges the racist, sexist and colonial discourses of the traditional ethnography while its structure and visual style experiment with textual forms. In rejecting the modes of ethnographic distancing which have marginalised First Nations in Canadian documentaries made by non-Native directors, *The Learning Path* takes a subjective and embodied approach. Todd's use of memory and reconstructions of the residential school experience allow for a more experiential, emotional, autobiographical and visceral representation of historical events. This places the film into the category of what Bill Nichols, in his essay 'The Ethnographer's Tale' (originally published in *Visual Anthropology Review*, spring 1992, and re-printed in his book *Blurred Boundaries*), calls performative documentary, a blurring of the boundaries between the 'real' and the 'performed' through which the forms of objectification, distancing, voyeurism and victimisation often inherent to documentary can be overcome. The several examples of dramatisation in the film reinforce this performative element. Where emotional responses and experiences cannot be easily expressed in interviews and observational segments actors perform them. Dramatisations in *The Learning Path* are almost exclusively without dialogue or narration, creating a dreamlike state of remembering.

This thumbnail sketch of the different documentary genres into which *The Learning Path* falls provides a point of departure for a closer reading of its narrative elements. The film tells the stories of three First Nations women: Eva Cardinal, a teacher of Cree language and traditional knowledge in the Edmonton public school system, Dr Anne Anderson, a language expert who has published several Cree texts and dictionaries while teaching adult language classes from her own cultural centre, and Dr Olive Dickason, a Metis woman who writes and teaches First Nations history at the University of Alberta. Each of these elders is introduced in the opening minutes of the film, but their personal stories of the past are framed by accounts of the new educational institutions and practices they are promoting for their communities. After a series of short interview segments with each woman speaking to the camera about her own educational vocation, the film takes us to a morning at Ben Calf Robe School, a Native high school in Edmonton, where we see interviews with teachers there. Returning again to its female subjects, *The Learning Path* follows a three-part structure that explores their memories of childhood and residential school education, examines the role of their mothers and other elders in their lives, and presents observations of each engaged in their current teaching and research activities. The film closes with another example of new educational models for Aboriginal people, this time with a visit to Onchaminahos School in the rural First Nations community of Saddle Lake. There is almost no narration or description in the film to tie the personal memories and observational footage together and at first the connections seem tenuous and the transitions disjointed. As the film progresses, however, the viewer begins to understand how the three women's experience of forced assimilation and cultural persistence is the common ground upon which new educational paths are being traced.

Todd has carefully crafted the autobiographical accounts in *The Learning Path* as scripts for personal and cultural transformation. Through the medium of film, these individual stories become part of collective memory, following traditional Aboriginal protocols in which leaders and elders are remembered for their strength, values and positive impact on the community. Todd herself contributes five separate voice-over commentaries in the film, though none of these is much more than one-minute long and these are the only instances of narration in the entire 59-minute film. Despite this relative silence, Todd's own voice becomes the fourth subject in the film. She is the absent interlocutor in conversation with her participants, inflecting and directing their stories around key ideas and issues. The narration in the film never tells us what the camera sees; it only offers brief contextual statements, questions and introductions. Midway through the film Todd asks the central political and moral question around which *The Learning Path* revolves: how can the elders accept the injustices perpetrated by church and state in the residential schools and on the reserves? While each woman provides her own account of brutality, abuse and exclusion, none expresses the kind of anger that arises in the film-maker's words at the moment when she refuses to absolve the Canadian government for the harm inflicted on First Nations peoples under its assimilation policies. Thus Todd's own voice becomes part of the structural device of the storytelling circle. She adds her overtly politicised interpretation of the past to the personal memories of the older women and the film arrives at a composite narrative from which the audience may draw its own conclusions.

The documentary does not dwell at length on the painful past of the residential school experience, but it gives substantial weight to the women's own memories of this period. Eva Cardinal gives one of the most compelling accounts in *The Learning Path* as she visits the now empty school in which she was boarded as a child. The observational footage of Eva at the school is prefaced by a brief dramatisation set in the 1940s era, of a young girl walking along a frozen prairie road with her grandmother. Both wear warm winter coats, hats, mittens and beautifully beaded moccasins. The point of view alternates between the movement of their feet along the snowy path and a medium shot of them moving towards the camera. The older woman speaks quiet reassuring words in Cree to the girl as an ominous black car approaches along the road. It stops and a white male Indian agent gets out. Shot from behind, without seeing his face, we hear him say, 'I have to take the child', and observe the oddly dispassionate parting of the two, as the child looks out the rear window of the departing car. No context, translation or subtitles are provided for the scene. Unless the viewer speaks Cree, she simultaneously experiences the strangeness of a foreign language and senses the unbridgeable cultural gulf between the white agent of the state and the grandmother and the girl. It is at this moment in the film that the contrast between the warmth and security of the Aboriginal family and the anonymity and hostility of the white world is most convincingly conveyed. The director has chosen to shoot the segment in Cree in a way that disorients non-Native viewers while in effect refusing them access to the private grief of the child's loss.

This scene cuts immediately to Eva's memories of arriving at boarding school, with a shot of her on the steps of the empty building. In an echo of the preceding dramatisation, Eva recalls her own confusion and uncertainty as the nuns spoke English to her on her first day, issuing instructions that she could not understand. No description or location of the school, nor any factual information about the length of Eva's stay is provided, and the film creates a continuing sense of a child's disorientation as Eva's voice is juxtaposed with observational segments shot in colour in the present and a montage of black and white images which are meant to evoke the past. The camera, in a high-angle shot, follows Eva as she mounts the stairs; the visit is clearly triggering harsh memories for her, the angle makes her seem small and vulnerable. Eva's description of daily routine at the school is carried over a slow sequence of lyrical images. A black and white pan of an empty corridor shifts to a colour shot of Eva in an empty room. A black and white image of bare, grimy windows cuts to a colour shot of Eva looking out the windows as she remembers hearing the sounds of her people passing on horseback on the nearby road, not being able to go out but longing just to see them go by. Then, in one of the more frequently discussed sequences in *The Learning Path*, we see black and white impressions of a woman in nun's habit, shot from the rear, drifting down the corridor, then shot from the side through a doorway, sitting on a chair in an empty room. We never hear her speak or see her face, but her dark presence seems to haunt the bright sunlit empty rooms as Eva moves through them recalling her experience at the school.

Following this sequence, the camera moves in on Eva's face as she describes her loneliness and her powerful desire to learn, but it halts and retreats to a medium shot as she begins to weep. A series of desolate grainy black and white images of chipped and stained sinks in a bathroom are accompanied by an echoing dripping tap that fades in over the sound of Eva crying. While Eva's emotion and despair are apparent in her voice, the filmmaker draws back from a gratuitous focus on her anguish. The respectful withdrawal of the camera in the present-day footage, in combination with the imaginary reconstructions in black and white, give visual substance to Eva's memories while avoiding the impersonal third-person description and ethnographic distancing of conventional documentary form. As Eva speaks of the past, the silence of the child in the dramatic segment, like the silence of Eva's own childhood, has finally been broken.

The Learning Path is not a documentary about victimisation or oppression but an account of survival and renewal. The film bears witness to injustice, but it does not present the women's pain for the viewer's voyeuristic gaze. Rather *The Learning Path* uses autobiographical accounts as a means of displacing the outsiders' perspectives so familiar to us from archival and documentary images of Aboriginal people. As Dr Anne Anderson recounts her childhood encounters with predatory priests and vindictive nuns, for example, her voice accompanies archival footage of young Native girls preparing for bed and saying their prayers in a residential school dormitory. Anderson's commentary takes the viewer beyond an invitation to pity the Aboriginal children who were exposed to this abuse to offer a sophisticated moral critique of the structures of religious hierarchy that allowed it to occur. Anderson explicitly contrasts the nuns' mean-spirited and inhuman behaviour to her own Cree mother's generosity and respect. In another instance, the film opens with a series of anonymous testimonials by Native speakers recalling their experience of persecution in mainstream schools into which Native children were integrated after the residential schools closed. Voice-overs describing the racial slurs and acts of violence that characterised the Native experience in these mainly white schools accompany a series of black and white images of Native children in school corridors and playgrounds. While the images could be drawn from the 'assimilationist' propaganda common to the NFB films of the 1950s and 1960s, like *No Longer Vanishing* (Grant McLean, 1955) or *Because They are Different* (Jack Ofield, 1965), the voices tell another story of race hatred and exclusion in Canadian society. The combined effect is not to produce pathos, but to present a powerful moral and political critique on the terrain of the personal and autobiographical.

The director uses the voices of her female subjects to add new layers of meaning to the archival images of Aboriginal children in residential schools included in the film. The women's voices are strong and confident; they tell stories of transformation and agency as they moved past the painful experiences of childhood into their present activities as teachers, researchers, authors and elders. *The Learning Path* focuses on the importance of individual healing and recovery in First Nations communities and demonstrates that Aboriginal identity is not some irretrievably lost object but a constantly evolving narrative of memory and the experience of change. The film follows each woman as she comes to terms with her own past and with the historical violence of colonialism. All three explore the influence of mothers, grandmothers and sisters in their path to teaching and learning and in the cultural continuity of their communities. The importance of parents, elders and community ties are illustrated with still images of earlier generations from archives or family albums, with brief dramatisations of life on the trap-line or learning to do beadwork, and with observational segments of visits home.

In its last half, *The Learning Path* moves with confidence toward a new educational future, presenting its subjects at work in classrooms, cultural centres and libraries. We observe Anne Anderson teaching an adult language class, Eva Cardinal demonstrating how to how to make pemmican and bannock to a rambunctious primary class, and Olive Dickason discussing precolonial indigenous trade patterns with a group of Native youth. Throughout the film we see contemporary First Nations people in various aspects of the educational process. Young people participate in a Cree sweet grass smudge ceremony in a typical high school classroom or join a round dance in the gymnasium. We see very young children learning Aboriginal languages in the classroom context as we see adult learners master the same vocabulary. In the Native-run schools she profiles, Todd interviews women teachers who argue for the value of mainstream curriculum taught within an Aboriginal cultural context. The residential schools left Native people with a legacy of racism and abuse, often without even providing the same basic academic skills as non-Native schools. *The Learning Path* does not present a one-size-fits-all solution to the failure of non-Native educational models for First Nations communities, but explores a range of different learning possibilities from primary to post-secondary, from large urban centres to remote reserves.

There is evidence in this film and others by Loretta Todd that adherence to the narrative codes and cultural protocols of Aboriginal storytelling not only changes the structure and style of documentary, but also affects its production practices. Carol Kalafatic, in an essay partially about Todd in the book *Gendering the Nation*, suggests that Todd's respect for the protocol of the storytelling circle allows each participant in the film to speak without interruption or explanatory narration. In disrupting the viewer's expectations of the conventional documentary or ethnographic film, Loretta Todd also explicitly resists the will to knowledge of the dominant society. Of the non-Native viewer she has told Lawrence Abbott in an interview for the *Canadian Journal of Native Studies*, in spring 1998: 'There is an expectation that we're there to explain the metaphysical world or the natural world, or to explain our hurt, our angst, our pain. To me that defines a power relationship in that they're the ones who need to know and we're there to serve their need to know.' She has described her films as a deliberate effort to decolonise the documentary, to provide accounts of Aboriginal people's experience that do not reconstruct the dominant gaze or replicate the forms of surveillance imposed upon Native people by invading outsiders. *The Learning Path*, like Todd's later films, is full of motion as the camera moves around its subjects, interviews are shot from oblique angles, and observational footage is shot from the side of a room or from behind a subject. With her preference for dramatisation as a means of conveying emotional experience in her films, Loretta Todd has carefully negotiated the tension between communicating Aboriginal perspectives on historical events, moral positions and political beliefs without allowing the non-Native viewer to easily control and appropriate this knowledge.

Screened at many film festivals in the United States and Canada, *The Learning Path* marked Loretta Todd's emergence as an influential voice in Aboriginal Canadian film. She has followed *The Learning Path* with a series of documentaries: *Hands of History* (1994), *Forgotten Warriors* (1997), *Today is a Good Day: Remembering Chief Dan George* (1998) and *Kainayssini Imanistaisiwa: The People Go On* (2003). These films share a similar focus on the connections between personal vision and cultural renewal and are marked by her signature visual story-telling style. Todd's documentaries demonstrate an acute political sensibility, but one that never overwhelms the integrity of her subjects nor offers simplistic resolutions to the contradictions of contemporary Aboriginal experience. Her infiltration of the Canadian cultural memory is well under way and her recent films, like *The Learning Path*, constitute a vital record of First Nations knowledge and collective identity in their own right.

Marian Bredin

THIRTY TWO SHORT FILMS ABOUT GLENN GOULD

FRANÇOIS GIRARD, 1993

François Girard's *Thirty Two Short Films About Glenn Gould* (1993) opens with a shot of Gould (played by Canadian actor Colm Feore) walking towards the camera, from extreme long shot to long shot, over a frozen lake; it closes with the reverse: he walks away, back into extreme long shot, at sunset, over the same lake. Considering these bookends by themselves, we may take the implication to be that the Glenn Gould of this oddly formed little film is ultimately unknowable. That compiling his biography – like Charles Foster Kane's biography and like so many modern biographies – is akin to assembling a puzzle without all the pieces. After all, in the final accounting, this film is not 32 short films at all. If we include the opening and closing credits we come to a total of 33. Strike those, and we are left with 31; there is quite literally a missing piece.

At the age of 13, when Gould played with the Toronto Symphony Orchestra, he was a prodigy and star attraction. By 24, when he released his seminal recording of Johann Sebastian Bach's *The Goldberg Variations*, he was a worldwide celebrity. Filmmakers François Girard and Don McKellar – a francophone/anglophone creative partnership – made use of this cultural association between Gould and *The Goldberg Variations* when they sought a structure to tell his biography. Bach's composition is made up of an aria, thirty variations on that aria, and then the same aria repeated. Thirty-two pieces. Those thirty variations are divided so that every third is a canon, and each successive canon is a full step higher. This is just the beginning of a geometric musical puzzle which includes inverted answer forms, dances and fugues. It was Glenn Gould – Canadian pianist, genius, future radio documentary producer, icon and wingnut – who took this composition for harpsichord and successfully interpreted it for the piano, re-presenting what was generally considered a dry exercise in music theory to an audience highly receptive to its texture, wit and mysterious emotional resonance. The challenge for the filmmakers was to attempt a similar transcription. But even though *Thirty Two Short Films About Glenn Gould* is permeated by mystery and the subjective haziness of emotion, it is ultimately a film about communication and clarity. Our return to where we began is not an admission of the monumental elusiveness of knowing a great human being. It is instead, like *The Goldberg Variations*, an experience of the same singular subject represented many times, and though in the end we watch our subject recede to the horizon, this is not because this life we have followed has resisted interpretation. It is this clarity of address, intent and thought which makes the film 'Gouldian', and accounts to some extent for its impressive critical, commercial and cultural success. *Thirty Two Short Films About Glenn Gould* is arguably, even today, still the most widely known and identifiably Canadian film ever made.

Each short 'film' is separated by black and each is named, sometimes enigmatically, by a plain title card. These vignettes are a combination of fictionalised re-enactments, documentary interviews with Gould's friends, and avant-garde sequences set to Gould's music. In part because of this regimented structure, and also because the vignettes are indeed very short, the effect is one of thirty-two films matched to thirty-two ideas. That is to say, each vignette is involved in making a single point; we understand that we are involved in searching for the point; we have time to digest this point; and the film moves on. The point of a vignette may not be entirely clear, but at the very least we understand that this vignette will connect somehow to others. For such an unconventional film, it demonstrates a powerful forward momentum as we are lured into a certain state of viewing receptive to discrete, yet ultimately cumulative, ideas. The film insistently rewards us with insights.

These insights are strategically timed. Consider the progression of the first four vignettes following the opening 'aria'. First we have 'Lake Simcoe', the most conventionally biographical segment in the entire film. Here, and for the only time, Gould's precise and lucid music is replaced, and instead we hear the swooning and menacing orchestration of the overture to Wagner's *Tristan and Isolde*. The camera is appropriately overwrought, and cranes and dollies around a lakeside cottage where Colm Feore as Gould – emulating the pianist's warmly enunciated radio voice – regales his early childhood. This is the setting for the odd and hardly credible relationship suggested between the young Gould – the little gentleman, well coiffed and smartly dressed, sitting in the house and crying softly to the radio – and his almost peasant parents, who drift through the cottage in flannel and plaid. The little Gould is almost uncanny, a little lonely monster in a quiet and still, nearly wordless, eternally autumnal childhood.

Our introduction to the adult Gould comes in the next vignette, '45 seconds and a chair'; this might be our image of the man – the genius – who narrated 'Lake Simcoe'. This 45-second track-in to a close-up of a seated Feore, poised to recreate a well known photograph of Gould, is the most thrilling moment of the film. It is a virtuoso performance, and links convincingly a faultlessly timed dolly across a worn wooden floor and Bach's 'Two Part Invention #13 from

Two and Three Part Inventions' as played by Glenn Gould. It might remind us of Michael Snow's 45-minute zoom across an empty apartment in his experimental film, *Wavelength* (1967). For anyone sensitive to this potential allusion, the apartment and Gould take on a nearly mythic connotation – and myth in Canadian film is a complex, rare and thorny form, and thus powerful when it is sensible. This is Gould at his most dashing and mysterious. I always find it disappointing when he lowers his eyes at the end, but it is a gesture that links this intimately to performance. This might feel like a moment of deference, if not a moment of pompousness, as we find ourselves face to face with a legend, a master over even this medium of cinema – and indeed, Gould's piano will seem, as the film progresses, more and more like the perfect accompaniment to the jittery start and stop of the film camera mechanism. This is a genius in his time, and the Glenn Gould we might recognise from what we have gleaned from the little we hear second-hand in the gap between Canadian culture, low and high.

While this vignette is avant-garde and even confrontational, the next – in dramatic juxtaposition – is a traditional and very straightforward documentary interview. Violinist Bruno Manseignon, speaking of his own false first impression of Gould, swiftly and convincingly dismantles the image of an unassailable genius we have been nurturing, just as the documentary form itself does the same to the heightened and impressionistic style with which we have so far been negotiating. Manseignon, as if to come to our rescue, describes how to get past the eccentricity, the first impression and media of Glenn Gould, to discover the man's real wit and humour. This affectionate deconstruction carries over into the next vignette, entitled 'Gould Meets Gould', where, as if to corroborate Manseignon, we witness Gould's humour. We have one of Gould's celebrated radio self-interviews recreated with a little cinema trickery and a very game Colm Feore. Gould asks himself all the big questions and Gould answers them, and while his argument is intriguing and idiosyncratic, it is not the argument that captivates us but its delivery: the modesty, the fussiness, the pranksterish self-awareness, the good humour. It is a sensation that solves the man, and thus the man is solved for us fifteen minutes into the film. We have been presented one image, the image of an unassailable genius, and then we have admitted – an admission bolstered by the form of documentary – that this is a problematic first impression. The film does not challenge this second impression. The humorous Gould – and the humorous film – takes over entirely for the duration, and at no point is Manseignon contradicted. What remains, for us, is to consider our second impression.

Gould is not – according to this film – a mess of contradictions. The mystery of Gould's real biography is that in 1964, for no apparent reason and with no warning, he retired from live performance. We have all sorts of 'Rosebud' theories, and though Gould has, in writing and interview, intellectually justified his choice, the documentary personalities we hear in this film are unconvinced by the justification. But these justifications are beside the point: the debris of aggressive interpretation. And this might be the film's most notable quality: the film manages, insistently, to debunk explanations without ever amplifying mystery. In a vignette called 'Questions', Gould is asked a series of point-blank queries complete with implied answers – at no point does he answer. The sequences ends with a question we have been anticipating, 'Are you a homosexual?', and the next vignette is the reading of a letter Gould wrote expressing his unrequited love for a nameless young woman. While not an irrefutable answer, it is satisfying to the cinematic-intellect of the viewer, as if the film is savvy to the interpretation-games we play – the ideas we most often nurture, we think, in secret – and is forward about the part it plays in manipulating how we 'read' what is going on. And, more importantly, by its transparency of argument, it manages to undercut a paparazzi-psychology, the familiar methods of interpreting biography. We watch biography to find a 'solution' to a man's life, and in the greatness of that life and in the straightforward mathematics of the solution, we hope to find ourselves implicated, even just a little. *Thirty Two Short Films About Glenn Gould* does not give us a solution to Gould, and though it offers many, it never adequately refutes them. It manages to make all 'solutions' not just inadequate, but irrelevant. This can be seen in the vignette called 'Pills', when Gould recounts his medicinal drug regime, each previous pill creating side-effects counteracted by a subsequent pill: the overall sense is not of an out of control drug user, but an elaborate system of ups and downs all cancelling each other out. No solution there. We move on. The paths and patterns we use to interpret the film are the ways we will interpret the man; the film – despite its status as an odd and difficult 'art film' – has made the way very straightforward. This becomes appropriate to our gathering sense of a 'Gouldian' aesthetic, and this aesthetic – more than anything – is what the film wishes to communicate.

The way Gould played the last aria of *The Goldberg Variations*, a near note for note repeat of the first, but played slowly and carefully, with a little bit of languor in unexpected places, accounts a bit for the popularity of his interpretation. Gould's ending is reflective, and we are left with the melancholy task of looking back over where we have been – namely, the last thirty variations on our first encounter with the aria – and slowly a synoptic sense is formed, a unity is resolved behind us and before us. It was this same aria that we hear now that was expounded over the last hour, and may have even been unrecognisable, but here it remains, and returns, complete. *Thirty Two Short Films About Glenn Gould* works the same way. But in the case of

17

Gould – who is the aria, whose life is the variation – the return of the aria comes at the end of his life. Knowing this, we are waiting for 'theme' to find us a way out, offer some insight into and over death. It comes in the metaphoric potential of the two Voyager space probes: launched by NASA in 1977, designed to leave our galaxy and carry with them, among other arguments for humankind, a short Bach prelude performed by Glenn Gould. And as we hear Feore's narration (no longer as Gould), describing the space launch, and as we watch Gould recede over the ice and snow, we cannot help associating him with that lonely spacecraft as it disappears from all human thought and into pure imagination. The meeting, in the darkness, of Voyager with an extraterrestrial fumbling with a NASA-engineered remote control, pushing play, and hearing Bach as interpreted by Glenn Gould, leaves us to consider what sort of life would include such a metaphoric escape from death, and that would discover, in its own personal and unique form of transcendence, not heaven, but precisely the same life lived. The same solitude. Because there is the distinct and infinitely more plausible possibility that the spacecraft will simply drift for an eternity alone. And it is in our state of reflection upon this profound and ultimate image of solitude, that the theme of solitude – the title of one of the middle vignettes, and our only other visit to the frozen lake featured in the 'arias' – becomes clearly the most important and consistent thread of the film, the unifying idea. The image of the Voyager spacecraft, this image of humankind's achievement, this vessel of our greatness, is also one of our own solitude. In the life of Glenn Gould, this solitude is not loneliness but 'singularity'. 'Loneliness' is for those left stranded and alone by catastrophe; they have lost, and wander an allegorical landscape of still and watchful memory. The 'singular' are those who live appropriately in a place indifferent to personal history, like the vast and horrible Canadian landscape and the imagination that is there in awe. It is 'singularity' – the uniqueness of Glenn Gould – that is reinforced by this film. In this sort of singularity there is an uncommon and not well understood manifestation of greatness.

There is an almost Freudian fascination with water in the film – death seems present even from the beginning. Images of a melancholy Lake Simcoe are matched to shots of the River Elbe; we see Gould soaking his arms up to the elbows in a backstage sink; the first two of the three vignettes detailing Gould's last years – 'Motel Wawa' and 'Forty-nine' – both take place by bodies of water. 'Motel Wawa', where Gould is alone in a northern retreat doing a phone interview (a recreation of an interview with Elyse Mach) about life after death, ends with a slow track-in, past a wool-gloved Gould clutching the phone, and out to a windswept lake. This vignette is perhaps the loneliest in the film: the light seems clearly late afternoon, Gould's companion on the phone seems nearly imagined. Water, as a symbol, of course, also suggests the unconscious, mystery, flux. But Gould's conversation is a discussion about probability, about the eminent (to him) reasonableness of the fact of a life after death. As the camera pushes out to the water, Gould intones, 'after all, don't you think, it seems infinitely more plausible than its opposite: oblivion'. As we look out over this bleak landscape and experience this sense of close-ness to an earthly oblivion, it is hard not to remember the first shots of Lake Simcoe, where we began, and the possibility of this same image of dark water as a beginning rather than an end. For Gould, this philosophy of the afterlife is not a 'deliberate self-reassuring process' – indeed, Gould seems to be saying that though he accepts the idea of an afterlife, there is nothing intrin-sically reassuring about it. Other than the fact of its existence. The vignette featuring a snippet of Norman McLaren's film *Spheres* (1969), also seems to take place in an almost liquid realm: globes of water blend, part and reform over a shadowy landscape. Here we have once again this image of a singular thing and its variations, the inevitable return, finally, to that single simple shape existing for a moment before it disappears over the horizon.

As we think back over the images of solitude we might be able to make better sense of the vignette entitled 'Leaving', when Gould, driving alone – in the rain; this is the last vignette before his death – happens to hear himself on the radio. He rushes to a back-alley phone booth and calls his cousin, pushing the telephone out of the booth so she can hear the car's radio and share his astonishment. Suddenly, it is as if, in a dark city street, Gould, the alien, met up with his own recording. This is a vision of spiritual communion for a man who created himself in solitude and in solitude searches for himself, and the affirmation of his life of searching will be the moment when he finds himself out here, and finds himself searching. If Gould's escape from death, his beyond, is to be sent into space in the form of a recording, then he is also the one to receive it. This is a life, as violinist Yehudi Menuhin puts it in interview, that is 'self-created'. This is entirely keeping with the Canadian vision of life with philosophic hardship, where the human soul is a small problem for hobbyists, where the big themes are uttered into a prairie winter wind already bundled in quotation marks – 'ambiguity', 'eternity', 'art', 'solitude' – and subject to radical deconstruction. Gould becomes not an artist, as we might understand 'artist', but a hobbyist intent on his routine and all that is attendant to the pursuit of his hobby. And his hobby is communication; his goal is to be in his own audience. The numerology and minutiae that dominated Gould's life are not an expression of a radical Gnosticism, a debilitat-ing fear, or the supernatural, but an appropriate science for a fatalistic man much more clear on mortality and the value of the small talismanic gestures of this life than those raging artists that confuse the feelings of imminent death with feelings of mastery over it. Fear and doubt exist, and accompany, necessarily, each insight, but they are so familiar, and become so irrelevant. The effect of seeing the singularity of Gould represented is not to feel separated from him, but to understand the contours of what a greatness is like that is unaccompanied by the myth of its own origin; instead it is a variation on a still intact wholeness. *Thirty Two Short Films About Glenn Gould* communicates clearly and is a great film.

Mark Sinker writes in the July 1994 issue of *Sight and Sound* that *Thirty Two Short Films About Glenn Gould* is 'Canadian … in its cool, intelligent, elegant non-conformity'. For a Canadian, this description of Canadian intellectual character is almost too good to be true. Doubt settles in. Sinker goes on: 'It fits the memory people seem to have of Gould, and the fascination with the unselfish self-absorption, his wayward intellectual clarity, his easy, slightly fussy open-mindedness.' Sinker is a Gould fan, and though he praises the film he ultimately decides that its impressionistic, episodic structure is unable – even by imitation – to accurately communicate what he felt was the pianist's greatest quality: his radical classical music iconoclasm. That is to say, Gould's greatness as an artist and human being. Sinker thinks that a narrative film, and by implication, a more conventional film, would have done that better.

This is a complex problem for Canadian film: how can we locate what is uniquely and positively Canadian when 'Canadianness' seems predicated on a reticence to ever claim greatness for itself? There is in the familiar conception of greatness, as we have inherited it, the idea that 'greatness' necessarily excludes some of us, and thus brings loneliness to the excluded. François Girard's follow up film, *Le violon rouge* (*The Red Violin*, 1998) not only reworks the themes of greatness and loneliness through the 'biography' of the titular instrument, but as a 'work of art' itself, it attempts for a level of greatness unknown to the insistently modest and insular *Thirty Two Short Films About Glenn Gould*. *Le violon rouge* is the work of the same creative team – director, writer, producer, cinematographer – and was produced by Rhombus Media, a small Canadian company that managed to create for itself, by the time of *Thirty Two Short Films About Glenn Gould*'s release, a reputation as the 'top brand' in classical music-based short subjects and documentaries sold almost exclusively to television. *Le violon rouge* becomes representative of an attempt to translate the technical skills and themes demonstrated in *Thirty Two Short Films About Glenn Gould* into a form likely to reach a much wider audience. While this is not a new goal for Canadian film, *Le violon rouge* emphasises the potential for a new sort of global cinema that the resolutely multi-cultural Canada is in the perfect position, ideologically, to profit from, and had not, historically, made much effort to exploit. This has a lot to do with the new reality of art film spending, as reported by Rhombus Media's Niv Fichman to Marc Glassman: 'Much to my surprise, commercial studios in Los Angeles treat our kind of things with enormous respect. They're dying for something cultural, not in the sense that they would take a documentary on Schoenberg, but they would consider a film about a violin over three hundred years and in five languages.' Video artist and scholar Brenda Longfellow – whose most well-known work, *Our Marilyn* (1989), is an investigation of a woman and her media that is not far removed from *Thirty Two Short Films About Glenn Gould*, and represents where her aesthetic sympathies lie – finds the trend outlined by Fichman problematic, and *Le violon rouge* dissatisfying on several levels. She writes that *Le violon rouge* represents a 'cautionary tale regarding the way in which artistic vision is complexly renegotiated and modulated within the context of a market-driven international co-production'. Because *Le violon rouge* represents a new form of Canadian (big-budget) storytelling, and because it was only moderately successful financially while *Thirty Two Short Films About Glenn Gould* was wildly successful culturally (and, because of its miniscule budget, also very successful financially), it might very well also represent, to the brutally self-justifying Canadian culture industry, the impossibility of a truly Canadian vision ever reaching a mass audience invested in narrative films built around the idea of greatness.

Thirty Two Short Films About Glenn Gould's 'Canadianness' comes most immediately from a circulation of signs associated with the two most Canadian of public institutions: the Canadian Broadcast Corporation (CBC) and the National Film Board of Canada (NFB). The work of genius animator Norman McLaren (vignette 21, 'Gould Meets McLaren'), the unmistakable idiosyncrasy of Canadian radio (where Gould's music is still a fixture and his profound documentaries still an inspiration), and even the mealy voice on a crystal-cold day of Knowlton Nash, CBC nightly news anchor from the mid-1970s to the late 1980s (vignette 22, 'The Tip', when Gould plays the stock market), are all so distinctive to anyone raised in Canada in the last half of the last century that the film feels almost embarrassingly personal. In its fragmented and yet precise structure, the film shares the feel of both an NFB experimental film and a CBC radio documentary. While these forms might be distinctly Canadian, they are so amorphous, so hard to pin down, linked more fully to biography rather than a history of shared national impression, that they do not, cannot, share the universal demands of 'culture'. *Le violon rouge* strove to find a place for Canadian film in the 'glittering museum' of profitable high art. But what it sabotaged in the process was precisely the essence of locality – of private history – which was so present in *Thirty Two Short Films About Glenn Gould*, and so ably made sensible the singularity of one exceptional man's biography. But while the local history presented by *Thirty Two Short Films About Glenn Gould* may never make a convincing and complete picture of a national greatness – and we may be dumbfounded why the phantoms of Canadian identity haunt even straight-forwardly successful films like this – it helps to remind us where missing pieces are most likely to turn up, and what, even missing, they might mean.

Adam Rosadiuk

KANEHSATAKE: 270 YEARS OF RESISTANCE

18

ALANIS OBOMSAWIN, 1993

In the hot summer of 1990 in Oka, Quebec, the most famous media text was a photograph. A masked Mohawk warrior stood face to face with a French-Canadian soldier. Another photograph revealed that the two men were circled by a group of armed Mohawks, and a third photograph further revealed that the Mohawks were surrounded by a much larger group of armed Canadian soldiers. It would be hard to find a better example of how perception is determined by point of view and adequate information. It is the ability of Alanis Obomsawin to position the viewer both within these circles and at the circumference that demands our attention. Confrontation, and the ensuing difficult negotiations between the First Nations community and the so-called 'white settler' community, has been the overriding subject of the films made by this experienced Aboriginal filmmaker.

Obomsawin was born in New Hampshire, a member of the Abenaki nation, but soon after moved with her family to the Odanak Reserve, near Sorel, Quebec. Her father was a hunting and fishing guide, while her mother was a traditional healer. At age nine, she moved again with her parents to Trois-Rivières, where, at school, as the only Native child, she bore the brunt of racial prejudice. She recalled the history curriculum with its focus on 'martyred priests being tortured to death by Indians'. Her school experiences energised her social activism. As she puts it, 'That was my fight from the very beginning, to fight for changes in the educational system concerning our people, and I wanted to see our history being taught and to try and do our own programs and get it in there as part of the curriculum.'

Her interest in the arts and social activism resulted in a Canadian Broadcast Corporation (CBC) profile in 1965, and this showcase alerted National Film Board of Canada (NFB) producers Wolf Koenig and Bob Verrall to engage her services. She has been connected to the NFB ever since. Her two main films in the 1970s were *Christmas at Moose Factory* (1971) and *Mother of Many Children* (1977), which focused on children and women in a variety of First Nation communities, detailing their experiences and way of life. In the 1980s, her work became more political. *Incident at Restigouche* (1984) recounted the raids by the Quebec provincial police on the Mi'kmaq Reserve on the Restigouche River, ostensibly to inspect salmon over-fishing. This film was followed by *Richard Cardinal: Cry From a Diary of a Metis Child* (1986), the tragic story of a Metis boy, who was moved around foster homes over twenty-five times before he committed suicide. With hindsight, both of these films on institutional abuse, ignorance and neglect, prepared her for her most challenging project, and the main subject of this chapter.

Obomsawin's film *Kanehsatake: 270 Years of Resistance* (1993) is an important contribution to the education of non-Aboriginals, in Canada and abroad, concerning the issues of Native land claims in general, and the character of the Mohawk community in particular. It is an NFB production, and it reveals the traits of that institution's aesthetics – historical context conveyed by an edited compilation of news footage, photographs, drawings and verbal re-enactment of speeches, interwoven with the filmmaker's voice-over combined with contemporary and follow-up interviews with the 'star actors' involved or near to the action of the 78-day 'crisis'. In addition, and what makes the film unique, is that it is *the* major visual work available of what went on behind the Mohawk barricades in the conflict that erupted in the summer of 1990 near the town of Oka in Quebec. Obomsawin was one of the few media personnel, and perhaps the only Aboriginal one, who stayed the course, specifically in the last month when the confrontation was that between the Canadian army and the Mohawks. Her departure from inside the encampment a day before the Mohawks voluntarily 'exited' necessitated the arrival of the NFB lawyer to ensure that her footage would not be confiscated.

The film is a critique of federalism or of the modern Canadian state, and its relationship to the respective parts that make the whole (this is at the centre of Jerry White's argument in the book *North of Everything*). Canada is an enormous country and is extremely difficult to govern. Governance is achieved by asymmetrical compromises. The three levels of government – federal, provincial and municipal – all have clear responsibilities on paper, but they also have numerous overlapping interests. The Oka uprising, resistance or crisis, a noun choice depending on your political view, is a potent illustration of how all these governments, in addition to the touted independence of the courts, cannot always address specific textures of the so-called mosaic of Canadian society, with its official policy of multiculturalism.

In this context, the governance of the Aboriginal community in Canada is often fraught with problems. Native affairs come under the direct jurisdiction of the Federal government, but this refers specifically to natives living on reserves. Kanehsatake is a Mohawk village and not a reserve. Therefore, it came under municipal jurisdiction with regard to land planning.

The community had close connections with the nearby reserves of Kahnawake and Akwesasne, the latter straddling the US/Canadian border. Why Kanehsatake was not a reserve with clear property rights is rooted in a history of grievances and wrongs that added to the tension. A fair degree of blame can be laid at the door of the Catholic Church and its Sulpician Order, who ruled over the Mohawk community from the first settlement in Kanehsatake in 1721 (hence Obomsawin's reference to '270 years of resistance'). The Mohawk had been displaced from Montreal proper to this outlying area, and they were promised that they would have title to the land. But the Governor of New France, as it was then called, actually saw the move as a Catholic mission of conversion for the Sulpicians to effect, and no written documentation granting the Mohawks the land was ever produced. When, in the nineteenth century, French-educated Mohawks discovered this travesty, they demanded the departure of the Sulpicians and their land claims began. Many of the Mohawks were imprisoned. One of the significant results of this conflict was a mass conversion of the Mohawks from Catholicism to Protestantism. In 1875, a Methodist church that had been built in Kanehsatake was torn down by a court order obtained by the Sulpicians. The Mohawks preferred English as a second language and Protestantism, and naturally this set them apart from the Catholic French-Canadians who had bought land from the Sulpicians and became the Mohawks' neighbours. The Protestant character of the Mohawk community generally even resulted (in Ontario) in the creation of a few Loyal Orange Lodges.

The Mohawks began in March 1990 to blockade the dirt road that led to the nine-hole golf course, on which land was the 'Pines', trees that had been planted by the Mohawks' ancestors and where a Mohawk cemetery existed. By early July despite the Mohawk objections to developing the land for an extension of the golf course and a luxury housing project, the municipal government had won a court injunction to remove the blockade. The Mayor and town council of Oka must have asked (there is still uncertainty over who is responsible) the Quebec provincial police, the Sûreté du Québec (SQ), to act, even though the Quebec cabinet minister responsible for Native affairs, John Ciaccia, was sympathetic to the Mohawks and repeatedly asked the mayor to shelve the development project. One assumes the premier of Quebec, Robert Bourassa, and his Public Security Minister, Sam Elkas, with the knowledge of Tom Siddon, the Federal Minister of Native Affairs, and possibly even Brian Mulroney, the Canadian Prime Minister, knew of the proposed action. It is also possible that none of them took seriously the Mohawks' feelings on the matter, and were unaware of the SQ's risky plan to clear the road.

As we see in the film, narrated by Obomsawin, the SQ arrived in force in the early morning of 11 July. Confronted by Mohawk women and their children on the road while some armed Mohawk men watched from the bush, the SQ lobbed gas canisters towards the protestors. The wind changed and the gas drifted back against the SQ. Armed Police started advancing and running and tripping, a shot went off, and then there was an exchange of hundreds of bullets in less than thirty seconds. At the end of it, Corporal Robert LeMay was dead, and the SQ retreated leaving many of their cars and station wagons, which the Mohawks dutifully pressed into service as a barricade. In his book *The Oka Crisis*, John Ciaccia later described the SQ action, echoing remarks by writer Mordecai Richler in his book *Oh Canada! Oh Quebec!*, as resembling the Keystone Kops. But as Ciaccia also pointed out, a man had died (whether by a Mohawk or SQ bullet remains unclear), and the situation had become critical. The tragedy is further enhanced with the knowledge (unknown, I assume, to Obomsawin at the time) that John Ciaccia had asked Tom Siddon in April 1990 to buy a small parcel of land in Oka that would effectively end the development plans. The Quebec cabinet could also have declared the area a 'Zone of Intervention', also preventing municipal development, but neither provincial nor federal governments saw it in their interests to act at the time.

Part of the reluctance was the fact on the ground that the Mohawk community of Kanehsatake did not have a widely agreed line of authority in its own population. There were also ongoing problems in all the native communities with illegal gambling and the smuggling of cigarettes. There was an elected leader in Kanehsatake, a process of first-past-the-post favoured by the federal Department of Indian and Northern Affairs, but there was a sizable group of tradi-tionalists who saw that kind of election as an imposition of non-Aboriginal culture. Through the whole standoff, the elected chief of Kanehsatake was based outside of his community, and he appears to have had little influence on the negotiations. Meanwhile, Mohawks in the nearby reserve of Kahnawake, on hearing of the attack, blocked all roads into its land, including the important Mercier Bridge that normally handled 65,000 vehicles a day into Montreal. It was a long, hot summer, with the threat of a catastrophic series of violent events. From the outside, some hostile media reported on a large arsenal of weapons at the disposal of the Mohawks, their militarisation, their presumed threat to blow up the Mercier Bridge, their flouting of Canadian law, and so on. Acts of racism by residents of Chateauguay and by white supremacist groups who had arrived on the scene (burning Mohawk effigies, stoning a convoy of fleeing Mohawk families while the police stood by and watched, preventing food and medicine reaching the embattled

Mohawk communities, all of which we see in the film) made Quebec look momentarily like 1930s Germany.

One of the most startling, humorous and telling images in the film is the efforts of a native Protestant minister, with the Bible aloft in his hand, attempting to cross the barbed wire separating the Canadian Army from the Mohawks. Three French-Canadian soldiers put their bodies between the wire and the minister to make it clear that he could not pass. It is almost a scene out of a Sartre or Beckett play. For the historically minded, it was a nuanced rerun of the conflict between the Sulpicians and the Methodists in the late nineteenth century. What is remarkable for anyone who watched the daily media reports is the fact that Obomsawin's camera is behind the wire, in a space that the minister cannot reach, and one the army could then not control. The physiological and psychological impact of a religious figure who is cut adrift both from the camera and from his flock, defamilarises the scene, clearly announcing Obomsawin's sympathies for the Mohawks. This sequence also tells us that the conflict is about land and where that land's ownership lies. Later Aboriginal/white conflicts in the 1990s at Ipperwash, Ontario and Gustafen Lake in British Columbia, and the media attention they garnered, were no doubt heightened by the 'event' that Oka represented.

Serious though the subject matter is, Obomsawin humanises the Mohawk warriors, and humour is used often in the film. We hear John Ciaccia declare that no food will be prevented from crossing the barricades, but Obomsawin's camera shows that even the Red Cross vehicles encountered major difficulties in obtaining access. We watch with equal incomprehension with the Mohawks as the Army put a barbed wire perimeter in the water surrounding the native land, as if they would seek to leave the land over which they are fighting. On the other hand, one feels sympathy for the soldiers who are simply following orders in encircling the Mohawks to smaller and smaller pieces of land. This gradual diminishment of space in itself is a suitable metaphor for the historical reality of the Aboriginal experience. Ironically, the Mohawks' last stand is in and around the 'Treatment Centre', suggesting to the audience a very Canadian version of the American 'Remember the Alamo' slogan. It is fairly clear that it is not the Mohawks that need treatment, but those on the other side of the wire. Many of the amusing sequences, often exhibiting army doublespeak, are accompanied by electric guitar chords, while the rhythm of normal Native life is sometimes accompanied by traditional drumming, and even flute. The discordant guitar-playing is interesting, as one can read the guitar as a sign of modernity versus the traditionalism of the drum, but one can also see the guitar as part of the counterculture movement of the 1960s (an influence, no doubt, on Obomsawin's generation), thereby implying that not all modernity is unhealthy for the Mohawk community.

What Obomsawin cannot and does not quite capture is the weakness of federalism generally at this point in time in the Canadian body politic towards Quebec. In June 1990, the Meech Lake Accord, which was intended to bring Quebec into the constitution of Canada by recognising the province as a distinct society, was unable to be ratified in the Manitoba Legislature (which required unanimous consent for the accelerated approach to constitutional changes demanded by the talks) when Elijah Harper, a Native MLA (the provincial equivalent of an MP), objected. When a Peace Camp opened near the barricades, Harper was one of the invited speakers (we see him very briefly at the beginning of the film). To many Quebecers, the failure of Meech was another humiliation at the hands of English Canada, and even more painful as it appeared that the Aboriginal objections were a useful and convenient smokescreen for other provinces' doubts about the Accord. The failure of the subsequent Charlottetown constitutional agreement and the closeness of the 1995 referendum in Quebec gave a greater sense of the overall weakness of federalism. The Oka crisis opened up that weakness to a worldwide audience. Mulroney and Siddon did not want to enflame further French-Canadian passions, and this may explain why they posted French-Canadian soldiers up against the Mohawks in the first instance. Equally apparent was the weakness of John Ciaccia, an Italian-Canadian (or allophone as some Quebecers would say) in steering negotiations and events. He was, at his own admission, a minority in the Quebec cabinet. One wonders if his allophone status aligned him too closely to the English-speaking Mohawks in the minds of mainstream Quebecers. And, it also has to be said that Premier Bourassa seemed ill equipped, as he was in 1970 during the Front de Libération du Québec (FLQ) crisis, to deal with violent confrontations. John Ciaccia reveals in his book that the Oka crisis prevented Bourassa from dealing with health problems, and he later died of a cancer that could have been treated successfully if detected early. Mulroney was also weakened at this time – the failure of Meech was a major blow for the bilingual Quebecer, who had won election in 1984 with the promise to Quebecers to remove the 'humiliation' of the 1981 patriation of the constitution, which occurred without Quebec's signature.

Obomsawin's film is strong, however, on the visceral impact of the standoff. We are introduced to the 'stars' of the Mohawk warriors, who have nicknames like actors – 'Lasagna', 'Spudwrench', 'Wizard', 'Psycho', 'Stonecarver', 'Blondie' and 'Mad Jap'. Film theorist Bill Nichols, in his essay 'The Voice of Documentary', points out that the 'string of interviews' film is prone to view characters as 'stars' and that the filmmaker tends to interview people with whom she agrees. This is clearly the case here, but Obomsawin would see this as her purpose as an aboriginal filmmaker. She does not interview Canadian Army soldiers or officers – that is left to excerpts from footage shot by other news agencies. Since she was the object of racial insults from the Canadian soldiers, who apparently would call her 'Squaw', during the time behind the barricades, her decision is understandable personally, if not professionally. The partisan documentary is not unusual at the NFB, but notions of 'balance' are always the concern of broadcasters, as evidenced by the CBC's reluctance to screen the full version of the film, although they eventually relented. The film was shown on British television before it was seen on Canadian television. On the other hand, she does not shy away from reporting that a number of the Mohawks were guilty of ransacking temporarily abandoned houses.

As Zuzana Pick has articulated, the film 'validates history and locates identity in tradition, thought and culture to imagine a Mohawk nation grounded in the spiritual connection with the land'. Yet it has to be countered that there is a specific weakness at the heart of Obomsawin's work. One may accept that the native community desires to have tradition, spiritualism and a rural or semi-rural way of life front and centre, but the reality of modern Canada is that it is urban, suburban, mobile, consumerist, capitalist and individualist. She chooses not to explore at any great length the internal dissensions within the Kahnesatake community, including profiling the elected chief. If only a small percentage of the Kahnesatake community are traditionalists, should their positions be presented as universal views? Certainly, we cannot argue with the high percentages of natives in Canadian jails, their crimes often fuelled by alcohol and drug addiction, which in turn have been fuelled by historical disadvantage, including land expropriation and abuse in forced residential schools. Like Obomsawin, we are often asking what is the way forward for these communities?

It is hard not to be overwhelmed by the problems and issues of many First Nations peoples in Canada, and Obomsawin's films are perhaps best understood theoretically by taking to heart Julia Lesage's observations in her article 'The Political Aesthetics of the Feminist Documentary Film'. Here Lesage outlines that the 1970s documentaries made by women exhibited 'biography, simplicity, trust between woman filmmaker and woman subject … little self-consciousness about the flexibility of the cinematic medium.' We see this implicit trust with men and women subjects in the three follow-up films to the Oka crisis that were made by Obomsawin: *My Name is Kahentiiosta* (1995), *Spudwrench – Kahnawake Man* (1997) and *Rocks at Whiskey Trench* (2000). The first film is a classic throw-back to the 1970s films that Lesage discusses. We listen to the on-camera explanations and experiences of one of the Mohawk women who were detained after the Oka standoff ended. As she only gave her Mohawk name, the court kept her in captivity for four more days before releasing her. It is a good example of the consequences of lack of recognition and respect, which Obomsawin's film seeks to remedy. Less successful in keeping on the Oka message is the film *Spudwrench*, which profiles the life of Randy Horne, one of the men behind the barricades, and who was beaten very severely by Canadian soldiers. Horne is presented as this hard-working high-steel worker and key provider for his family in Kahnewake. His life is traditional up to a point. The movement of many Mohawk men into the dangerous life of high-steel work (the men travelled all over North America to build skyscrapers) was a response to lack of opportunity on the reserve. Horne seems to have achieved a balance between his life on and off the reserve. Then again, his wife and family have had to live with his constant absences, and perhaps this is why Obomsawin spends a good amount of time on other high-steel workers to convey that sacrifice more strongly.

Obomsawin's later film *Rocks at Whiskey Trench* is a re-examination of the rock-throwing incident near the town of Chateauguay in August 1990 when, under fear of army attack, elderly women and men and children were driven out of the Kahnawake Reserve to supposed safety. Their 75-car convoy, after being held up by the police, was stoned by the residents of Chateauguay. It is a highly emotional event caught on tape, and Obomsawin replays the scene continuously as many of the participants on the receiving end of the stones remember their experiences. Throughout the film, Obomsawin's aim is to display the dignity of the (mainly female) Mohawks, while also providing a history lesson, thereby establishing that the Mohawk grievances are many and real. There are a number of uncomfortable scenes – for example, a mother relays how her young daughter had been hit with a stone, and then had to be rushed to hospital, while her now teenager daughter cries beside her. That fine line between empowering people to tell their story, and the tendency to unconsciously label them as victims without agency is ever-present. It is somewhat of a relief to hear the filmmaker as narrator at the end of this fourth film on the Oka crisis and its aftermath that it is believed that lessons were learned, and that the future is somewhat more positive.

It is clear that without Obomsawin's 1993 film, the history of Oka circa 1990 would be dominated by Mulroney's assertion, reproduced in the documentary, that the armed Mohawks were criminals and illegally wielding weapons. One of the most bizarre comments, also reproduced, came from Robert Bourassa who justified the Army's entrance as a defence of democracy. To many observers, Quebec's inability to take the heat out of the situation with the Mohawks in the first month of the conflict was more evidence of the need for Quebec to stay in confederation. On the other hand, the separatist Parti Québécois argued that because Bourassa was a federalist and ceded responsibility of native affairs largely to the federal government, a solution was inevitably slow to arrive, falling as it did among too many jurisdictions. Obomsawin's implied thesis in her visual treatment of the event was that attention must be urgently paid to Aboriginal land claims and to their traditional way of life. The last decade and a half has seen progress on these issues, and Obomsawin's work, though aesthetically unadventurous, has had a major political and social impact on those who have and will become treaty negotiators.

Brian McIlroy

DEAD MAN

19

JIM JARMUSCH, 1995

The central character in Jim Jarmusch's 1995 neo-western *Dead Man*, a Blackfoot-Blood Indian named Nobody, was just a child when British soldiers kidnapped him. He was exhibited in a Buffalo Bill-type travelling show, educated in English boarding schools, finally escaping and making his way home, where he found himself unwelcome by his tribe. Now, Nobody wanders the wilderness, an outsider walking between two worlds.

Set in the Pacific Northwest in the 1870s, *Dead Man* is a tale of displacement, disorientation and alienation that helps audiences imagine the 'Wild West' as an indigenous character may have perceived it. By offering an indigenous perspective on western expansion, Jarmusch challenges a central premise of the Hollywood western: that the white man's presence in the Americas was justified and/or preordained. That alone makes *Dead Man* a rare and significant film. That Nobody, played by the Canadian actor Gary Farmer, is such a memorable character helps make it a great one. Nobody serves as a prism through which Jarmusch expresses a radical vision of the Wild West: radical, at least, to anyone familiar with the Hollywood western.

In *Dead Man*, the Europeanised West is characterised by greed, chaos and cruelty, a striking departure from the heroism, nobility, order and redemption that American pop-culture materials typically assign stories about the North American West. Writing in *Cineaste* in spring 1996, Kent Jones stated it well: '[In] *Dead Man*, there is no American West. There is only a landscape that America the conqueror has emptied of its natives and turned into a capitalist charnel house.' Jones added that 'even during the heyday of the "anti-western", there was nothing as bluntly dismissive of the United States of America's very existence as Jarmusch's cinematic poem of bitterness … Jarmusch has thrown out the template and crafted a new one based on the idea that the only real moral conflict lies with the fact of America itself.'

Though shot in the US by an American director, *Dead Man* was never welcomed in the States, largely, one suspects, because of its radical politics and disdain for the standard elements of the western genre. Jarmusch financed the film without American money. Upon *Dead Man*'s release by Miramax in 1996, many American movie reviewers seemed either dismissive or mystified. (Roger Ebert rated it with one and a half out of a possible four stars; Rita Kempley of *The Washington Post* described its 'revisionist message … gussied up in flip metaphysical finery'.) The film quickly disappeared from stateside moviehouses. But *Dead Man* developed a loyal following among some critics and in international film circles following its premiere at the Cannes Film Festival. Jonathan Rosenbaum wrote a book on the film for the British Film Institute's 'Modern Classics' series, and the film won the 1997 European Film Award for best foreign film – the first work by an American director so honoured.

Dead Man is also a film that, due to Farmer's participation, has Canadian roots. Farmer was born in 1953 near Brantford, Ontario, not far from the US border, and educated both in Canada and in the US. His work has taken him throughout the continent – from Toronto, where he first made his name as a stage actor, to Hollywood, were he has been a steady presence in movies and on television shows, and through Mexico, where he filmed *The Gift,* his 1999 documentary about the importance of corn to indigenous cultures. Through his work, Farmer has said he seeks to dissolve notions of borders and boundaries, and he recognises the relevance of *Dead Man* throughout the American continent: 'Colonisation didn't just happen in the USA', Farmer said in a phone interview. 'It happened in Canada. It was the same interests, hand in hand, the same people who exploited us. When it comes to indigenous people, there's no difference between Canada and the US. And there's no border for me – not as Gary or as an actor. I'm a North American.'

Jarmusch wrote the part of Nobody with Farmer in mind after seeing the 1989 film, *Powwow Highway,* directed by Jonathan Wacks from the novel by David Seals. Farmer stars as Philbert, a good-natured spiritual warrior who agilely navigates the tricky racial and cultural territory of modern America (and, perhaps, could be seen as a prototype for the deeper, more pointedly subversive Nobody). Farmer's first discussions with Jarmusch about *Dead Man* took place in Farmer's rural Canadian home. 'I was living in an isolated place in central eastern Ontario – Kingston, in the bush', Farmer told me. 'Jim called me and said he'd like to visit, and I said sure. He flew to Toronto and for two or three days we just talked, and he told me the story of the film. We walked around – I had 400 acres of unadulterated bush and trees and rocks – then when he was leaving, he gave me the script and said, "Why don't you have a read? If you want to do it, give me a call".'

Jarmusch prepared for the film by immersing himself in Aboriginal literature and history and chose in Farmer an authority in the complex issues of indigenous representation. A member of the Cayuga of the Six Nations of the Grand River, Farmer has worked as an actor, a teacher, an activist and a media maker. His career took shape on stage in the late 1970s and 1980s and he starred in the premiere of Tomson Highway's groundbreaking play *Dry Lips Oughta Move to Kapuskasing* (1989). That same year, *Powwow Highway* won an award at the Sundance Film Festival and Farmer was nominated for an Independent Spirit Award, a success that opened the door to more film and television work. His best-known roles include the recovering alcoholic Albert Joseph in Chris Eyre's landmark *Smoke Signals* (1998), for which Farmer received another Independent Spirit nomination; Gary Ledbetter's *Henry & Verlin* (1990), for which Farmer received a Genie nomination for Best Actor; John Greyson's *Lilies* (1997); Frank Oz's Montreal-set *The Score* (2001); and the Spike Jonze-Charlie Kaufman mind-bender *Adaptation* (2002).

Farmer's behind-the-scenes career has been equally impressive. In 1993, he started Aboriginal Voices, an organisation dedicated to encouraging Native-produced media in a variety of forms. The organisation's projects included *Aboriginal Voices*, a bimonthly magazine that Farmer edited; the network Aboriginal Voices Radio, which continues to broadcast in major markets throughout Canada (Farmer founded it with help from the filmmaker Alanis Obomsawin); and the Aboriginal Voices Festival, which brought together artists, musicians, performers and filmmakers. Farmer also served as the executive producer of *Buffalo Tracks*, a talk show hosted by the actor Evan Adams, who played Thomas in *Smoke Signals* and Seymour in Sherman Alexie's *The Business of Fancydancing* (2002). *Buffalo Tracks* was broadcast on the cable channel Aboriginal Peoples Television Network. In addition to *The Gift*, Farmer's filmography as director includes *The Hero* (1995), *What the Eagle Hears* (2000), *21 Days* (2002) and *Scratch and Win* (2004). Farmer's reputation as a tireless spokesperson for respectful depictions of Native people – as an actor, Farmer said he always takes a principled stance on issues of Aboriginal history and identity – has not always helped his Hollywood career. He frequently turns down roles that he feels mischaracterise Native people and confronts and challenges directors about their portrayals of Native cultures.

Before filming *Dead Man*, Farmer said that he and Jarmusch discussed, in detail, Nobody's identity and actions. While Jarmusch did not yield on every argument, Farmer said he felt that he had actively participated in the shaping of the film's attitudes towards indigenous cultures and people: 'I always have been a protector of indigenous reality and I never give way, so Jim and I, as good friends as we are, had a fair amount of difficulty and challenging times making this film. I'm a realist when it comes to cinema, and I don't like fabrications of things that can be real. I didn't want to perpetuate specific stereotypes, and wanted to make sure the film had a cultural integrity, because of the job that Hollywood had done [in portraying Native peoples]. For example, there was a scene where Johnny [Depp's character] and I got drunk, and I said that I didn't see the purpose of it.' Jarmusch ultimately deleted that scene. After helping revise the script, Farmer set off with Jarmusch and the cast and crew to photograph *Dead Man* in Arizona, Nevada and Northern California.

The story follows William Blake (Depp), a white accountant who travels to the far edges of the American empire for a job that no longer exists. He is drawn into a gunfight, is shot in the heart, but survives enough to escape into the wilderness. Blake meets Nobody who, during his British education, was mesmerised by the work of another William Blake – the visionary poet and artist. Thinking this new William Blake to have a spiritual connection to the poet, Nobody escorts him to a place where he can depart for the spirit plane.

In another filmmaker's hands, *Dead Man* would probably have slipped into the comfortable conventions of the western genre. Jarmusch, however, dodges the clichés without ever seeming preoccupied with them. He fills his West with the unexpected, including cannibals, drag queens and peyote trips, and filters it all through Nobody's tragic personal history. 'My blood is mixed', Nobody tells Blake. 'My mother was *Ohm gahpi phi gun ni*. My father is *Abso luka*. This mixture was not respected. As a young boy I was often left to myself … White men came upon me. They were English soldiers … They hit me on the head with a rifle. Everything went black. My spirit seemed to leave me. I was then taken east in a cage, to Toronto, then Philadelphia, and then to New York … on a ship across the great sea over to England. I was paraded before them like a captured animal. Exhibited. So I mimicked them, imitating their ways, hoping that they might lose interest in this young savage. But their interest only grew … I made careful plans and I eventually escaped.'

As Nobody replays his life story for Blake, his experiences are reflected with brief flashbacks – the capture by the soldiers, the study of European texts and, finally, the devastation of his home by invading European settlers. 'I saw many sad things as I made my way back to my people', Nobody tells Blake. 'Once they realised who I was, the stories of my adventures angered them. They called me a liar: *Exaybachay*. "He Who Talks Loud Saying Nothing". They ridiculed me, my own people. And I was left to wander the earth alone. I am Nobody.'

The story of imprisonment, exploitation and displacement is harrowing, but Nobody recites it carefully, as if stating it for the historical record. Nobody 'is hardly one of those warm and fuzzy spiritual gurus familiar from *Dances with Wolves* [1990] and similar New Age westerns', Jacob Levich wrote in *Film Comment*. '[He] hates white men, and the reason for his hatred is implicit throughout the film. Although *Dead Man* contains no melodramatic portrayals of the victimisation of Native Americans, the *mise-en-scène* is littered with evidence of genocide – ruined tepees, abandoned villages and charred corpses – and Nobody speaks matter-of-factly of the distribution of smallpox-infected blankets by smiling white traders.'

Farmer said he drew on his own experiences with American culture as he created Nobody. 'Nobody paralleled my own upbringing – as a child, growing up in Buffalo, I got the same American education that everyone else did, an education void of any knowledge of Aboriginal culture, except whatever I could tell them – I was the expert. This was my own colonisation.' By so doing, he makes Nobody seem modern, and helps turn him into a container for *Dead Man*'s complex, layered politics and attitudes toward history. For example, Nobody's disdain for white men (his signature line is 'stupid fucking white man'), is overcome by his admiration for the work of the poet William Blake. 'You were a poet and a painter', he tells the accountant William Blake with an unmistakeable glee. 'And now you are a killer of white men … your poems will be written with blood.' Blake the artist was a visionary and radical, and so, at least in Nobody's eyes, is Blake the accountant. The new Blake, if Nobody has his way, will like his namesake turn renegade against a corrupt culture.

Though he received second billing to co-star Johnny Depp, Farmer serves as *Dead Man*'s emotional centre. Writing in *The Nation*, Stuart Klawans described Farmer's performance in *Dead Man* as 'slyly eccentric in his reading, with a bear's combination of lumbering power and amused curiosity. Farmer gets most of the film's best lines and much of the best business. The role gives him room to act insolent and wry, high-flown and wised-up by turns, and Farmer makes the most of his chances, playing out Nobody's tragedy in gruffly comic style.' Farmer creates, with Nobody, a character that is distinct in nearly every way from the typical Hollywood 'Indian'; he is educated, insightful, flexible and highly capable; he is multilingual, fluidly recites English-language poetry, proves himself well-versed in Native ceremony, and recognises the significance of being chosen to escort the accountant Blake on his spiritual journey.

Farmer described Nobody's personal journey in *Dead Man* as the evolution from exclusion to inclusion, from separation to unity. As he leads Blake through barren forests, past the mercenaries who hunt him, and to the ocean, where he will depart for the spirit world, Nobody calls on the help of the Makah tribe, thereby becoming a bridge between tribes and cultures. 'Nobody was a victim of the cultural clashes of eighteenth century, but he knew both sides well enough to survive', said Farmer. 'He's been expelled [from his tribe] because he's been socialised by the white man, but he retained enough skills and knowledge of the medicines and the techniques to survive in the environment. I can totally relate to that, having been educated in the white man's ways.'

As Farmer points out, Nobody also has found his way in the wilderness: 'Nobody isn't suffering – he's prospering, but he's prospering on his own. Look how big he is, look how well he's fed … He's healthy enough to get Blake, this medicine man, to the place he needs to be. To me, Nobody was extremely worldly among the indigenous people. When watermelon got here, the seed spread around the continent in five years – the trade routes were extremely sophisticated. That's why it was imperative for Nobody to speak so many languages. Nobody was a pan-Indian … he thrives out there on his own. His pain is in seeing all of the people suffer, whether his tribe or not.'

In creating the character of Nobody and the tribal elements in the film, Jarmusch engaged in a substantive dialogue with Farmer and cultural consultant Kathy Whitman, who is of Mandan-Hidatsa heritage, about the details of indigenous life during the 1870s. Farmer consulted with his Crow and Blackfoot relatives and with Cherokee friends in preparation for the role. 'It's a real challenge, as an actor and as a human being, to invade a culture that has been so exploited and to take more from them, for the sake of entertainment', he said. 'I know something about Blackfoot and Crow but nothing about their spiritual realities, and Jim supported me in going and learning. That's something I insist on in any film if there is anything to do with ceremonial life. That's not something that's up for grabs.' Farmer also learned and spoke the various Native languages in the film, including Makah, Crow and Blackfoot, in scenes that Jarmusch chose not to subtitle. 'I wanted it to be a little gift for those people who understand the language', Jarmusch told Jonathan Rosenbaum in *Cineaste*.

Jarmusch's attempt to capture a level of verisimilitude in the indigenous languages, architecture, clothing and ceremonies is another of *Dead Man*'s gestures that is both simple and radical; few directors have taken the time to depict indigenous tribal life as something richer than the monolithic Indian culture that Hollywood helped invent. 'We are very, very careful with details and try to stay as true culturally as we could', Jarmusch said during a press conference following the film's Cannes premiere. 'In Hollywood, for example, in John Ford's film *The Searchers* [1956], you have Navajos called Comanches and playing Comanches, but they speak Navajo in the movie. So, westerns in America have often treated Native Americans as though they were some kind of mythological creatures.'

The decision by Jarmusch and Farmer to try and offer respectful depictions of Crow and Makah culture is revolutionary only because Hollywood's track record has been so abysmal. In nearly every way, commercial films featuring indigenous peoples have offered a very narrow focus of indigenous lifeways and history. The North American West, as seen on the big screen, has been the sole domain of white European-American directors, only a handful of whom have even made the attempt to acknowledge indigenous perspectives. As Hollywood tells and retells the same story – white men overcome moral dilemmas as they heroically 'tame' the Wild West – the single, most important element of western expansion is ignored. That, of course, is the genocide of indigenous peoples.

While debate continues about the size of the indigenous population in 1492 – a debate that is heavily weighted with politics – respected scholars have estimated that the Native population in North America was reduced over the subsequent four centuries by more than ninety per cent due to disease, warfare and systematic killings. The indigenous people who did survive were displaced from their ancestral lands. The estimates of numbers may vary, but there can be no doubt that the Europeans' westward march took an incalculable human and cultural toll, extinguishing countless thriving societies.

While Jarmusch does not explicitly explore the history of European genocide of indigenous people, that history provides a strong subtext in *Dead Man*. From the senseless killing of buffalo (frontiersmen use rifles to pick them off them from a train) to the burned-out remains of an Indian village, the destruction of Native America flows through the film like a just-forgotten nightmare. 'If America – the continent of America… – is haunted by the genocide that presided over its conquest, one thing that makes *Dead Man* a haunted film is a sense of this enormity crawling around its edges, informing every moment and every gesture', Rosenbaum writes in his book on the film.

Not only has Hollywood obscured the genocidal history of the North American West, it has consistently depicted indigenous peoples as lesser beings, and thereby justifies their mistreatment. The pop-culture stereotypes – the Indian as savage, as princess, as monosyllabic subhuman, as noble victim – were initiated in the pulp fiction of the 1800s and remained in full force, thanks largely to Hollywood movies and television, through at least the 1950s. With no real connection with history, these works of fiction invented indigenous people the same way that science fiction films of the 1950s invented extraterrestrials. 'During the first three centuries of contact between Indians and whites, the image of the Indian, although confused and fictional, nevertheless had an empirical reference point – the experiences of people on the frontier who encountered Indians', the esteemed Sioux theorist Vine Deloria wrote in 1980. 'Beginning with the Wild West shows and continuing with contemporary movies, television and literature, the image of Indians has radically shifted from any reference to living people to a field of urban fantasy in which wish fulfillment replaces reality.'

More than a hundred years after first filming of indigenous life (Thomas Edison's company made shorts of Pueblo people as early as 1898), Hollywood has yet to provide more than a few fully actualised Native characters. Nobody is such a figure. He is simultaneously flesh-and-blood and mystical, solemn and sarcastic, disaffected and deeply passionate. Jarmusch and Farmer never idolise Nobody, who can also be ridiculous – in one scene, he tries on William Blake's hat and seems to mimic the chattering of a typical white man. But he is also the only character in *Dead Man* who seems to belong where he is. 'There is no mastery here among the white men, as there is in most westerns', Kent Jones in his *Cineaste* review, 'no instinctive understanding of the land. There is only mute incomprehension or violently aggressive dominance ... and it is as if there are no alternatives available to dislocated intruders.'

Jarmusch was not the first director to challenge Hollywood's clichés of the West. Once the western's tropes were well established – the white, heroic gunfighter, the savage Indians – other films began to tinker with the elements. From a relatively early stage, filmmakers, including Victor Schertzinger, with the 1929 film *Redskin*, created films that presented indigenous people as something other than caricatures. By the 1960s, a stream of revisionist westerns and anti-westerns inverted the form, making, for example, the Indians the heroes and the cowboys the villains. One notable strain of this is the Indianerfilme, a curious and popular Eastern European genre that posited Indians as socialists, living peacefully, communally and in harmony with the land, rising up only to resist the white cowboys, depicted, not unreasonably, as greedy, land-grabbing capitalists. Among the 1960s and 1970s Hollywood portrayals that were sympathetic to indigenous perspectives (though, to varying degrees, misguided) included *Little Big Man* (Arthur Penn, 1970), *Tell Them Willie Boy Is Here* (Abraham Polonsky, 1969) and the silly but popular *Billy Jack* (Tom Laughlin, 1971). Advancing the cause ever so slightly in the 1980s and early 1990s were Kevin Costner's *Dances with Wolves* and *Thunderheart* (Michael Apted, 1992). *Dead Man,* however, stands apart from these films in part, as Rosenbaum points out, because of its presumption of a Native viewership.

'Responding to the question, "What would (or might) a Native American spectator think of this representation of Native Americans?", the most likely answer in most cases would surely be, "I never thought of that"', Rosenbaum writes in his book on *Dead Man*. 'And the reason such a thought would not be entertained is that the presence of Native American spectators as part of American society and therefore as part of the American audience is seldom taken into account. ... the existential innovation of Jarmusch, simple yet crucial, is to acknowledge that he inhabits the same universe as Native American spectators who might happen to see *Dead Man*.'

One fears that describing *Dead Man* solely in terms of its political or sociological impact robs it of its essence. At no point does Jarmusch's film feel like a socio-political tract – this is an ethereal, at times violent and strikingly visual work of cinematic art that operates simultaneously on sociological, self-referential, historical and poetic planes. J. Hoberman, in his *Village Voice* review, gave *Dead Man* perhaps the finest recommendation a poet-filmmaker can have, calling it 'the western Andrei Tarkovsky always wanted to make'. Though *Dead Man* challenges Hollywood's precepts of the West, it is equally important as a personal expression by a filmmaker who has never been bound by cinematic fashion. Jarmusch himself described *Dead Man* during his Cannes press conference: 'The film really is about, on the most simple level, the idea that our physical life is a brief kind of voyage. We travel through it – it is fragile – it could end at any moment. We don't know what happens afterwards. We see a lot of things that are cruel, that are beautiful, that are incomprehensible, that are very amazing.'

Jacob Levich, in *Film Comment*, described some of *Dead Man*'s many layers:

Just beneath *Dead Man*'s surface, a verily conventional outlaw narrative, lies a visionary allegory of the soul's progress from physical death to spiritual transcendence. And that's not all: its themes include a blessedly unsentimental attempt to grapple with the historical substance of westward expansion — in particular, the destruction of native populations and cultures — and a fresh, unusually perceptive take on what many see as the genre's central thematic concern, the Wilderness vs. Civilisation dichotomy.

At the end of *Dead Man*, Nobody is shot and apparently killed by the last surviving bounty hunter. This gunfight happens in the background, as William Blake drifts in a canoe off to sea. Farmer was frustrated with Nobody's death, especially happening, as it did, in a seemingly offhanded way. Even Jarmusch, who over the course of his career has proven himself particularly resistant to cliché, engages in a popular one: the indigenous character dying in service of a white friend. But Jarmusch obviously had second thoughts about killing Nobody. Though Nobody was shot and died in *Dead Man*, in the Pacific Northwest in the 1870s, he manages to make a curtain call, more than a century later, in another Jarmusch film – the 1997 martial-arts genre-bender *Ghost Dog: The Way of the Samurai*. In that film, set in present-day New York

City, Nobody appears and speaks his signature line – 'stupid fucking white man'. This intertextuality positions Nobody as a mythic figure – the enduring Aboriginal, still comfortably out of place, direct and articulate in the face of grim circumstance. That scene also acknowledges how badly Jarmusch and Farmer, like the rest of us, wish that Nobody was still around. Thanks to his cameo in *Ghost Dog: The Way of the Samurai*, we can have a glimmer of hope that Nobody's journey of reconciliation and unification continues.

Jason Silverman

EXOTICA

ATOM EGOYAN, 1994

Exotica (1994) is the masterpiece and summation of a decade of feature filmmaking for Atom Egoyan. From *Next of Kin* (1984) through *Family Viewing* (1987), *Speaking Parts* (1988), *The Adjuster* (1991) and *Calendar* (1993) to *Exotica*, Egoyan turned out a succession of formally abstract, narratively contrapuntal films of tremendous stylistic and thematic consistency. Repeatedly drawn to a tight cluster of subjects including family relations, ethnicity and history, perception and memory, and the technologies and human uses of visual representation, these films combined subject matter of melodramatic, sometimes almost operatic, emotional intensity with a filmic apparatus of abstract detachment and coolness.

Most of the films depict characters in a state of emotional confusion or outright distress who are trying to negotiate their way out of unhappiness through some ritualised behaviour or symbolic process that seems quite rational to the subjects but looks very strange and even incomprehensible to the viewer. Egoyan usually has a small handful of separate characters all behaving like this, their projects related in some way to each other and increasingly intersecting as the film proceeds. The initially baffling behaviour of the characters is gradually elucidated, their commonalities revealed, and the action culminates in a series of doublings and treblings so insistent that the viewer at last understands the meaning of the film – and understands it as a set of patterned themes of almost game-like abstraction. But the abstractions of these films are, to repeat, imbedded in human situations of strong emotional pull.

Here are some of the things presented in *Exotica*'s narrative: extensive striptease, homosexuality, impregnation by contract, interracial sex, lesbian parenthood, surveillance, smuggling, corruption, blackmail, adultery, incest, paedophilia and child sex-murder. The content of the film is largely made up of sex, 'deviant' sex and sex crimes. And yet the ultimate subject of the film is the internal states of loss and compensation experienced by the characters, and the words that best describe the feelings the film finally inspires are sweetness and sadness. Much of the action takes place at an up-market strip club, the Exotica, where the greasy-haired and tank-topped emcee, Eric (Elias Koteas), saves his most poetically lubricious commentary for the routine of Christina (Mia Kershner), who dances in a pre-adolescent schoolgirl's outfit to the strains of Leonard Cohen's anthem of cynicism 'Everybody Knows' ('Everybody knows that the dice are loaded/Everybody rolls with their fingers crossed/Everybody knows that the war is over/Everybody knows that the good guys lost'). Her most devoted onlooker is thirtysomething Francis (Bruce Greenwood), as middle-class-white-male as the rest of the clientele, who visits every other day and always invites her to table dance. During his visits to the club, he hires his young niece Tracey (Sarah Polley) to babysit for him, but there is no child or any other inhabitant in his house. In another part of the forest (one should perhaps say 'jungle' in view of the film's emphasis on that 'exotic' climate), Thomas, the owner of a tropical pet-shop, is smuggling macaw's eggs through Canada Customs strapped to his body. In his free time he cruises potential gay partners at the ballet through a ritual of buying two tickets, scalping one of them to a likely-looking guy, and then returning the money after the performance with the story that the tickets were given to him and he does not feel right charging for them.

In the first part of the film viewers are baffled by what connection many of the people and events have to each other, but connections begin to show themselves gradually, then inexorably, as the action proceeds. What seems arbitrary turns out to be determined and even overdetermined. And, in a parallel movement, the guesses we make about how things are connecting and why people are acting as they do form another unfolding process (like a striptease, as Egoyan himself has remarked in the film's press kit), which, however, is full of misdirection and false clues, so that we find ourselves constantly having to revise our guesses, often drastically, in the light of new information, right to the last scene of the film. This is a scenario familiar from some of Egoyan's earlier films, notably *The Adjuster*, carried here to climactic heights. At the end of the film the pieces have all locked together to paint a picture complex in itself and full of reverberations and further suggestions that leave the viewer still working on the puzzle.

Connections in the film are equally complex. Eric is a former lover of Christina's, accounting in some measure for his tone of longing as he introduces her in the club. Professionally, Francis is an auditor working for Revenue Canada; he appears at Thomas's shop to examine the books pursuant to the government's suspicion that Thomas is running a six-figure-a-year smuggling operation. Zoe (Arsinée Khanjian), the owner of the Exotica, is in a romantic relationship with Christina, but is carrying a baby implanted under contract by her lover's former lover, Eric. A man (Calvin Green) Thomas brings home from the ballet one night turns out to be a customs agent who saw him at the airport bringing his eggs into the country. Francis's little daughter Lisa was abducted and killed by somebody; the police at first thought Francis might be guilty and while questioning him told him his wife was having a long-time affair with his brother Harold (Victor Garber) – who is Tracey's father, crippled in a later car accident that killed Francis's wife. In the club, Eric anonymously provokes Francis to touch Christina during a table dance, and then brutally throws him out when he does. In turn, Francis offers Thomas a clean slate with the government in return for going to the club and asking Christina some questions. As the film moves towards its end, it becomes clear that Eric met Christina when both of them were volunteers in the hunt for Lisa's body: Eric was the one who found the body, and the body was clothed in exactly the outfit that Christina now uses for her dance routine. And last of all, we find in a flashback that when she was a teenager Christina babysat Lisa for Francis, and that she felt great appreciation for Francis as an ideally affectionate and interested father (Christina's own father, it is hinted, is far from ideal). Christina does mention to Eric earlier, during the flashback of their first meeting, that she used to babysit the girl they are searching for, but the viewer does not know this girl is Francis's daughter, and cannot bring things together to explain Christina's relationship to Francis until near the end of the film.

This catalogue is only part of the dense skein of connections, of a complex counterpoint of repetitions and resemblances that reaches all the way down to locations (the Exotica club, Thomas's hot and humid pet-shop, the Caribbean neighbourhood where Harold and Tracey live), props (the parrots in Thomas's shop, in Harold's apartment and on Eric's control board at the club), gestures (the touch on the abdomen that Zoe keeps soliciting for her unborn baby, repeated by Francis's touching of Christina during her dance), actions (the surveillance conducted by customs officers and by backstage minders or voyeurs at the Exotica), motifs (the eggs strapped like ovaries onto the gay Thomas's abdomen, the baby sprung from the ovaries of the gay Zoe's abdomen), themes (fertility, parenthood, childhood and their relation to sexuality) and much more.

In this sense, *Exotica* is a feast for the viewer, a film to be sifted over and decoded and speculated about. Viewers who are not particularly sympathetic to Egoyan often object to this kind of woven connectedness and repetition as too self-consciously clever, as jejune. The test is whether the network of tropes and concealments and revelations is mustered to a purpose beyond hermetic formal virtuosity, and here the other side of the film's equation – the side of human crisis and the drama of affect – provides the necessary substance. For the movement of the film is to conjure up and then exorcise demons of destructiveness. Sexual victimisation, catastrophic emotional loss, personal betrayal and vengeful anger are all ravaging forces that maim people psychologically. Francis, Christina and, to a degree, Eric are all casualties of these forces, and *Exotica* is largely devoted to tracing how they got to be that way, the bizarre and usually inappropriate coping-mechanisms they have devised, and in the end a possible path to redemption.

The process of redemption – for the characters, and for the viewer who also sees bad vistas everywhere – is one of gradually understanding that there is more love in the world than there seems to be (Egoyan has given a shorthand description of this recurring perspective in his work, saying in the film's published screenplay that 'If you have to sum it up, love can still conquer all'). The film moves, broadly, towards a prospect of horror which then transforms itself into a prospect of compassion and tenderness. The most spectacular example of this movement is the way that Christina's dance and Francis's consumption of it evolve in the viewer's mind. At first sight the dance is sold by the performer (Christina) and the *raisonneur* (Eric) as frankly transgressive – paedophilic – and seemingly must be consumed in this way. The message of her accompanying song therefore seems to be: all the good values have been defeated, there is no justice or love in the world, so you might as well indulge your worst appetites. Eric's commentary drips with cool lust, and also exemplifies a philosophy that exalts the girl-child's 'freshness' and 'innocence' as qualities agonisingly remote from the current experience of the mature male clientele which yet can only be re-attained by an act of sexual depredation. The first clue that what is going on might not be so straightforwardly appalling as it seems is the look on Francis's face as he watches Christina – a look not of desire but of suffering. Francis's behaviour is gentle and sympathetic, and it is hard to maintain an attitude of aggressive suspicion towards him. As we watch the mime repeated during Christina's table dance, her attitudes too seem confusing. 'How could anyone think I could hurt you?' he asks her repeatedly, a remark that has one meaning (murky) in the context of a paedophilia-miming sex-dance and another (crystal clear) after we hear the history of Francis and his daughter and the police suspicions.

Similarly, Eric's underhanded attempt to get Francis to touch Christina seems at first simply an act of malicious jealousy, but later is seen as a kind of 'Patient Griselda' test by a sympathetic onlooker to reaffirm the total sexlessness of this apparently transgressively-sexual ritual. Thomas ends up helping Francis in his plan to kill Eric not because Francis is threatening to send him to jail, but out of pure sympathy. All the selfishness and corrupt appetites – Francis's, Christina's, Eric's, Thomas's – are refigured like this, and the four-fold repetition looks like a benediction and a formal pattern both. That is Egoyan at his most characteristic.

Let us examine the Francis/Christina relationship a little more closely. Viewing it in the light of the film's eventual revelations of past events, we can make the following analysis. Christina, in her dance, mimes a 'bad-girl' childhood, using the same schoolgirl uniform

Lisa was dressed in. In other words she presents both Lisa and herself-as-a-child in an overtly sexual form; Francis in turn confronts this dual representation as a father and as a heterosexual male. His child (in the form of the mature but pretending-to-be immature Christina) makes an incredibly overt appeal to his sexual instincts, phrasing these also as paedophilic. The purpose of this is to allow Francis to disavow any such desire. Even if his daughter were physically mature and making explicitly sexual overtures to him, he would not respond – he would protect her and she could trust him and be safe with him.

Christina's motives are even more difficult to parse. Pity for the suffering Francis is certainly there, but, as she tells Thomas, there is more to it: 'I need him for certain things, and he needs me for certain things.' What Francis is providing for her – other than money – is not clear, and really cannot be clear until the final scene of the movie, which reveals Francis-the-father-of-Lisa as the teenaged Christina's idealisation of a father (with the further implication that there is something wrong with her real father). The young Christina gives signs of being very unhappy, to the point that Francis senses something more than routine neglect and tells her she can always talk to him. In the last shot of the film she is seen walking slowly into her upper-middle-class Doric-pillared house, a building that somehow seems sinister for all its solid respectability. These moments are suggestive, but it is only in the context of Christina's dance-contract with Francis that her childhood problem may be clearly identified – like the missing, to-be-solved-for number in an algebraic equation – as sexual abuse at the hands of her father. As Christina is Francis's murdered, sexually-abused daughter, whose sexuality could never deflect his good parental love ('how could anyone think I could hurt you?'), so Francis becomes the projection of Christina's father, or rather the person her father should have been, to whom an explicit sexual appeal is made by his daughter. Even if she had made an overt sexual appeal to her father, he would not respond – she could trust her father, he would protect her and not harm her or make her a victim. Both of them 'soothe' each other (to use Eric's term), through a scenario where the suggested or implicit sexuality of each of them is explicitly dramatised and then controlled and denied and transformed into pity. In Eric's words, 'She'll protect him – she's his angel.'

In this way, *Exotica* carefully, almost surgically, removes much of the transgressive sexuality it has dangled so insinuatingly before the viewer's eyes. Christina's dance, Francis's consumption of it and the salacious commentary by Eric are all subjected to a process of desexualisation. The movement even has its comic apotheosis when the heavily pregnant Zoe, having fired Eric for unprofessional behaviour, takes up the microphone herself to provide a commentary to the strip dancers that is ludicrously incompetent in the business of inflaming male desire – so that the Exotica club itself has become desexualised to a degree. And yet the movement to purification and grace is hardly complete or unshadowed. Nothing can truly redeem the past: the horrible death of a child, Francis's atrocious sufferings, Christina's appalling childhood. In the present, and for the future, Eric has been fired from the club and the love of his life hates him and is involved in a gay domestic relationship with his former boss. Francis is only a few minutes' distance from an attempted murder, and has completely betrayed his professional responsibilities in order to co-opt Thomas's help in his strange plans. And Christina continues to dance to 'Everybody Knows' and to believe that the world is shit. The central trio of Francis, Christina and Eric are still dysfunctional persons or close to it. To describe the conclusion of *Exotica* as a happy ending, therefore, would be completely misleading.

More fundamentally, the transgression cannot truly be removed from *Exotica* because it is in some shadowy way essential to the constitution of the characters and the action. That is, if at first sight transgression is everywhere, and at second sight it is redeemed and evaporates, at third sight it continues to leave a faint, ambiguous stain even after it has been washed away. In subsequent viewings of the film, when all is known, there remain disturbing things in Eric's extreme anger towards Francis ('that asswipe!') after he has lured him into touching Christina at the table, and in his augmented recitation of his 'innocence' patter as he sits in the empty club after closing time:

> What is it that gives a schoolgirl her special innocence? Is it the way they smell? The sweet smell of their perfume and their hair? The aroma of fresh flowers? And all that other stuff that hasn't been fucked up by late nights and a lot of bad food. Is it their gestures? The way they move … the way their body still holds on to some semblance of self-respect, and dignity. And they wrap their beautiful legs around you, tight, holding on, looking at you, you looking at them…

Clearly Eric is talking here about the Christina he is in love with, but this is inseparable from a discourse of paedophilia, especially when it is accompanied by a flashback to the field where the two of them met, and found the murdered body of Lisa. Francis's decision to exorcise any suspicion that he could have had predatory incestuous/murderous feelings towards his little daughter by immersing himself continuously in an atmosphere of erotic stimulation and fantasy, too, hints at the presence of something like the feelings he is attempting to deny. It is not so much that he might have had incestuous feelings towards his daughter; it is more as if he is aware at some level of an erotic attraction to Christina even when she was his under-age babysitter, and that this somehow connects to his catastrophic loss. And for Christina there is something similar: perhaps simply the babysitter's erstwhile crush on Francis, perhaps also the damaged sexuality of the abused child that finds both sexual arousal and sexual disgust in avatars of the abusing parent. None of this is to detract from the state of relative grace to which the film finally wins through. On the contrary, these reflections on the permanence of damage and distortion simply emphasise how tangled the thicket of suffering and desire is, how great a victory, *any* victory, is over those powerful forces that so indelibly mark its victims. In the end *Exotica* remains suspended over a Manichean bipolarity of human motives and feelings, where we must look at both sides of the polarity simultaneously and life as a result becomes undecidable.

This undecidable double view is exemplified in a number of ways, but it is nicely encapsulated in one small trope: the Exotica's outlandish two-way mirrors (in the shape of curvaceous females) that allow people in the club's back rooms to spy on 'private' table dances. According to one story (that of Zoe's mother, the founder of the club) these two-way mirrors were built for the protection of the dancers, allowing an onlooker to make sure nothing bad was developing at the tables; according to another (Eric's), they were financed by 'this very rich guy' who paid for the privilege of anonymous voyeurism. Christina unhesitatingly chooses the second interpretation, although there is no way of determining the truth. This is just one of the film's miniaturised metaphors of its own condition of antithetical impenetrability.

Egoyan's films repeatedly stage the spectacle of people working to subdue and control the messier and less predictable aspects of their lives through a process of instrumentalisation and substitution. Central characters in *Family Viewing*, *Speaking Parts* and *Calendar* compulsively use video representations to mime solutions to their private crises of desire or suffering; characters in *The Adjuster* use classification (censorship categories) and quantification (insurance adjustment) in similar ways. In *Exotica* huge swatches of the central action are *substitutive* in this way. Indeed it is impossible to describe the Christina-dancing/Francis-watching/Eric-commenting cluster without talking about a voodooistic re-enactment of trauma in forms so strangely altered as to be unrecognisable at first. Most of the time in Egoyan's cinema these substitutions, however understandable, do not work in the long run, give rise to severe distortions of behaviour and feeling and are clearly identified as bad strategies. In *Exotica*, they have this same aspect (think especially of Francis and Tracey), but the situation they are palliating is so awful that any kind of healing (or 'soothing') seems preferable to just suffering endlessly.

The substitutive process is very widespread. For example, one of the most persistent tropes in *Exotica* is the way characters use the substitute of money to regulate and ritualise acts of kindness or favour. Francis pays Christina for soothing him by dancing for him in the guise of his dead daughter (as she says to Thomas, 'paying me to do him this favour'), and he pays Tracey for babysitting a child who is not there. These are transactions where money is paid for emotional services. This is at first puzzling to viewers, but eventually felt as something innately perverse: the two realms are incommensurate. Compassion is precisely something you cannot buy or sell, and should not try to. Thomas acts in a similar way in fetishising the business of giving ballet tickets away after lying about his own cash layout to get them. But for him it seems like an attempt to reverse the activity of transforming emotion into cash, of substituting cash for emotion. Instead he pays out money to buy the token of affection (the tickets) and then converts that deed, within himself, into 'let's not soil this occasion with money' generosity. No wonder the contract between Francis and Thomas is so strange: Francis will commit a crime for Thomas (concealing his smuggling) if Thomas commits a crime for Francis (surreptitious tape-recording, then abetment of homicide). As Francis says 'you do this favour for me and I'll do that favour for you'. Things like these should not be traded. Adding together all these actions – and Christina's, and Eric's – the notion of 'doing a favour' becomes seriously twisted. Everyone is acting as they do for very strong reasons: their projects are all understandable and often, indeed, moving. Despite the ugly tinge of sexual crime that surrounds almost everything, the spectacle of their bizarre rituals and substitutions produces in the viewer the response not of distaste but of wonder and compassion.

Exotica's negotiation of its seductive maze of themes, tropes and situations is perhaps the most virtuosic performance in this arena of any of Egoyan's films. That is a strong statement, given the degree to which so many of them have dedicated themselves to this pursuit. *Exotica* is also, I would say, the film that most satisfyingly balances this formal play with a dramatic and psychological substance: with transgressiveness of subject matter and with characters of greater roundness and depth. And never has Egoyan found such a luxurious and powerful set of visualisations to complement the narrative. Prowling, stalking dolly shots have a long history in Egoyan, and in *The Adjuster* there is also a richness and density of *mise-en-scène* that is newly impressive. But in *Exotica* the filmmaker is able to match and redouble the transgressive sensuality of aspects of the narrative – above all the Exotica, crammed with errant desires and obscure repentances – with a sensuality of colours and textures and sinuous camera movement to an extent unprecedented in his cinema. The undersea coolness and shadow of the club, heated by the decor-accents of a tropical forest, produces a beautiful and caressing environment, and its visual interventionism is echoed in many of the other locations as well, notably Thomas's pet-shop with its fish tanks whose waters seem to glow with different unlikely colours, and Harold's and Tracey's apartment, surrounded by strong West Indian colours (and reggae music). At times Egoyan dares audacious strokes of *mise-en-scène* such as the repeated windshield reflection of a neon-sign lightning-bolt that seems to penetrate Francis's skull as he sits in his car outside Tracey's house, or Thomas's aforementioned eggs-as-ovaries. In short, the film is a virtuoso exercise in every dimension. It also puts the capstone to a certain kind of filmmaking for Egoyan. His subsequent projects, without ceasing to manifest many identifiable Egoyan characteristics, have been adapted from others' stories (*The Sweet Hereafter* (1997) and *Felicia's Journey* (1999) from novels by Russell Banks and William Trevor, respectively), or set abroad with non-North American actors (*Felicia's Journey*), or addressed to world-historical issues on a much-expanded scale (*Ararat* (2002)). They have, in other words, escaped the gravitational pull of Egoyan's first model of the feature film, that unique personal model whose members were full of unmistakable family resemblances. If *Exotica* is indeed the last of these, it is an eloquent farewell.

William Beard

ROBERT LEPAGE, 1995

Robert Lepage's *Le confessionnal* (*The Confessional*, 1995) is a film about blindness and its cognates that delves into the spaces of memory to bring to light hidden secrets and forgotten histories. Its primary narrative, set in two discrete yet tightly interwoven time frames, 1952 and 1989, circles around a secondary storyline that involves the making and viewing of a film – Hitchcock's *I Confess* (1953). That Lepage develops his film's politics around a complex dialectic of seeing and being seen, not seeing and being blinded, drawing, photographing, performing or filming, being imaged and being imagined, is significant. As Lepage himself has noted, what is at stake in the film is modernity itself: 'Imagine … an insular society of French origins, and what is more, Catholic, turned inward upon itself, witnessing the arrival of the great Hollywood machine', he says in the press package, 'In a symbolic manner, it can involve the transition to modernity, with all the re-questioning … that involves.' The film frames Quebec's modernity in relation to visual orientations and practices, specifically the collisions and conflicts that the arrival of the technologies of television and film generate between religious, oral-textual and secular, spectacular ways of seeing. But the film's own visual practices formulate a pointed critique of this modernity and the effects it has on the individual subject, on history, and on knowledge itself. By paying attention to the visual themes and motifs around which the narrative develops and the film's logic and aesthetics, it is possible to uncover some of the epistemological dimensions that colour the film's national-allegorical dimensions. As the film explores a variety of representational practices that affect our conception and experience of space, of subjectivity, and of logic itself, it seeks to come up with new conditions of knowledge and new possibilities of being.

In the year 1952, a voice-over narrator explains in the film's opening sequence, three important events made an impact on life in Quebec: the appearance of the first television sets, the re-election of Premiere Maurice Duplessis and the presence of Alfred Hitchcock, who chose the city to be the backdrop of his new suspense thriller. The list develops an argument in two visual registers – technological and social – that together enunciate the primary forces colliding as Quebec society enters into modernity. The arrival of television and film – Lepage's 'Hollywood machine' – marks the end of an oral-textual culture centred in the public sphere around the

Church's masculine sacred liturgy and in the private sphere around the kitchen table's feminine gossip best exemplified by the character of the motor-mouth aunt. In its place is the mass media's presentation of life as an immense accumulation of spectacles, along with the primary symptoms of this discursive reorganisation: the mediation of the real, the de-contextualising of knowledge and, for the entranced beholder of the spectacle, a radical sense of alienation. In the list of Pierre (Lothaire Bluteau), however, the arrival of television and the filmmaker in Quebec frames a third event – the re-election of Maurice Duplessis as premier of Quebec – that seems not to belong to the same order of things. And yet closer examination reveals that it too has everything to do with vision. Duplessis' reign is often referred to as 'La Grande Noirceur' or 'The Great Darkness' because of the way he struggled against the industrialisation, urbanisation and secularisation of the province, promoting instead a very conservative social order. Like the examples of film and television, this example also frames a particular 'way of seeing', as John Berger might say. Discourses about modernisation are often starkly utopic or dystopic: they either celebrate or condemn the development of mass media and culture industries at the expense of traditional cultures. What is fascinating about the list that opens *Le confessionnal* is the way it avoids simplistic binary oppositions that would idealise one over the other. Its tripartite structure suggests that modernity holds in tension practices that are conservative and inward-looking with practices that are conservative and outward-looking. Lepage's point in this film is that the culture industries of television and film perpetuate 'darknesses' every bit as much as the practices of Duplessis, the Church and the talk at the kitchen table do. By revealing the way phenomena are embedded in one another and thus avoiding any representation of history as a narrative of progress, the list ultimately allows for a more complex mapping of the factors that shape Quebec society and individual subjects.

So what are the effects of this history of social and media technologies on individual subjects? For the Lamontagne family in *Le confessionnal*, their personal inheritance of Quebec's peculiar legacy of modernity produces symptoms of blindness. Many writers have commented that within the modern Western paradigm, to observe is to exercise a kind of power over the object of vision. Here, however, the gaze of the observers has turned inward, generating a vicious circularity that produces passivity and alienation in both seer and seen. This is as true of the characters in the narrative's past tense as it is of the characters in the present tense. Within a world of darkness and blindness, the introspective and ultimately repressive logic of the confessional is as devastating as the spectacular and expressive logic of the strip-club's private booth. Neither permits productive forms of sociality.

Within the family, blindness is posed as a moral-epistemological problem, the consequence of a practice of seeing that separates subject from object and observer from observed. Françoise (Marie Gignac) wants a baby, and aunt Jeanne d'Arc (Lynda Lepage-Beaulieu) wants her daughter to be a star. These two young matriarchs are so caught up in their narcissistic fantasies they turn a blind eye to the sufferings of their charge, Françoise's 16-year-old sister Rachel (Suzanne Clément). The very model of a Sadean protagonist – that is, parentless, vulnerable and extremely beautiful – Rachel epitomises the state Laura Mulvey describes, in her famed essay 'Visual Pleasure and Narrative Cinema', as 'to-be-looked-at-ness'. Objectified by all who behold her, she is unable to return the gaze or speak. To resist her state of abjection, however, Rachel wages a battle for invisibility. Pregnant and refusing to identify the father, she struggles to conceal her body, avoids eye contact with everyone, and finally commits suicide to remove herself altogether from the devastating economy of the gaze. But even decades later, Rachel is pursued and her secrets probed as her descendants pour over photographic images of her to uncover the mysteries of the past.

Rachel's son Marc (Patrick Goyette), adopted and raised by Françoise and her husband Paul-Émile (François Papineau), also works to make himself invisible. Because he has no clear picture of his origins, he lives his life in retreat – passive, powerless, in the dark spaces on the margins of society. In the film, he is represented as a liminal figure; he is notably absent from the father's funeral ('il n'est pas trouvable', their cousin André remarks; 'he isn't findable'), is next only briefly glimpsed running away from the hotel room of a john, and when he is finally 'found', he is almost entirely obscured by steam deep in the recesses of a gay bathhouse. Marc's cousin and adopted brother Pierre is a painter, and therefore possesses special powers of vision. He takes on the task of curing Marc's condition of lost-ness by mapping out the coordinates of his time past and present. As Manon (Anne Marie Cadieux), the mother of Marc's son, proclaims: 'To know where you're going, you have to know where you are', and, by extension, where you come from. But Pierre looks to images – to representations and mediations – for answers to his questions, and so his maps have very little relationship to Marc's embodied experience of the world. As he pours over televisual, cinematic and photographic evidence to find clues to the mystery of Marc's paternity, it becomes increasingly clear that Pierre remains blind to the truths of his own body (his vertigo is a symptom of diabetes that shows the connections between him, Marc's son and their father), as well as to his brother's suffering. The stakes of Pierre's pursuit of vision without insight are high. Marc, like his mother, withers under so much scrutiny and finally disappears into suicide.

An example of the way Pierre's visually-oriented project of mapping ultimately fails to connect thought with experience occurs early in the film. Pierre, attempting to bridge the emotional distance between himself and his brother, traces their name, Lamontagne, in Chinese on a napkin with wine. Pierre draws the horizon line, and the summits of the mountains, and remarks that with the removal of one line within the image, his inscription becomes the sign for river. With this drawing of their patronym in red wine which metonymically and metaphorically represents blood shared and spilled, Pierre makes an argument for the interconnectedness of things. He demonstrates how meanings can contain others meanings hidden invisibly within them, and thereby shows that absence can be as full as presence. Marc's response, 'Mais c'est quoi le rapport?' ('but what's the relationship'), topples the entire edifice. Marc wonders about the relationship between river and mountain in Chinese script, but it is clear he is also expressing his doubts about his own relationship ('rapport') with the Lamontagne family. Most important, his query implicitly formulates a counter-argument to Pierre's. Not all forms of knowledge and experience can be connected, not all rifts bridged, Marc seems to (but of course cannot) say. By returning the symbolic abstractions to the literal, Marc maps out part of the conceptual space that is missing from Pierre's worldview, one that is resolvedly literal, embodied, grounded in experience rather than in mediations. Sadly, Pierre is unable to accommodate this alternative map into his own system.

The most important case of blindness in the film, however, is the father's: his is the source and model for all others. For Paul-Émile Lamontagne, blindness is a physical reality. At the beginning of the film, we are told that he has died of the diabetes which blinded him, and that his house shows the signs of his neglect. At the end of the film, however, his physical blindness is granted important symbolic, mythic resonances. Paul-Émile offers a story to Alfred Hitchcock, who is a passenger in his taxi, as possible material for a new suspense film. It is the 'story of a couple', more of a confession than a film pitch:

The wife is unhappy because she hasn't had any children, so she doesn't feel like a real woman. So one day she asks her younger sister to live with them. The wife is always sick and depressed, but the sister is very beautiful and full of life. The man tries to resist her but he can't so they fall in love. The problem is soon after she becomes pregnant. They are desperate because they don't want to hurt the wife so they disguise the situation and make it look like it is another man who is the father. When the child is born, the sister cannot bear the guilt so she kills herself.

Hitchcock listens, and asks what happens to the man. Paul-Émile replies: 'He cannot bring himself to love this child so when he sees all the suffering he has caused, he plucks his eyes out.' Hitchcock's retort, underlining the speaker's allusion to Sophocles' *Oedipus Rex*, is 'That's not a suspense story. It's a Greek tragedy!' This intertextual flourish indicates at once Paul-Émile's guilt and his sense of the inevitability of both his actions and their consequences. But his confession in a taxicab to the high priest of the cinema of a story that culminates in his own metaphorical blinding, like the confessions made to Catholic priests in the confessional, remains a secret. The truth of his family comes to light, but only briefly in a place where it will remain hidden from those who need to see it most.

Blindness is thus a way of referring to the way gaps between knowledge and experience are perpetuated over time, and to the toll such gaps wreak on human lives. When the film suggests that blindness is hereditary, it refers to the diabetes this father has passed on to his sons and grandsons, as well as to the fact that repressed secrets are responsible for the family's broader problems. But it also captures the 'darkness' perpetuated by their traditional and modern cultural practices' de-contextualised, disembodied, abstracted ways of seeing and being.

Lepage takes this theme of blindness and makes it into a structuring principle. The film's narrative is told in two time frames, 1952 and 1989, that intertwine with and strive to illuminate one another, but remain fundamentally detached. The film's past tense neither represents the memory of those in the film's present tense, nor does it represent what the present time's inquiry into the past has yielded. Likewise, much of what is represented in the past tense of the film remains just beyond the apprehension or comprehension of those in the present who are investigating it. Yet although there is this disconnect between the two storylines that remain at least partially blind to one another, the past continuously seeps into the present-tense narration of the film, leaving its indelible traces in peoples' lives, under their skin, and in the spaces they inhabit. The past cannot be summoned by nor subordinated to the gaze of the present, but colours and frames it nevertheless.

A recurring image again taken from the register of the visual captures this sense of history's layering of the then and now: paint, a medium which both obscures and reveals the traces and absences of what lies beneath. Pierre attempts to create a *tabula rasa* in the neglected house he inherits from his father. Despite his application of several different primary colours of paint, he is unable to fully cover up the traces of the photographs that once hung on his walls, which seep through layer after layer. But Lepage's motif of paint and the traces that bleed through it does more than simply point to the complex ways in which the past and the present, things forgotten and things remembered, all interconnect. It is a metaphor for the relationship between the conscious and unconscious mind, and for the relationship between cogitation and repression that is set into play most explicitly in the titular and archetypal scene of confession where hidden things are brought into consciousness only to remain secreted. It is also a metaphor for everything that is problematic about an epistemology based on the supremacy of sight; many things of great importance are, of course, invisibly hidden beneath the surface of things.

Despite the film's attention to the things that are not seen, or cannot be seen, and despite the way its present and past times interpenetrate without having full knowledge of one another, *Le confessionnal* offers an astonishing sense of *déja vu*. The camera's mobility through time as well as space yields a constancy of experience. Structured around audio, visual and narrative repetitions, this is a film with an almost dizzying circularity. Spaces repeat. Characters in both the present and the past tense of the film haunt the same restricted locations: the nearly gothic architecture of the Chateau Frontenac and the church, the long sterile hallways of the Lamontagne house, and the inside of the car. Spaces also echo and recall one another. The confessional with its narrow space and Cartesian grid-like grill is recalled in everything from elevator doors to shutters to private dancing booths in strip clubs to sauna ceilings. Symptoms and states repeat as well: diabetes, with its vertigo, weakness and eventual blindness appears in three generations; children cut off from their parents seek solace in the arms of older men in at least two. And all of these spaces and states themselves repeat the scenes and themes of the film within the film – Hitchcock's *I Confess*.

The effect of the constancy of embodied experience and space despite the passing of time, despite the machinations of modernisation, and despite the boundaries of fiction and reality is uncanny – *unheimlich* – that is, we experience something that is disorientingly familiar. The film mobilises the three main categories of the uncanny Freud identifies in his 1919 essay: things which relate to the notion of a double such as multiplied objects and involuntary repetitions of acts; castration anxieties expressed as loss of the eyes; and a feeling associated with losing one's way. For Freud, these elements in conjunction with intellectual uncertainty form a visual aesthetic and a subject matter that can provoke a 'quality of feeling' connected to the deepest, most intimate core of the human subject because it makes us behold the things that are most familiar to us in new frames. Lepage finds in Freud's notion a logic of images and narrative that can work to undermine the structures of knowledge he wishes to criticise.

Lepage's investigation of the secrets of the Lamontagne's familial home in the city of Quebec exploits the primary double meanings of *unheimlich*. In *The Uncanny* Freud writes that 'starting from the homely and the domestic, there is a further development towards the notion of something removed from the eyes of strangers, hidden, secret'. Like a haunted house, the Lamontagne's apartment's closed doors have concealed terrible deeds – adultery, childbirth out of wedlock and suicide – which, demanding to be known, even bleed through washes of crimson paint. In this place, we experience anxiety and dread because of the sense of inevitability the repressed will return and the returned will again be repressed.

The film's reworking of Hitchcock's famous shower scene reveals the psychological dimensions of the uncanny. Lepage's scene of bloody carnage takes place in a bathtub in which a male body is the object of what seems to be a razor's violence. Françoise is taking a bath to relax her nerves, and she invites her husband who is shaving his beard to come close so she can take his shaving foam off. She pulls him into the tub, and while they are jostling about, laughing, the tub suddenly fills with blood. Our first thought is that he has brought the razor in with him, and that we are witnessing an accidental castration. Only later do we learn that the blood is Françoise's from a miscarriage. According to Freud, 'anxiety about one's eyes, the fear of going blind, is quite often a substitute for the fear of castration'. What connects castration and blindness in Lepage's revisiting of Freud's notion of the uncanny is masculine guilt. In *The Uncanny* Freud explains: 'When the mythic criminal Oedipus blinds himself, this is merely a mitigated form of the penalty of castration, the only one that befits him according to the *lex talionis*.' Evidently, castration would befit the philandering Paul-Émile, who, less like Oedipus and more like some Sadean villain, has taken advantage of his 16-year-old sister-in-law. But in this film, anxiety about castration and impotence is also a substitute for broader epistemological fears – of knowledge become sterile and insight that reveals nothing – that emerge from the social conditions of Québécois modernity.

In addition to these sources of the uncanny – involuntary repetitions, losing one's eyes, being castrated – Lepage exploits the uncanniness of losing one's way, which is, in effect, another problem of vision and knowledge. I have already alluded to Marc's private emotional lost-ness and Pierre's attempts at mapping. These instances are merely emblematic of larger disorientations. At both the beginning and end of the film, a voice-over narration, rendered incantatory through its repetition, connects the film's problems of direction and vision to the historical. On the soundtrack, Pierre narrates 'In the city where I was born, the past carries the present like a child on its shoulders', while on the image track, we see a bridge behind which the city of Quebec is partially hidden. The soundtrack conjures the central trope from the old debate between the ancients and moderns about knowledge and its progress. In both Bernard of Chartres' statement of 1126 – 'We are dwarfs standing on the shoulders of a giant and thus able to see farther than the giant himself' – and Isaac Newton's reformulation in 1675 – 'If I have seen further, it is because I was standing on the shoulders of giants' – clarity and depth of vision are the consequence of the present's connection with the past. Lepage's substitution of the image of an adult and child for these mythic images of dwarves and giants indicates his conviction that the unit of the family is the most important place where past, present and future meet. In the final scene of the film, Pierre carries his deceased brother's child on his shoulders, and for an instant, we believe that the disconnect between past and present has finally been resolved, vicious circles will cease repeating, and vision and insight will end the family's plague of blindness. Yet the final images of the film fall entirely within the register of the uncanny and produce the strongest sense of uneasiness. Pierre takes the child *off* his shoulders and encourages him to teeter dangerously on the railing of the bridge. Accompanying this image of disequilibrium is the sound of the little boy's giggles, but the laughter is eerily ambiguous. This scene of journeying home, like the scene it repeats at the beginning of the film, is neither joyous nor celebratory. The image of the boy's grandmother's suicidal jump from this same bridge years earlier bleeds to the surface of our memory, and we realise that the existential condition of lost-ness has neither been resolved for the family nor, by extension, for Quebec.

The prospect of this final disequilibrium which so clearly undermines any sense of the narrative's own teleology need not be understood as a sign of Lepage's cynicism about the entire project of modernity. As mentioned above, the film explores a variety of representational practices that affect our conception and experience of space, of subjectivity, and of logic itself, and in so doing, seeks to come up with new conditions of knowledge and new possibilities of being. These conditions and possibilities are, however, not shown directly. There are no easy answers in this film about blindness, no quests that can lead straightforwardly to vision and insight. Indeed, Lepage's entire project seems to hinge on his criticism of an Oedipal hubris; if we believe we can probe the darkness for its secrets, if we believe our powers of vision are connected to insight, we are mistaken. In place of this hubris and the tragedies it wreaks, Lepage makes a case for what Samuel Weber, writing about Freud and Kant in his book *The Legend of Freud*, calls 'that peculiar state of knowing without knowing'; the film's two 'lost' central characters, Rachel and Marc, possess this state of knowing, and for brief moments so too might Pierre on the night he gets drunk and is tattooed, Manon ('Mowse') when she is holding her sick child, and Paul-Émile when he is telling his story to Hitchcock. In these scenes, Lepage demonstrates a knowledge of the body that can counter the abstractions of visually-oriented cognitive systems as well as their superficiality, and a knowledge of experience that can anchor mediations and representations. The film as a whole, moreover, produces this elusive state of 'knowing without knowing' for the viewer through its disturbing and haunting images of castration and blindness, its unpredictable doublings, its representation of lost-ness and its intellectual uncertainties. There may be no cure to the moral and epistemological dilemmas of the family and society – modernity is too much with them. Nevertheless, by cultivating disequilibrium and lost-ness, Lepage maps out the very space he believes a modern Quebec occupies, and by showing the problems that are inherent in the way we see, Lepage turns blindness into its opposite.

Monique Tschofen

EARTH

DEEPA MEHTA, 1998

The 1947 Partition of India has not been a topic for many Western filmmakers, even though the devastating massacres and violence between independent India and Pakistan have been described as India's Holocaust and account for one of the largest forced migrations of population in history. Before the British left India, the British Labour government, along with the Muslim League and the Indian Congress Party, split India into a Hindu-dominated India and a Muslim-controlled Pakistan that saw over ten million people forced from their homes and over a million people massacred out of religious fervour. Friends and neighbours turned on each other and women and children became targets of brutal assaults for eradicating communities from their homes and cities.

Indo-Canadian filmmaker Deepa Mehta, with her 1998 film *Earth*, personalises the global issues of sexuality and nationalism via this bloody history, and thereby situates epic topics at the level of ordinary mundane people. Kass Banning, in her essay 'Playing in the Light: Canadianizing Race and Nation', identifies Mehta as a truly 'independent transnational filmmaker' by virtue of her unique position as a filmmaker that transcends both authorship and genre into cross-cultural identifications and meanings. Mehta's films are uniquely Canadian, but more significantly they are the embodiment of the emerging trans-national genre of films and filmmakers.

Earth is based on Bapsi Sidhwa's novel *Cracking India*, an autobiographical account of the partition of India seen mostly through the eyes of eight-year-old Lenny and focuses on the group of friends and suitors around her *ayah* Shanta. As rumours of India's division begin to actualise, the group of friends begin to separate into their respective religions of Hindu, Muslims and Sikhs. Lenny's family is the Sethna household, an affluent family of Parsees who remain neutral, but their neutrality leaves them uncomfortably in the midst of escalating hostility between their friends and neighbours. The story behind the Parsees in India is that on coming over from Persia a millennia ago, the Indian prince said his country was too full to accept any newcomers and presented the Parsees a bowl of milk brimming to the top as a symbol of India. However, the Parsees stirred in some sugar and sent the milk back saying that they will be like the sugar in the milk: sweet, but invisible. The Parsees' neutral yet middle position marks a perfect alignment for Mehta the filmmaker, as she also becomes involved with the devastation of others but remains on the periphery. Two scenes exemplify the Sethna's position during the partition of India: first, as their family car drives through the crowded streets of the market place, an oncoming group of pro-Pakistan marchers envelop the vehicle. Even though the car and the marchers move in opposing directions, the Parsees' neutrality renders them invisible as well. They cannot take any one particular side without betraying someone close to them, but this in-between stance is also suggestive in its discussion of the responsibility for the ensuing chaos.

The main story, however, rests on the two young Muslims – Hasan the masseur and Dil Navez the ice-candy man (respectively played by Rahul Khanna and Aamir Khan). These two men are competing for the affection of Shanta (Nandita Das), the Hindu nanny and maid of the Sethna household. As the day of Independence nears, it is not only the country that gets divided, but also families from their homes and friends amongst each other. Although Mehta does not deal with the conflicting tensions prior to 1947 and the complex political motivations involved, the film acts as both a humane testament to a tragic moment in India's history and as a highly stylised interpretation of the tragedy of Partition and does not try to hide its heavy-handed symbolism. Similar to her earlier film *Fire*'s (1996) mythologically-derived names, Shanta connotes the meaning of *peace* in Sanskrit. As Shanta is the main preoccupation for most of the characters in the film, this anti-separatist film deals with the desire for peace during India's time of chaos.

The film begins with young Lenny (Maia Sethna) colouring of a map of India in an array of different colours accompanied by a voice-over of adult Lenny (Bapsi Sidhwa) discussing the arbitrary line of division left by the British that would scar India as a continent forever. Her colouring is interrupted as we immediately see Lenny's crippled leg as she moves into the adjoining room where her curiosity propels her to smash a plate into irreparable pieces. Her seemingly unmotivated action is loud and violent as even she recoils from her own senseless action. As Lenny is questioned about her actions by her mother, she asks back, 'Can one break a country?' Clearly Lenny does not understand the eminent division of India, but her confusion over the ensuing violence and separation to come frames our own viewpoint of the film. Lenny's penchant for the truth also frames the beginning and the end of the film along with the voice-over of Sidhwa, but the role of truth-telling also speaks of Mehta the filmmaker as telling the basic truths of separation during the partition of India. In *Earth*, Gandhi and

Lord Mountbatten are merely names dropped in hushed conversations. Mehta has chosen to de-mythologise India using conventional narrative cinema, but her cinematic techniques do fit in with the concerns of many transnational filmmakers, especially in her emphasis of the ephemeral and liminal.

During a dinner party at the Sethna household, a heated argument begins between Mr Rogers, a white British officer and Mr Singh, a Sikh buffalo owner. As emotions begin to rise, the camera floats continuously back and forth conveying the rhythm of a ticking time bomb – and the conversation does explode as Rogers' insults draw Singh to attack him across the table with his fork. After everyone has settled down, Roger prophetically mutters, 'This bloody country. It's the only home I know.' Although this line does not receive any special attention within the film, it should be noted that this line is the underlying thesis of the film. Everyone, no matter which religion they belong to, felt the effects of the partition that saw over a million people massacred at the hands of civil strife and millions more losing the only home they ever knew. Friends stopped speaking with one another and neighbours vanished in the night to become refugees across new borders that were being quickly re-drawn. Religion was used by the British to dictate the displacement of people from their homes and it is no coincidence that the lame leg that stifles Lenny's movement is a direct result of polio – a disease brought to India by the British.

Although the film does not deal with the escalating religious animosity pre-1947, Mehta does show her awareness of territorial struggle in a scene featuring Spring Festival kite-flying. This scene is interesting for two reasons: the first being that the soundtrack diagetically breaks in and out of the sequence and second that the rooftop will be once again visited, but the context of this second visit will be as different as day from night in contrasting the chaos that has overcome Lahore and its citizens.

First, the haunting original score by A. R. Rahman floods the scene as we see the action from high crane shots or long shots of other rooftops. There is minimal dialogue as the focus is on the vibrant colours of the scene and the music, but at one point Dil Navez begins singing along to the music that seemingly appears outside the diagetic action. It is not unfathomable that the music came from a record player, but in other scenes in the film, Mehta purposely establishes the victrola player as the source of music in the beginning of the park sequence and in the ballroom dancing scene between Lenny and her mother. Therefore, it can be argued that the intrusion of the soundtrack into the main diagesis is purposeful here to identify Dil Navez apart from the rest of the characters.

The scene begins with Dil Navez putting on his Muslim *Jinnah* cap as Shanta, Lenny and Imam Din (Kulbhushan Kharbanda) pay him a visit. The putting on and taking off of his cap is an action that will be repeated in key scenes later on in the film as well, indicating the motivations behind his actions as personally or religiously sanctioned. On the rooftops of Dil Navez's surrounding neighbours, Muslims, Sikhs and Hindus are all enjoying the festivities and are flying kites in the daylight sky. However, as Dil Navez teaches Shanta how to fly the kite in the sky while amorously flirting with her, another kite tries to cut theirs out of the sky. He proceeds to take over and cuts the other kite instead to general applause. In this bold and light-hearted sequence, Dil Navez has proven that he is a character who will fight for his territory and who also has the ability to win. His character changes most drastically over the course of the film from a charming cad into being angry and deceitful, but he is also the one Lenny likes the most. In fact, the original title of Sidhwa's novel was *Ice-Candy Man* and Mehta uses the Dil Navez character as an emotional barometer for the pace of the entire film: when he is rational and charming, Lahore appears to be merry and cosmopolitan, but when he loses his sisters to a brutal massacre and his desire for Shanta is not returned, Lahore is lost in its internal violence and chaos. During an earlier discussion between Dil Navez and Shanta as he walks her and Lenny from the park, he tells her it does not matter that she is a Hindu and he a Muslim because, 'In God's eye, we are all equal.' This has a resounding effect on the remainder of the film as it suggests that only in human eyes has difference become intolerable.

As the partition of India divided a country based upon religious nationalism, the group of close friends around Shanta also begins to show cracks in their friendships with one another. In their first visit to the park, we see Shanta and Lenny abruptly leave on account of an on-going politically-charged discussion about Muslims and Hindus. However, the next time the group of friends meets again, the park itself has transformed; Muslims, Hindus and Sikhs have begun keeping to themselves, but only the group around Shanta remains the same. The deterioration of this small close-knit community of mixed religious backgrounds represents the country as a whole as individuals become divided amongst each other and themselves. The close group of friends' desire for peace has shifted from jovial jesting and friendly debates into restless anxiety and derogatory slurs against each others' faiths. As each can only sit back and watch their country break into two and anticipate the power struggle between the Hindus and the Muslims over land, fissures appear at the level of everyday interactions.

The first slur made by the Muslim butcher about the Hindi diet is greeted with silence, and raucous laughter from the speaker himself. However, this quickly escalates into tension when the group of friends is next gathered around for a meal. The butcher's hostility first turns onto Lenny who he accuses as acting too much like the English. Once reprimanded, his anger is unleashed on the boy who comes to clear his plate away. Finally, the tension erupts between the friends who cannot stop from debating fiercely whether the Hindus or the Muslims will receive Lahore. There is a sense of tension and pride as this city is all of their homes, but they all know only half of them will be able to remain. Once again, Mehta's camera floats back and forth between opposing arguments, this time between the butcher and Sher Singh the zookeeper. Hasan tries to pacify the situation with reason by saying, 'We share the same language, food, and enemies.' Since they are gathered around talking, eating and fighting with each other, this line points to their common bond and also to the source of the their conflict. They have lived as brothers for centuries, but now that each may be given their own independence, each will fight for what they believe is rightfully theirs and theirs alone. Hasan and Dil Navez appear to be the only two abstaining from conflict and so it is no coincidence that they are the only two who are officially courting Shanta. However, as Shanta begins to show preference for the gentle-hearted Hasan, Dil Navez's jealousy corresponds to his involvement with mob violence and the unraveling of the city's chances of achieving a peaceful outcome.

The turning point for Dil Navez comes as he waits for his sisters to arrive from Gurdaspur, which has just been given over to India. As he and others wait during a twelve-hour delay, the stationmaster tells him, 'Trust in Allah, brother.' The train rolls in, but shrieks and screams are heard as the train doors open to massacred bodies and sacks of women's amputated breasts. These ghost trains went back and forth in Punjab slaughtering thousands of people as India and Pakistan were about to awake to independence, but 'an independence soaked in our brothers' blood'. The apocalypse has begun and mob mentality has completely taken over as all hell has broken loose. Shanta, Lenny and Hasan go to visit Dil Navez, but this time, the view from his rooftop is of Muslims and Hindus fighting one another to a backdrop of a fire-brazen Lahore in deep contrast to the earlier Spring Festival. Perhaps as the most violent gesture in the film, Shanta holds Lenny as they stand in-between Hasan and Dil Navez and watch in horror as a Muslim man is torn in two by the Hindu mob in police jeeps. Bombs are going off in the Hindu tenements and firefighters arrive quickly, but they are Muslim and spray petrol instead of water onto the buildings housed full of people. There were not even civil servants left in Punjab, but only those fighting only for India or Pakistan. Lenny later mimics the horror she has witnessed and asks her cousin Adi to help her tear one of her dolls in two. As the doll rips open, Lenny cannot understand her actions and weeps in frustration, echoing the first scene when she does not understand how one can break a country and smashes a plate on the floor. She still does not understand and her cousin asks her, 'Why are you so mean if you can't stand it?' But how does anyone, let alone an eight-year-old child, understand the senseless massacres in their city streets? At the wedding of her friend Papoo, after the discovery that she is being married off to an old man, Shanta appeases Lenny's concern by explaining, 'Fear is making people do crazy things.' Lenny's ten-year-old friend has been married off to an elderly Christian dwarf to save her and her family, but all Lenny can do is give her friend a doll as a present that gets snatched away along with her innocence. Mehta uses the viewpoint of Lenny not unlike Harper Lee's use of 'Scout' Finch in *To Kill a Mockingbird* to simplify extremely serious issues and to highlight the situation through the heightened sensitivity of an innocent child's eyes. The child-like naïveté of the situation is echoed once again when Lenny and her cousin encounter an orphaned Muslim boy. Without missing a beat he tells them that he found his mother hanging naked in a Mosque tied by her hair and asks if they want to play marbles. The escalating violence remains incomprehensible even as Lenny sees a gun in her parent's bedroom. Only the gun remains in its box, an object that automatically signifies violence, but in this film seems oddly out of place. That is because the violence that Mehta explores goes deeper than the cold distant killing of firearms. The violence during the partition was mostly hand-slaughtered massacres carried out by raging mobs fuelled by a long dormant hatred that goes far back into history. This violence was not sudden nor was it new, but it did need a catalyst such as the arbitrary line of division over people's homes to further fuel a deeply-seeded conflict. Along with the ghost trains, there were many attacks on women, since they are bearers of the enemy's future generations and symbols of fertility.

As Shanta and Lenny cower in terror and fear from this ungodly spectacle, Dil Navez watches and his passionate hatred is mirrored in the blazing fires in the city below him. Hasan has gone down to see if he can help and Dil Navez takes this opportunity to express his need for Shanta and to ask for her hand in marriage. The metaphor of the lion in the cage has been repeated throughout the film; the lion that Lenny is so afraid of in the beginning, but which has been promised to be guarded by the zookeeper and the butcher has figuratively been unleashed. The lion is the animal inside all of us, waiting for the cage to open, and Dil Navez needs Shanta to control the animal inside of him. He is trying to hold onto the last remnants of peace left within him, but it is too late. Shanta remains silent to his proposal and his gesture of peace is only accepted by little Lenny. The scene conveys a sense of impotence on both Dil Navez and Shanta's part after the brutal violence witnessed from below suggests all words and actions are futile to stopping the escalating madness. Mehta sets the discussion between Shanta and Dil Navez in front of a large, clearly symbolic cage of audible doves. As Shanta sits against the cage unable to respond to Dil Navez's requests, it becomes clear that peace is simply no longer an option.

After Shanta rejects Dil Navez's marriage proposal, she turns to Hasan who she plans on fleeing Lahore with to get married. We discover that Hasan has been hiding Sher Singh the zookeeper in his house as the group of friends are slowly leaving their homes or converting to Islam in the now Muslim-controlled Lahore. As Dil Navez laments that he needs Shanta to watch over him and to keep the animal inside him from escaping, Hasan has been protecting the lion keeper in his own home. By this point, Shanta has made it clear that she wants only Hasan and as they consummate their love, Lenny peeking through one window sees Dil Navez glaring from another window. In the following scene, Dil Navez walks off to the side of the house, removes his cap, wipes away a tear, and puts the cap back on. We see that his heart has been broken and he expresses his emotion specifically after removing a symbol of his faith, but the fury in his eyes immediately following sees him put his cap back on suggesting his subsequent vengeance will be personally motivated, but carried out in the name of Allah. This reaffirms his earlier argument to Shanta that in the eyes of God they are all equal, but that it is the human heart that cannot be appeased.

Before the mob of Muslims storm the Parsee household looking for Hindus and Sikhs to persecute, there is a calm before the eye of the storm. Lenny and Hari the gardener, who has converted to Islam and has had to cut off his *dhoti* pigtail and changed his name to Himmat Ali, go for a walk in the empty streets. Lenny asks about the whereabouts of her *ayah* and at this eerily calm moment, everyone becomes concerned with the whereabouts of Shanta, but they are unable to find her or peace anymore. As they walk along the deserted streets, they come across the slain body of Hasan on the side of the road and it is at that moment we begin to hear the chanting mob in the background. Hari looks on in disbelief at Hasan's lifeless body and asks, 'What have they done to you, my friend?' The 'they' he refers to no longer represents anything reasonable, as Hasan was likely killed for hiding Sher Singh, but that he was a Muslim killed by other Muslims is only a reflection of the madness. Also, as Hari has converted, he too is now a Muslim contemplating the killings that continue to go on after independence.

As the mob surrounds the Parsee household and Shanta has hidden herself in her madam's bedroom, the mob has become diluted with power and uses this opportunity for humiliating and terrorising the clearly outnumbered Parsees and their servants. A familiar face emerges from the mob, and it is the butcher who demands to know the whereabouts of the 'Hindu nanny'. He is no longer an admirer or even a stranger, but a clear representation of the drastic change that has taken place among the people. It is Imam Din, a respected elder Muslim and servant, that challenges the mob, but as the crowd does not believe Shanta has left and becomes restless, Dil Navez breaks through the crowd and shoves them out of the way. Lenny runs up to him and he offers her a treat, but first asks where Shanta really is. After all the violence and human atrocities and disappearance of friends and neighbors that Lenny has witnessed, she has remained as honest as she was in the first scene of the film and confesses the hiding spot of Shanta. Whereas she was praised in the beginning for telling the truth, Dil Navez turns his back on her and motions for the mob to go inside the house. Shanta is dragged out as the members of the Parsee household are held back and trampled over by the mob. In the chaotic stampede that follows, Shanta's *sari* has been half torn off and she is never to be seen again by Lenny who never recovers from her grief over betraying her *ayah*. In the novel, Lenny's betrayal of her *ayah* leads her to obsessively look for Shanta everywhere. It turns out she has not been killed, but turned into a prostitute and unhappily married to Dil Navez. In the film, however, Mehta leaves Shanta's fate ambiguous – peace has not died, but has been torn away from Lenny forever. The adult Lenny has not gotten over her guilt nor has she comprehended the result of all the violence. The only thing she does know is that when she lost Shanta, she lost a large part of herself.

As Mehta resides in Canada but enjoys shooting in India, her strong affection for her mother country translates onto the screen through her liminality as a transnational filmmaker. More so in *Earth* than in *Fire*, the external landscapes are captured and celebrated with more screen time and more notably, the characters progressively speak more in Hindi than in English (the languages spoken in *Earth* are Hindi and English, along with Urdu and Punjabi, but I cannot confirm or deny the presence of four distinct languages). The role of language plays an immensely important part in the representation of culture because language is also rooted to the earth of its speakers. In *Earth* especially, the film begins with an even mixture of English and Hindi, but as the narrative progresses and the story is no longer about the British occupation but about the people of Lahore, the native tongue is almost exclusively the only language spoken by the end. Earlier comments about English being the greatest gift given by the British to India is strongly ironic now. A country torn in two and a people divided, it is their language that still unites them, for better or for worse.

Amy Fung

ATANARJUAT: THE FAST RUNNER

ZACHARIAS KUNUK, 2001

Zacharias Kunuk's *Atanarjuat: The Fast Runner* is the first Inuit-produced, Inuktitut language, feature-length dramatic film, and, after winning the Caméra d'Or at the Cannes Film Festival in 2001, it achieved widespread popular and critical success. It is not, however, a museum curiosity, but the culmination of twenty years of media production on the part of its producers, Igloolik Isuma Productions, which together provide a complex engagement with the concept of time in relation to culture and place. Indeed, the history of media practices in northern Canada can be understood, in part at least, as a critical response to the dominant presence of broadcast television (this is dealt with in Jerry White's chapter on *Asivaqtiin* (*The Hunters*) in this volume). While the temporal structure of commercial television is consistent with the ideological function of entertainment, *Atanarjuat* draws upon oral tradition in order to communicate Inuit history across time through an articulation of place. This engaging communicative process forces a re-imagining of present-day life in the north through the linkage of contemporary media practices with the pedagogic and communal value of oral culture.

The claim that movies *take place* in time signals the close relation between the temporal and the spatial, a relation that is central to philosophical investigations of the ontology of the moving image – a line of inquiry that is usefully mapped onto the central role of film in conceptualising the history of the twentieth century, particularly in the popular imagination. To say that *Atanarjuat*, or any film, is fundamentally about time is to draw attention to the artifice of cinematic representation and the gap between representation and reality. But 'time' is literally a production tool in contemporary digital video (the medium with which this film originates) which is technically described as a time-based medium because computerised editing software locates and manages images through a sequential time-code audio signal. This temporal and technological 'base' is the ground upon which the superstructure of culture and community is constructed.

When the concept of time is invoked in modernist art cinema, it is, following Gilles Deleuze's arguments in the book *Cinéma 2: L'image-temps*, set against the physicality of place and offers, instead, a cinematic journey into dream and memory, offering an image of thought that may relate to place but is also understood as providing access to a depth of meaning beyond the physical surface. Of course, this perspective necessarily understands clock time as a cultural invention for the administration of society and is consistent with the ideological function of a linear narrative of history as progress. Inuit culture and tradition provides an alternative means of understanding the relationship between time and space, as between community and meaningful cultural continuity. Time and space are integrated in the formation of culture while in dominant Euro-centric critical theory, space is conceptualised as static and undialectical while time is privileged as the vehicle for history. The necessity for the deconstruction of a culturally-specific ideological use of time must not elide alternative conceptualisations in which the temporal and the spatial are integrated and integral to each other.

Atanarjuat, based on a thousand-year-old Inuit legend, is the story of conflict and discord emergent with the entrance of individualistic greed into the community. The nomadic community of Igloolik is visited by a shaman, Tuurngarjuaq, who challenges the leader, Kumaglak, leading to the latter's death, upon which the subsequent shift in power divides the community and ostracises one of its members, Tulimaq, who is subsequently plagued by bad luck as a hunter. The survival of his family depends upon his acceptance of the scorn and meagre rations from the mean-spirited new leader Sauri. Tulimaq's sons, Aamarjuaq and Atanarjuat, grow up to be excellent hunters and, respectively, the strongest and the fastest in the region, bringing an end to the family's bad luck but also continuing the rivalry with Sauri's clan. This antagonism culminates with Atanarjuat's love for Atuat, a beautiful young woman betrothed to Sauri's son Uki. The survival of the community is threatened by the lust for power and control on the part of Sauri's clan, particularly represented by the cruel persona of Uki, but also by Atanarjuat's own double transgression of marital norms – first by openly coveting Atuat, and later after marriage, by his infidelity with Uki's sister Puja. Here, the communal need for order is set against individual desire on the part of both Uki and Atanarjuat. A southern-based audience must set aside the privileging of Atanarjuat over Uki in the framework of an individualised conflict of good against evil – a framework which must be understood as arbitrary and ideological rather than integral to narrative. While this conflict clearly exists, and while Atanarjuat is more appealing as a character – kind, good-humoured and physically attractive – the film also forces us to reconcile individualism with the continuity of community, a process existent in time as well as in place.

The value of the story is in communicating the need to privilege the needs of the group over that of the individual through presentation of the grim consequences of ignoring this message. There is evidence of four thousand years of continuous habitation in the area of Igloolik, where the film was produced. This culture was able to survive by communicating its historical and cultural narratives through oral storytelling and it is with this communicative legacy that the film engages. The cultural function of the oral tradition is temporal continuity and, in the case of the Inuit, that continuity has a primary relationship with the landscape. Just as the gap between thought and place useful to modernism is inapplicable in an understanding of Inuit culture, so too is that between time, space and history. For the Inuit, history is not built up with a succession of generations; rather, the spirit life of those who have come before are present and engaged with contemporary experience. This fact is explicit in the shamanistic practices with which the film begins and concludes. The function of shamanism and the relation between body and spirit is not simply a Sunday fairytale but integral to cultural meaning, that this belief system has been almost entirely marginalised with twentieth-century assimilation and the colonising intrusions of Christianity marks the value of this film in the restoration of tradition; that is to say, of continuity through time and in space.

While conventional museum images posit aboriginal culture as static and locked into the distant past, in fact the nomadic culture of the Inuit by definition cannot be simplified as static even if contemporary circumstances are marked by permanent settlement. This cinematic rearticulation of cultural myth contributes to the vitality of contemporary Inuit culture while simultaneously confounding disciplinary distinctions between film and video, documentary and drama, fiction and history, traditional storytelling and mass culture, as well as the relation between the local and the global. The intervention against dominant uses of media is made clear in Igloolik Isuma's statement of intent prepared for an earlier television series called *Nunavut* ('Our Land') made to coincide with the formalisation of the new territory within the nation-state. In that script they state that: 'From the *Iliad* to *Hamlet* to *Star Wars* to *Star Trek*, conventional Western narrative requires emotional conflict, often with violence, to be recognised as drama. In the European tradition, the conflict *is* the story, and without one we assume there simply isn't a story there at all. However, this is a cultural assumption that different cultures may not share.' What the statement makes explicit is the relation between cultural representation and the claim to territory, set against the system of colonisation as it has been written over the land.

Atanarjuat does provide an intense dramatic experience in accord with the Western narrative tradition, but it resists reproducing the naturalisation of culturally-specific temporal and spatial conventions. Likewise, it functions as a document of traditional practices of pre-contact life on the land. Extended scenes reveal practices of food preparation and shelter building, while the setting and costumes also provide a visual record of the material context of the narrative. In this way, the film provides the cultural continuity that once would have been maintained orally and in the lived integration of tradition with everyday practice. That continuity is not contained within the closed narrative but is renewed through the agency of craft practitioners involved in the making of the film and who are then able to share this knowledge with others in the community. As the production notes accompanying the film's DVD release indicate, extensive research in the design of the film included both the consultation with elders as well as thorough study of textual records and museum artefacts originating with imperialist white explorers. In this way, the film is re-appropriating Inuit culture, and closing the circle broken by colonialism. The accuracy of representation is a primary consideration for the producers, as an antidote to the stereotype marginalisation and misrepresentation of northern peoples in mainstream media culture beginning with Robert Flaherty's *Nanook of the North* (1922) and continuing into the present. We must understand this narrative of pre-contact life as emergent in the context of colonisation.

Similarly, the legend of Atanarjuat fulfilled multiple related functions in Inuit culture, including the entertainment value of storytelling as well as that of historical narrative. The story must be compelling and engaging for it to have survived over time, and the survival through time of tradition and community depends upon the communication of cultural values. In this way, the Euro-centric distinction between objective history and fiction are confounded. While *Atanarjuat* is a fictional film, Atanarjuat is a real being within Inuit traditional culture. He embodies the threat to community survival posed by individualist-based discord, and the resolution of this narrative provides a necessary articulation of the continuity of communal identity – a continuity through time that is fundamentally based on survival upon the land. In the published screenplay for the fiction film (edited by Gillian Robinson), there is a photograph of a bench-like stone near the settlement of Igloolik known as that upon which Atanarjuat would sit during hunting expeditions. Likewise, the specific locations of the legend are known in the community, and this cultural map is integrated with hunting and settlement practices.

In contrast, the conceptualisation of the north through southern eyes is of an undifferentiated frozen mass sparsely populated by a vanishing primitive people characterised by a life of humourless grim survival. What the film demonstrates is the complexity of culture as lived practice and the differentiation of characters in contrast to the dominant stereotype of either noble or bloodthirsty savage, in either case contained by the ideological assumption of disappearance. Of course, disappearance is predicated upon a southern Euro-centric perspective predicated upon a teleology of progress through which history is compartmentalised and the past is replaced by an ever-unfolding present. What *Atanarjuat* provides is a narrative through which the integration of past and present is felt in lived reality.

From the perspective of a non-Inuit audience, the film begins by thrusting into unfamiliar and undifferentiated territory and the first line of dialogue, 'I can only sing this song to someone who understands it', reiterates this discord. We are compelled to watch rather than expect didactic conventions of narrative to reproduce that which is already familiar to us. Producer and cinematographer Norman Cohn indicates that while the film is primarily dramatic entertainment and not, strictly speaking, an educational film. He told Jason Anderson, in the 11 April 2002 issue of Toronto's *Eye Weekly*, that 'it has to educate people *how to watch*. [As an audience, we then realise] that what [we are] watching is a culture that communicates by watching. So all of a sudden the way in which [we are] watching is actually culturally appropriate.' While earlier productions of Igloolik Isuma were made with Inuit as the primary audience and southern distribution as a secondary consideration, this film has proven to be successful with audiences throughout the world. While the film makes use of dramatic storytelling conventions, it also confounds assumptions of verisimilitude. What we see is set in the past but the experience of viewing forces a reconciliation with present reality. Moreover, while dominant canonical assumptions of Canadian cinema privilege social realism and the heritage of documentary production, *Atanarjuat* confounds these categories.

National cinema typically asserts unity and coherence through the marginalisation of non-mainstream narratives in order to proclaim a common identity. This approach naturalises the arbitrary political construct of the nation-state which has, in turn, mythologised the 'true north' as the vast empty expanse onto which national culture is written. Nationalist culture fulfils the ideological function of mythologising place in order to legitimise borders. However, if the origins of documentary in Canada are, following Grierson's establishment of the National Film Board (NFB), to show Canada to Canadians and to the rest of the world, the function of which is to insert colonial Canada into the modernist industrial economy; what *Atanarjuat* provides is recognition of the limits of national cinema. In order to gain production financing through Telefilm Canada, Canada's federal film and television funding agency, Igloolik Isuma had to challenge the ghettoisation of Aboriginal productions within a highly restrictive financing envelope in comparison with that which is available for feature films. While Canadian film financing is typically tied to token efforts of national distribution, for which distributors are subsidised irrespective of their actual efforts to get the film seen by Canadians, this film was inserted into the global media marketplace and the filmmakers refused to sign with a Canadian distributor until significant promotional efforts were guaranteed. Against the unifying fantasy of Canadian multiculturalism, what the film instead articulates is the experience of colonisation and resistance in a context which challenges and exceeds national borders.

The story is told through mastery of advanced digital video technologies (shot on digital Betacam format and then transferred to 35mm film for theatrical release), reflecting the producer's affinity with activist and artist uses of media unbeholden to conventions of cinema. In particular, the representational strategy consists of lingering close shots of the faces of the characters. It is the nuance of unspoken reactions that are as important as what is actually said, and is also indicative of the distinction between Inuit and southern approaches to meaning. In this way, the story which forces us to see Inuit culture and tradition also forces us to see cinema in new ways. Likewise, while conventional cinema privileges authorship as co-extensive with the singular identity of the director, the actual production practice of this film reflects the non-hierarchical and communal nature of Inuit culture. We see culture from the inside, as a process through which community and conflict is negotiated, and if the film begins by situating non-Inuit audiences as lacking an interpretive framework, it is because the conflict central to the narrative must be resolved through a process of learning and experience rather than in accordance with the static terms of tradition.

What we see is that traditional culture is not cast in the past and separate from present-day challenges; rather its integration with contemporary media forces a rethinking of the terms of both of these points of reference. The temporal trajectory of narrative cinema is predicated upon the continual unfolding of new information in the formation of character complexity and in the development and final resolution of conflict. What is key to this form is its containment within the temporal framework of the text to which the audience is positioned externally. Where narrative progress emerges with the continual unfolding of the new within the text, Inuit storytelling folds back and forth upon the experience of culture and history. Indeed, storytelling is the primary way of communicating history – where history is simultaneously about the specificity of place and the lessons needed for community survival within place. In this way, the arbitrary discord between metaphor and metonymy unravels. An Inuit audience is already familiar with the story of Atanarjuat; indeed, the film's director Zacharias Kunuk reports experiencing it as a frequently-told bedtime story. He told Kimberly Chun in an interview for *Cineaste* that 'It's a lesson about what happens to people when they act, and it has *everything* because when we were growing up, there was no school system, and the Inuktitut way of teaching was telling these stories. Then you start to choose how you want to lead your life.' The question then becomes how this particular version of the story functions in a contemporary context.

The story reveals life formed by the experience of the seasons rather than the clock, the rhythms of place are integrated with the rhythms of the body. The film begins in the darkness of winter, then cuts ahead in time to maturity of Atanarjuat and Aamarjuaq as grown men, but we see that the conflict through which Sauri has come to take leadership of the community continues to shape their lives. The central image of the film is that of Atanarjuat running naked across the open tundra, fleeing Uki and his cohorts who have just murdered Aamarjuaq in a revenge ambush. As in other key moments of conflict in the film, survival is achieved by a combination of physical effort and the intervention of the spirit world. Arguably, Atanarjuat's impossible run across the open ice field is a kind of suspension of time, following which his physical healing or rebirth accompanies a spiritual reconciliation (for having transgressed marital taboos) prior to his recuperation into society. This reconciliation is important in the original legend and is detailed in the film's screenplay, though it has been largely excluded from the final film. In traditional storytelling, variations of the legend are determined by the contingencies of present circumstances, and this variable structure further demonstrates the integration of past and present in accordance with the needs of the community. In this case, the compelling drama of the chase, familiar to cinema audiences, emphasises the individualised conflict of romance and jealousy through which the vitality of the legend is made manifest – though at the expense of a literal representation of the determining presence of the spirit realm in traditional culture (a presence which has itself been violently erased through the intrusions of Christianity). As Kunuk bluntly states in the published screenplay, 'Four thousand years of oral history silenced by fifty years of priests, schools and cable TV.'

The temporal relation between past and present is reiterated through the act of naming. To take on the namesake of a deceased family member is on the one hand an expression of cultural continuity, but it also has literal value. As a sidebar in the published screenplay explains of *Tugslurausiq*, or terms of address: 'When a loved one passes away, his or her name may be given to the next child to be born. The child will be addressed using the same kinship terms that were used when addressing the deceased person.' When Atuat discusses with Panikpak her anxiety about the arranged marriage with Uki, this elder refers to her as 'Little Mother' and quietly discourages the marriage. Several times in the film Panikpak calls upon the spirit of her deceased husband Kumaglak to intervene and her advice to Atuat is a similar intervention across time in order to restore order in the community. In this way one generation is not understood as replacing the previous but as being a literal embodiment of the past in the present.

The relation of names existing through time that is set up in the dialogue between Atuat and Panikpak is then manifest in the film's conclusion. It is a form of trial for Uki, his sister Puja and cohorts Pakak and Pittiulaq who must face the consequences for the harm their actions have brought to the community. The scene involves shamanistic reference to animal spirits in order to draw out and finally confront the bad spirit Tuurngarjuaq and draw to an end the discord created by the shaman ritual at the film's beginning. There is no distinction between lived experience and spirit life, and spirit life is not simply of the past; rather, it is populated by figures who have lived in an earlier time but who intervene in present reality. Following the banishment of Tuurngarjuaq's spirit the accused on trial are also sent into exile which, in these difficult physical conditions means that their ability to survive becomes severely compromised. While the film brings us into a world that is demonstrably far more complex than the stereotype of grim survival, it is the survival of the community that is privileged over that of individuals. The film then concludes with Panikpak calling to her dead husband Kumaglak whose name has been given to the son of Atuat and Atanarjuat. Kumaglak the child speaks in the husband's voice, asking Panikpak to sing his hunting song. In this way, Kumaglak, the community leader at the start of the film is returned to his position. This continuity through time via name and namesake is not to suggest the substitution of one for the other; instead, it posits the co-existence within one character of multiple identities.

In the film's climax, prior to this communal and temporal resolution, Atanarjuat has returned to Igloolik and takes revenge upon Uki, Pakak and Pittiulaq by luring them into his igloo under the pretence of clearing away the weight of ill-feeling through the sharing of food. He then steps outside, secures carved antlers to his boots in order to provide stability on the slippery ice surface he has created as the floor of the igloo, brandishes a club and returns inside. In the original legend as reported in the descriptions accompanying the published screenplay, Atanarjuat brutally murders his foes. In contrast, in the film Atanarjuat demonstrates his ability to murder and then brings the club down beside Uki's head rather than bashing it into his skull. We can read this transformation of the legend productively in the context of how storytelling elements are flexible and contingent upon the needs of the community. Here, Atanarjuat demonstrates his power first through force and then through the ability to withhold the violent consequences of that force. In this way, the cycle of violence is disrupted and the community is able to reconstitute itself. While this is a narrative rooted in tradition, it can be read allegorically as an indictment of the negative force of colonisation as well as a means of conveying Inuit history. The cinematic transformation of the legend makes use of southern-based systems of representation to re-claim culture as distinct from the experience of colonisation through which Inuit are produced as victims. In this way, the cinematic narrative becomes a means of reaching through time to re-invent the present.

Darrell Varga

BEARWALKER

SHIRLEY CHEECHOO, 2002

Let us begin *in medias res*. Two adult sisters sit in front of a television, a third sister enters the room and gesturing towards the TV comments with amusement, 'Oh, the Young and the Useless', presumably an ironic twist on the title of the American daytime soap *The Young and the Restless*. The sisters are Cree women, living on a reserve on Miniautlin Island circa 1976. The living room is unremarkable: a neat, modestly furnished working-class abode. As they catch up on the soap opera's plot points, the juxtaposition of their own circumstances and surroundings with the show's ridiculous drama comes into sharp focus. All the more so as the sisters have entered into a dark melodrama of their own, although not the sort of daytime television: Ella Lee has stabbed her husband to death, and the hallway from the living room is still covered with blood, a mess her sisters are helping her clean up. The hallway's spectacle is the blatantly uncanny element, but one which the sisters greet with a jaded equanimity. On the fridge in the adjacent kitchen, bloody handprints blend in with the children's proudly displayed school artwork, including their own handprints done in paint.

This scene's diverse strands – the uncanny domestic space, the spectre of violence, the droll humour, the sisters as a group of female support, the melodramatic impulse – saturate Shirely Cheechoo's *Bearwalker* (2000, originally titled *Backroads*) as a whole, and render it difficult to pigeonhole. On the one hand *Bearwalker* is unique within Canadian cinema in that it is the first fiction feature to be written and directed by a Native woman (Cheechoo, who also acts in the film). On the other, *Bearwalker* is isolated from both Cheechoo's earlier fiction shorts and, more generally, from the majority of indigenous Canadian cinema in that it appropriates a gothic/melodramatic model to frame its emotional, highly affective drama. Indeed, the film points this up by showcasing the sisters as critical consumers of melodrama. The American soaps are evidence of post-colonial domination in the realm of cultural production and exhibition, an ongoing concern in Native communities, especially in the televisual formats, but the soap's romantic and risible template is also a pleasure to be enjoyed (Ella Lee later admits that her fantasies centre on the romantic anodyne these shows offer), and actively critiqued and derided, which is a piece with the viewing pleasure.

That the film evinces influences more akin to George Cukor's *Gaslight* (1994) or David Lynch than to the National Film Board of Canada (NFB) follows a certain logic in so far as the film is not an NFB production. It was developed at the Sundance Institute, to which Cheechoo was invited following a Sundance Native Forum screening of her first fictional short *Silent Tears* (1997), a film that, like *Bearwalker*, evinces an interest in extreme circumstances and the bodily abject, but plays much more as a meditative, experimental piece than as a dramatic narrative. By contrast, *Bearwalker* appears to have been conceived with the mainstream, commercial market in mind; indeed, the film has been a festival audience favourite. But *Bearwalker* has not had a vibrant life beyond the festival circuit, and, to my knowledge, it has not had a theatrical release in either Canada or the United States, although I am not sure that this was ever the goal. The film's running time of 83 minutes suggests that it was geared for television viewing, and it did air on the Sundance channel. With the recent success of Zacharias Kunuk's *Atanarjuat: The Fast Runner* (2001), much utopian speculation has taken place as to the possible broad appeal of indigenous productions within Canada, but *Bearwalker*'s lack of attention from either the theatrical or television circuits suggests that distributors are still wary of Native productions that have neither the stamp of approval from Cannes nor the safe temporal distance of a historical setting to relieve the sting and immediacy of potential social critiques. (As an aside, it is worth noting that Cheechoo worked as an acting coach on *Atanarjuat*.)

Regardless, the film's exclusion from national distribution does not negate its crossover aesthetics. Like the fiction of Thomas King (author of *Green Grass, Running Water*), it employs recognisable generic strategies in which to situate its specific, local needs and investments. This equation is not reductive; indeed, a large part of *Bearwalker*'s appeal is the manner in which it navigates and incorporates both generic requirements and Native concerns (without falling into the porridge pleas of a bland but good-for-you socially conscious document), and, for the most part, the two work seamlessly, suggesting melodrama's resilience to act as the site in which tensions of gender, class, race and modernity can be articulated and, pointedly, not resolved.

The eponymous Bearwalker is a malevolent spirit of Cree tradition, a spirit that feeds on revenge and hate, and exacerbates both. The Bearwalker's manifestations in the film vary between a hovering, menacing fireball and, strangely, a black Model-T Ford. This second incarnation is especially indicative of Cheechoo's overall diachronic mode. The Model-T (first produced in 1908), a harbinger of modernity and an epitome of both industrial ingenuity and assembly-line monotony, blends into Native myth, suggesting both the incorporation of modern signifiers by traditional myth and a turn to the past which recalls the traumatic vanishing of Natives and

Native culture in the face of Canada's colonial modernisation. Film, another axis of modernity, also played a part in this vanishing through an intensive ethnographic practice that often froze Native culture in an imagined pre-modern state of grace, relegating it as a relic from the past rather than recognising its continuation in the present tense.

Again similarities can be drawn with Thomas King; Cheechoo is not interested in situating the present in relation to the legacy of colonial oppression, a gambit which does tend to conflate the orignary starting point for Native culture and history with the moment of first contact. King wrote in an essay entitled 'Godzilla vs. Post-Colonial' that

> while post-colonialism purports to be a method by which we can begin to look at those literatures which are formed out of the struggle between the oppressed against the oppressor, the colonised and the coloniser, the term itself assumes that the starting point for that discussion is the advent of Europeans in North America. At the same time, the term organises the literature progressively suggesting that there is both progress and improvement. No less distressing, it also assumes that the struggle between guardian and ward is the catalyst for contemporary Native literature, providing those of us who write with method and topic. And, worst of all, the idea of post-colonial writing effectively cuts us off from our traditions, traditions that were in place before colonialism ever became a question, traditions which have come down to us through our culture in spite of colonisation, and it supposes that contemporary Native writing is largely a construct of oppression. Ironically, while the term itself – post-colonial – strives to escape to find new centres, it remains, in the end, a hostage to nationalism.

King's thesis is provocative within the terms of postmodernity, suggesting a resituation of Cheechoo's strategy not as a disjuncture signaling the terms of cultural re-appropriation, but as evidence of culture's perpetual adaptation and adjustment which work both with and against the lines of power, and not strictly from the centre to the peripheries. The use of a melodramatic format of *Bearwalker*, points up rather than replicates the paradoxes in re-thinking post-colonialism by decentring colonial contact, and positing instead a Native voice that articulates itself attendant with rather than in opposition to cultural shifts and currents.

Most noticeably, Cheechoo proposes a contemporary drama which is refreshingly matter-of-fact in the manner it views the modernity/tradition influx. The valences are complicated, fluctuating and never straightforward, eschewing any expected positive or negative registers.

The Bearwalker of tradition wreaks havoc and demands sacrifice but also manages justice in a way that the official law and its enforcers (in *Bearwalker* the official law is decidedly corrupt), fail to do. In this sense, the Bearwalker of tradition intersects cleanly with the wish-fulfillment patterns of women's melodrama, suggesting a realm of abject, unarticulated power, forces outside of the realm of the Law and Language of the father, which achieves a form of justice even as it demands a sacrifice. And likewise, following the historical patterns of melodramatic tropes, vengeance and sacrifice are imbricated in a manner that both play out for and against the female protagonists. But if *Bearwalker* is able to balance modernity and tradition, the film's violence jars the usual melodramatic trappings, revealing a vulnerable, physical body that is in excess of its positionality on an imagined race/gender grid.

Bearwalker focuses on female communities; the film is unabashedly a woman's film and female suffering is at its core. But while, as mentioned above, it ably balances modernity and tradition, the spectre of gendered difference unbalances generic expectations, pointing up a violent excess that destabilises a neat relay between melodramatic heroines and contemporary Native women. Women suffer in melodrama, but visually their suffering is lovely to look at. Think of the death-bed scenes of Greta Garbo in Cukor's *Camille* (1936) or Bette Davis in *Dark Victory* (Edmund Goulding, 1939), or, more recently, Julia Roberts in *Steel Magnolias* (Herbert Ross, 1989). Conversely melodrama can also take a perverse glee in rendering women's deterioration as visually ridiculous. Think of Davis in *Mr. Skeffington* (Vincent Sherman, 1944), in which her journey to true love is paved upon a bout of diphtheria that leaves her body bizarrely ravaged. In both the former and latter examples, though, an aesthetic disconnect occurs that allows the female viewer to enjoy the image of female unraveling, not as a masochistic exercise but as an aesthetic spectacle that makes it *memorable* as such, but easily *forgettable* as narrative information within the context of the film as a whole.

Bearwalker has no such disjuncture. Its violence is difficult viewing, as is its image of Ella Lee's body which is increasingly battered, beaten and bruised throughout the course of the film. Her experiences with violence are numerous: she lives in an abusive relationship with her Native husband, who she eventually kills; she is beaten and raped by her white boss; physically and psychologically tortured, and finally fatally beaten by the white police officer who formerly had romantic, or at least sexual, designs on her. Chronologically the rape occurs and is shown first; formally, the scene is fragmented, at times shot with a red light that marks the intervention of male violence into the film, an intervention that is reflected formally and narratively. From this point on, though, scenes of violence are stubbornly, chillingly realistic. And from this point on, Ella Lee's body has no time to recover from one beating before another occurs, leaving her bruised and bloodied until her horrific death. Male violence is literally written on Ella Lee's body. Her body is the material evidence of the fractured relationships between the white and Native communities, between men and women, between classes, and between the sister's history and their present. The film is merciless in its attention to the physical results of abuse, but in this attention it refuses to allow the viewer an easy out to the usual melodramatic comforts.

The death of Ella Lee is a sacrifice that leads to the death of the corrupt police officer who killed her, but, more importantly, her death serves as the sacrifice that draws her younger sister back into the community. Unlike the three older sisters, Grace has left Miniautlin and works as a lawyer in Toronto; she returns, however, to help Ella Lee, who has been charged with her husband's murder, although Grace's law experience is land claims and not criminal defense. Her sisters mock Grace for her inability to speak Cree, but her line of work suggests an alternative method of maintaining Native-ness at the same time that it leaves her alienated from her sisters and their lives in Miniautlin. Disillusioned by the ineffectiveness of official channels (Ella Lee is killed while in police custody), Grace calls on the Bearwalker to avenge Ella Lee's death, and at the film's end Grace has decided to remain with her family and help out with the upbringing of Ella Lee's children.

Thus is the film's ambivalent relationship to community maintenance, which comes at a high price. The Bearwalker, like the more sociological explanations for community violence and domestic abuse, cannot be simply and easily expelled; it feeds on discontentment and resentment, waiting for a moment of crisis which will set it into action. The film's conclusion, then, is not a resolution, but a provisional moment that allows for a sense of closure, while still suggesting an uncertain, but hopeful future.

Within the context of Cheechoo's oeuvre, which includes both documentary and fiction works, *Bearwalker* is something of an anomaly. In her documentaries, Cheechoo tends to retain an earnest voice and vision that are considered characteristic of Native NFB film work. Her fiction, by contrast, has a macabre cast that cuts its earnestness and a visual style that suggests a knowingness towards the complexities that earnestness, however well intentioned, cannot completely combat. *Bearwalker* is an earnest film in that it is a serious film, but the performances of its lead actresses and its mordant humour suggest a knowingness and world-weariness that is absent in Cheechoo's documentaries. I am not suggesting that earnestness should be devalued, although it has often been used as a criticism of Native NFB films. But I am suggesting that the fiction format, and in this case, specifically, the melodramatic resonance, opens up a space that earnestness does not reach, a space that includes the restless affective energies of community building and destruction, and allows the difficulties a sophistication beyond dogmatic credo.

Documentary, of course, can also have this affective, restless political force, and in this regard I would like to move for a moment to another comparative paradigm, situating *Bearwalker* alongside Alanis Obomsawin's *Kanehsatake: 270 Years of Resistance* (1993). The latter is a well-known, acclaimed and controversial Canadian documentary about the Oka crisis (and the subject of a chapter in this volume by Brian McIlroy), in which a number of Mohawks of the community of Kanehsatake entered into a standoff with the Canadian Army, at Oka, Quebec. The film charts the standoff and, incidentally, the eventual evacuation of mainstream media reporters – before long Obomsawin's is the only camera rolling. Both films share an interest in female voices, masculinity in crisis and the problematics of a tripartite (French, English and Native) society attempting to define itself as a national unit. And in both films, the cracks and pressures of the situation result in violence and increased desperation on all sides. Indeed, *Bearwalker*, while wildly different form Obomsawin's piece, could be read, without stretching, as equally a response to Oka.

Finally, then, *Bearwalker* stands as a creative melding of personal, political and generic filmmaking; the assurance and confidence with which Cheechoo achieves this blend is admirable. As a director she has the goods, which does raise questions about both film production and distribution in Canada. Unconventional wisdom would suggest that distribution remains the final frontier of Canadian cinema, which may be true, generally, but Cheechoo's lack of Canadian support for continuing in the fiction feature vein posits that Canada's production problems could still use some ironing out (her most recent fiction feature, *Christmas in the Clouds* (2001), was made in the United States). Perhaps *Atanarjuat: The Fast Runner* will mark a watershed of sorts, and inject Canada's funding bodies with a willingness and vigour for producing Native features. But the results on that one are hardly a foregone conclusion. In the meantime, anyone interested in viewing *Bearwalker* may contact the filmmaker directly via the email address listed in the filmography.

Lysandra Woods

FILMOGRAPHY

EN PAYS NEUFS 1936
Director: Maurice Proulx
Producer: Ministère de la Colonisation et de l'Agriculture de Québec
Camera: Maurice Proulx
Editor: Maurice Proulx
Narrator: Maurice Montgrain
16mm print held at Cinémathèque québécoise, Montréal (www.cinematheque.qc.ca) and at the Archives nationales du Québec, Quebec City (www.anq.gouv.qc.ca)

CHURCHILL'S ISLAND 1941
Director: Stuart Legg
Producer: Stuart Legg (National Film Board of Canada)
Editor: Stuart Legg
Music: Lucio Agostini
Narrator: Lorne Greene; récitant/narrator (French version): Gérard Arthur
Video Mail Order: www.nfb.ca (VHS only)

LA FORTERESSE WHISPERING CITY 1947
Director: Fédor Ozep
Producer: George Marton/Roger Wood (Québec Productions)
Screenplay: Michael Lennox/George Zuckerman
Camera: Charles Quick/Guy Roe
Editor: Leonard Anderson/Douglas W. Bagier/Richard J. Jarvis
Music: Morris C. Davis/André Mathieu (from 'The Quebec Concerto')
Cast: Jacques Auger – Fr. / Paul Lukas – Eng. (Albert Frédéric), Nicole Germain – Fr. / Mary Anderson – Eng. (Marie/Mary Roberts), Paul Dupuis – Fr. / Helmut Dantine – Eng. (Michel Lacoste), Henri Letondal – Fr. / John Pratt – Eng. (Edward Durant, editor), Mimi D'Estée – Fr. / Joy Lafleur – Eng. (Blanche Lacoste), Armand Lebrun – Fr. / Mimi D'Estée-Eng. (Renée Brancourt)
35mm print held at Cinémathèque québécoise, Montréal (www.cinematheque.qc.ca)

POUR LA SUITE DU MONDE OF WHALES, THE MOON, AND MEN 1962
Directors: Pierre Perrault/Michel Brault/Marcel Carrière
Producer: Fernand Dansereau (National Film Board of Canada)
Camera: Michel Brault/Bernard Gosselin
Editor: Werner Nold
Music: Jean Cousineau/Jean Meunier
Made with the participation of Abel Harvey, Alexis Tremblay, Joachim Harvey, Louis Harvey and Léopold Tremblay
Video Mail Order: www.nfb.ca (VHS or DVD)

NOBODY WAVED GOOD-BYE 1964
Director: Don Owen
Producer: Roman Kroitor/Don Owen (National Film Board of Canada)
Screenplay: Don Owen
Camera: John Spotton
Editor: Donald Ginsberg/John Spotton
Music: Eldon Rathburn
Cast: Peter Kastner (Peter), Julie Biggs (Julie), Claude Rae (Father), Charmion King (Mother), Toby Tarnow (Sister), Ron Taylor (Boyfriend), Robert Hill (Patrolman), Jack Beer (Sergeant), John Sullivan (Probation Officer), Lynne Gorman (Julie's Mother)
Video Mail Order: www.nfb.ca (VHS only)

REASON OVER PASSION 1968
Director: Joyce Wieland
Screenplay: Adapted from the writings of Pierre Trudeau
Camera: Joyce Wieland
Editor: Joyce Wieland
16mm Rental: Canadian Filmmakers Distribution Centre, www.cfmdc.org

THE WINDS OF FOGO 1969
Director: Colin Low
Producer: Tom Daly (National Film Board of Canada)
Camera: Robert Humble
Editor: Edward Le Lorrain
Sound: Ted Haley
Featuring inhabitants of Fogo Island off the coast of Newfoundland.
Video Mail Order: www.nfb.ca (VHS only)

YOU ARE ON INDIAN LAND 1969
Director: Mike Mitchell/Mort Ransen
Producer: George C. Stoney (National Film Board of Canada)
Camera: Tony Ianzelo
Editor: Kathleen Shannon
Sound: Hans Oomes
Video Mail Order: www.nfb.ca (VHS only)

ON EST AU COTON COTTON MILL, TREADMILL 1970
Director: Denys Arcand
Producer: Marc Beaudet/Guy L. Coté/Pierre Maheu (National Film Board of Canada)
Camera: Alain Dostie
Editor: Pierre Bernier
Sound: Serge Beauchemin
Video Mail Order: www.nfb.ca (VHS only)

ASIVAQTIIN THE HUNTERS 1977
Director: Mosha Michael
Producer: Peter Raymont (National Film Board of Canada)

Camera: Mosha Michael

Editor: Mosha Michael

Music: Kowmageak Arngnakolak/Mosha Michael

Narrator: Mosha Michael

Video Mail Order: www.nfb.ca (VHS only)

MOURIR À TUE-TÊTE SCREAM FROM SILENCE 1979

Director: Anne-Claire Poirier

Producer: Anne-Claire Poirier/Jacques Gagné (National Film Board of Canada)

Screenplay: Anne-Claire Poirier/Marthe Blackburn

Camera: Michel Brault

Editor: André Corriveau

Music: Maurice Blackburn

Cast: Julie Vincent (Suzanne), Germain Houde (rapist), Paul Savoie (Philippe), Monique Miller (director), Micheline Lanctôt (editor), Pierre Gobeil (police), André Page (gynecologist), Michèle Mercure (Philippe's sister), Luce Guilbeault (patient), Christiane Raymond (disciple), Louise Portal (actress), Murielle Dutil (wife), Julie Morand (secretary), Leo Munger (victim), Jean-Pierre Masson (victim)

Video Mail Order: www.nfb.ca (VHS only)

SONATINE 1983

Director: Micheline Lanctôt

Producer: Pierre Gendron, René Malo (Corporation Image M & M, Ciné Ii, Films René Malo)

Screenplay: Micheline Lanctôt

Camera: Guy Dufaux

Editor: Louise Suprenant

Music: François Lanctôt

Cast: Pascale Bussières (Chantal), Marcia Pilotte (Louisette), Pierre Fauteux (Fernand), Kilment Denchev (Bulgarian Seaman)

Video Mail Order: Once published by Malofilm Vidéo (without subtitles), now out of print. Available from www.amazon.ca

FOSTER CHILD 1987

Director: Gil Cardinal

Producer: Jerry Krepakevich (National Film Board of Canada)

Camera: James Jeffrey

Editor: Alan Bibby

Sound: Alan Bibby

Video Mail Order: www.nfb.ca (VHS only)

I'VE HEARD THE MERMAIDS SINGING 1987

Director: Patricia Rozema

Producer: Patricia Rozema/Alexandra Raffé (Vos Productions, Téléfilm Canada, Ontario Film Development Corporation, Canada Council, Ontario Arts Council, National Film Board of Canada)

Screenplay: Patricia Rozema

Camera: Douglas Koch

Editor: Patricia Rozema

Music: Mark Korven

Cast: Sheila McCarthy (Polly Vandersma), Paule Baillargeon (Gabrielle St Peres), Ann-Marie MacDonald (Mary Joseph), John Evans (Warren), Brenda Kamino (Japanese Waitress), Richard Monette (Clive)

Video Mail Order: Available from Miramax on DVD, via www.facets.org or www.amazon.co.uk (region 1 only)

LE DÉCLIN DE L'EMPIRE AMÉRICAIN THE DECLINE OF THE AMERICAN EMPIRE 1986

Director: Denys Arcand

Producer: Pierre Gendrom (Corporation Image M & M, National Film Board of Canada, Téléfilm Canada, Société Générale du Cinéma du Québec, SRC – Société Radio-Canada)

Screenplay: Denys Arcand

Camera: Guy Dufaux

Editor: Monique Fortier

Music: François Dompierre

Cast: Dominique Michel (Dominique), Dorothée Berryman (Louise), Louise Portal (Diane), Geneviève Roux (Danielle), Pierre Curzi (Pierre), Rémy Girard (Rémy), Yves Jacques (Claude), Daniel Brière (Alain), Gabriel Arcand (Mario)

Video Mail Order: Available from Miramax on DVD, via www.facets.org (region 1) or www.amazon.co.uk (region 2)

THE LEARNING PATH 1991

Director: Loretta Todd

Producer: Cari Green/James Cullingham/Kent Martin/Peter Raymont (National Film Board of Canada)

Screenplay: Loretta Todd

Camera: Kirk Tougas

Editor: Frank Irvine

Music: Annie Frazer/John Kim Bell

Narrator: Loretta Todd

Made with the participation of Anne Starr, Bertha Twin, Jane Paul, Jessica Daniels, Lorelei Morin, Ray Fowler, and Veronica Lozo

Video Mail Order: www.nfb.ca (VHS only)

THIRTY TWO SHORT FILMS ABOUT GLENN GOULD 1993

Director: François Girard

Producer: Niv Fichman (Téléfilm Canada, Rhombus Media, Ontario Film Development Corporation, Canadian Broadcasting Corporation, National Film Board of Canada, Radio Televisão Portugal)

Screenplay: François Girard/Don McKeller

Camera: Alain Dostie

Editor: Gaëtan Huot

Video Mail Order: Available from Sony Pictures on DVD, via www.facets.org (region 1)

KANEHSATAKE: 270 YEARS OF RESISTANCE 1993

Director: Alanis Obomsawin

Producer: Alanis Obomsawin/Wolf Koenig (National Film Board of Canada)

Screenplay: Alanis Obomsawin

Camera: André-Luc Dupont/Barry Perles/François Brault/Jean-Claude Labrecque/Jocelyn Simard/Philippe Amiquet/Roger Rochat/Savas Kalogeras/Susan Trow/Zoe Dirse

Editor: Yurij Luhovy

Music: Claude Vendette/Francis Grandmont

Narrator: Alanis Obomsawin

Video Mail Order: www.nfb.ca (VHS only)

DEAD MAN 1995

Director: Jim Jarmusch

Producer: Demetra J. MacBride (12-Gauge Productions, Pandora Filmproduktion, Filmförderungsanstalt, Filmförder ung in Berlin-Brandenburg, Filmstiftung Nordrhein-Westfalen)

Screenplay: Jim Jarmusch

Camera: Robby Müller

Editor: Jay Rabinowitz

Music: Neil Young

Cast: Johnny Depp (William Blake), Crispin Glover (train fireman), Gibby Haines (man with gun in alley), George Duckworth (man at end of street), Richard Boes (man with wrench), John Hurt (John Scholfield), John North (Mr Olafsen), Robert Mitchum (John Dickinson), Milli Avital (Thel Russell), Peter Schrum (Drunk), Gabriel Byrne (Charlie Dickinson), Lance Henriksen (Cole Wilson), Michael Wincott (Conway Twill), Eugene Byrd (Johnny 'The Kid' Pickett)

Video Mail Order: Available from Miramax on DVD, via www.facets.org or www.amazon.co.uk (region 1 only)

EXOTICA 1994

Director: Atom Egoyan

Producer: Atom Egoyan/Camilia Frieberg (Téléfilm Canada, Ontario Film Development Corporation, Ego Film Arts)

Screenplay: Atom Egoyan

Camera: Paul Sarossy

Editor: Susan Shipton

Music: Mychael Danna

Cast: Bruce Greenwood (Francis), Mia Kirshner (Christina), Don McKeller (Thomas), Arsinée Khanjian (Zoe), Elias Koteas (Eric), Sarah Polley (Tracey), Victor Garber (Harold), Calvin Green (Customs Officer)

Video Mail Order: Available from Miramax on DVD, via www.facets.org or www.amazon.co.uk

Cast: Colm Feore (Glenn Gould), Gale Garnett (Journalist), Derek Keurvorst (Gould's Father), Katya Ladan (Gould's Mother), Devon Anderson (Glenn, Age 3), Joshua Greenblatt (Glenn, Age 8), Sean Ryan (Glenn, Age 12), Kate Hennig (Chambermaid), Allegra Fulton (Waitress), Gerry Quigley (Music Critic), and with the participation of Yehudi Menuhin

Video Mail Order: Available from Samuel Goldwyn on DVD, via www.facets.org or www.amazon.co.uk (region 1 only)

LE CONFESSIONNAL THE CONFESSIONAL 1995

Director: Robert Lepage

Producer: Denise Robert/David Puttnam/Philippe Carcassonne (Cinémaginaire, Confessionnal, Enigma Films, Cinéa, Téléfilm Canada, Société Générale des Industries Culturelles du Qué, European Co-Production Fund (UK), Channel 4 Films, Ministère de la Culture et de la Francophonie, Centre National de la Cinématographie, Quebec Government)

Screenplay: Robert Lepage

Camera: Alain Dostie

Editor: Emmanuelle Castro

Music: Sacha Puttnam/Stefan Girardet/Adrian Utley

Cast: Lothaire Bluteau (Pierre Lamontagne), Patrick Goyette (Marc Lamontagne), Jean-Louis Millette (Raymond Massicotte), Kristin Scott Thomas (Assistant to Mr Hitchcock), Ron Burrage (Alfred Hitchcock), Richard Fréchette (André), François Papineau (Paul-Émile Lamontagne), Marie Gignac (Françoise Lamontagne), Normand Daneau (The Young Priest Massicotte), Anne-Marie Cadieux (Manon), Suzanne Clément (Rachel), Denis Bernard (Narrator)

Video Mail Order: Available from Artificial Eye on VHS (PAL only), www.artificial-eye.co.uk

EARTH 1998

Director: Deepa Mehta

Producer: Deepa Mehta/Anne Masson/ Bobby Bedhi (Cracking the Earth Films Inc, Kaleidoscope)

Screenplay: Deepa Mehta (sased on the book *Cracking India* by Bapsi Sidhwa)

Camera: Giles Nuttgens

Editor: Barry Farrell

Music: A. R. Rahman

Cast: Aamir Kahn (Dil Nawaz), Nandita Das (Shanta), Rahul Khanna (Hasan), Maia Sethna (Lenny Sethna), Kitu Gidwani (Bunty Sethna), Arif Zakaria (Rustom Sethna), Eric Peterson (Mr Rogers), Kulbhushan Kharbanda (Imam Din), Pavan Malhotra (the butcher), Sunil Mehra (Toto Ramji), Navtej Singh Johar (Sher Singh), Raghuvir Yadav (Hari), Gulshan Grover (Mr Singh), Bobby Singh (Yousaf), Kabir Chowdhry (Cousin Adi), Lauren Walker (Mrs Rogers), Cinia Jain (Mrs Singh), Roshan Banu (Papoo), Radhika Singh (Muchoo)

Video Mail Order: Available from Zeitgeist on DVD, via www.facets.org or www.amazon.co.uk (region 1 only)

ATANARJUAT: THE FAST RUNNER 2001

Director: Zacharias Kunuk

Producer: Zacharias Kunuk/Paul Apak Angilirq/Norman Cohn (Igloolik Isuma Productions, National Film Board of Canada, Channel 24 Igloolik, Vision TV, Government of Canada Tax Credit Program, Government of Northwest Territories, Baffin Business Development Centre, Kakivak Association, Canada Council, Nunavut Tunngavik Inc, First Air, Canadian Broadcasting Corporation, Canadian Television and Cable Production Fund, Telefilm Canada – Equity Investment Program, CTF – Licence Fee Program)

Screenplay: Paul Apak Angilirq/Zacharias Kunuk/Norman Cohn/Herve Paniaq/Pauloosie Qulitalik

Camera: Norman Cohn

Editor: Zacharias Kunuk/Norman Cohn/Marie-Christine Sarda

Music: Christopher Crilly/(Ajaja Songs: Emile Immaroitok, Abraham Ulayuruluk)

Cast: Natar Ungalaaq (Atanarjuat), Sylvia Ivalu (Atuat), Peter Henry Arnatsiaq (Oki), Lucy Tulugarjuk (Puja), Madeline Ivalu (Panikpak), Pauloosie Qulitalik (Qulitalik), Eugene Ipkarnak (Sauri), Pakak Innuksuk (Amaqjuaq), Neeve Irngaut (Uluriaq), Abraham Ulayuruluk (Tungajuaq), Apayata Kotierk (Kumaglak), Mary Qulitalik (Niriuniq), Luke Taqqaugaq (Pittiulak), Alex Uttak (Pakak)

Video Mail Order: www.isuma.ca; also available on DVD, region 1 (from Alliance Atlantis, www.amazon.ca) or region 2 (from Optimum Home Entertainment, www.amazon.co.uk)

BEARWALKER 2002

Director: Shirley Cheechoo

Producer: Shirley Cheechoo/Phyllis Ellis/Christine K. Walker (Girls from the Backroads Productions Off Line Entertainment Group)

Screenplay: Shirley Cheechoo

Camera: Jonathan Brown

Editor: Lee Percy/Miume Jan Eramo

Music: Wendy Blackstone/Paul Hartwig

Cast: Renae Morriseau (Ella Lee), Sheila Tousey (Grace), Max Martini (Larry), Shirley Cheechoo (Ruby), Greta Cheechoo (Tammy), John Tench (Guy)

Video: Contact Shirley Cheechoo at scheechoo@hotmail.com

BIBLIOGRAPHY

The following bibliography serves two functions. Firstly, it gives the bibliographic information for material cited in the text of this book. Articles or reviews in daily and weekly papers and magazines have generally not been included; dates for such material are usually given in the relevant chapters. This bibliography also strives to serve as a guide for further reading. Those interested in pursuing some of the issues raised in this volume will find citations for books and articles not referenced in the text which they may choose to locate in the course of further research.

For a more exhaustive critical bibliography of writings on Canadian film, readers are advised to consult Loren Lerner (1997) *Canadian Film and Video: A Bibliography and Guide to the Literature/Film et vidéo canadiens: bibliographie analytique sur le cinéma et la vidéo*. Toronto: University of Toronto Press.

Abbot, Lawrence (1998) 'Interviews with Loretta Todd, Shelley Niro and Patricia Deadman', *Canadian Journal of Native Studies*, 18, 2, 340–4.

Anon. (1995) 'La première confession de Robert Lepage', *Séquences* (September–October), 180, 24–9.

Agee, James and Walker Evans (1960) *Let Us Now Praise Famous Men: Three Tenant Families*. Boston, MA: Houghton-Mifflin.

Aitken, Ian (1990) *Film and Reform: John Grierson and the Documentary Film Movement*. London: Routledge.

Aklil, Myriam (1991) 'Le Septième art de la Première nation', *L'Initial* (June), 19.

Alfred, Gerald R. (1991) 'From Bad to Worse: Internal Politics in the 1990 Crisis at Kahnawake', *Northeast Indian Quarterly*, 8, 1, 23–31.

Alioff, Maurie (1995) 'Haunted by Hitchcock: Robert Lepage's *Le confessionnal*', *Take One*, 4, 9, 9–15.

Alioff, Maurie and Susan Shouten Levine (1987) 'Interview: The Long Walk of Alanis Obomsawin', *Cinema Canada*, 142, 10–15.

Allor, Martin (1993) 'Cultural Métissage: National Formations and Productive Discourse in Quebec Cinema and Television', *Screen*, 34, 1, 69–75.

Anderson, Benedict (1983) *Imagined Communities: Reflections on the Origin and Spread of Nationalism*. London: Verso.

Arcand, Denys (1964a) 'Cinéma et sexualité', *Parti Pris*, 9, 11, 90–7.

____ (1964b) 'Des evidences', *Parti-Pris*, 7, 21.

____ (1986) *Le Déclin de l'empire américain*. Montréal: Boréal.

Armatage, Kay (1989) 'Joyce Wieland, Feminist Documentary and the Body of Work', *Canadian Journal of Political and Social Theory*, 13, 1–2, 91–101.

____ (1999) 'Kay Armatage Interviews Joyce Wieland', in Kathryn Elder (ed.) *The Films of Joyce Wieland*. Toronto: Toronto International Film Festival Group.

Armatage, Kay, Kass Banning, Brenda Longfellow and Janine Marchessault (eds) (1999) *Gendering the Nation: Canadian Women's Cinema*. Toronto: University of Toronto Press.

Baillargeon, Jean-Paul (1986) *Les Pratiques culturelles des Québécois*. Montréal: Institut québécois de recherche sur la culture.

Banning, Kass (1989) 'Surfacing: Canadian Women's Cinema', *Cinema Canada*, 167, 12–16.

____ (1999) 'Playing in the Light: Canadianizing Race and Nation', in Kay Armatage, Kass Banning, Brenda Longfellow and Janine Marchessault (eds) *Gendering the Nation: Canadian Women's Cinema*. Toronto: University of Toronto Press, 291–310.

Beard, William and Jerry White (eds) (2002) *North of Everything: English-Canadian Cinema Since 1980*. Edmonton: University of Alberta Press.

Bérubé, Bernard and Richard Magnan (1997) 'La distribution des films québécois aux États-Unis', *Cinémas* 7, 3, 31–59.

Bonneville, Léo (1979) *Le Cinéma québécois par ceux qui le font*. Montréal: Éditions Paulines and ADE.

Boulais, Stéphane-Albert (1987) 'Le Cinéma vécu de l'intérieur: Mon experience avec Pierre Perrault', in Pierre Véronneau, Michael Dorland and Seth Feldman (eds) *Dialogue: Cinema canadienne et québécois/Canadian and Quebec Cinema*. Montreal: Mediatexte, 161–72.

Brault, François (1982) 'Manifeste pour un cinéma vraiment national', *Possibles*, 7, 1, 83–7.

Brumble, David (1988) *American Indian Autobiography*. Berkeley: University of California Press.

Brunet, Michel (1976) *Notre passé, le présent et nous*. Montréal: Fides.

Buchanan, Donald W. (1965) 'The Projection of Canada', in Peter Morris (ed.) *The National*

Film Board of Canada: The War Years. Ottawa: Canadian Film Institute, 13–17.

Campbell, Maria (1973) *Halfbreed*. Toronto: McClelland and Stewart.

Carrière, Louise (ed.) (1983) *Les Femmes et cinéma québécois*. Montréal: Boréal.

____ (1986) Special issue: *Aujourd'hui le cinéma québécois, CinémAction*, 40.

Charest, Robert (1995) *Robert Lepage: Quelques zones de liberté*. Québec: L'Instant meme/Ex machina.

Ciaccia, John (2000) *The Oka Crisis: A Mirror of the Soul*. Dorval, Québec: Maren Publications.

Chun, Kimberly (2002) 'Storytelling in the Arctic Circle', *Cineaste*, 28, 1, 21–3.

Clandfield, David (1984a) 'From the Picturesque to the Familiar: Films of the French Unit at the NFB (1958–1964)', in Seth Feldman (ed.) *Take Two: A Tribute to Film in Canada*. Toronto: Irwin, 112–24.

____ (1984b) 'Ritual and Recital: The Perrault Project', in Seth Feldman (ed.) *Take Two: A Tribute to Film in Canada*. Toronto: Irwin, 136–48.

____ (1987) *Canadian Film*. Toronto: Oxford University Press.

____ (1989) 'Dialectical Interpretation: the case of cinéma direct and Pierre Perrault', *CineAction!* 16, 20–4.

____ (2003) 'Linking Community Renewal to National Identity: the Filmmaker's Role in *Pour la suite du monde*', in Jim Leach and Jeannette Sloniowski (eds) *Candid Eyes: Essays on Canadian Documentaries*. Toronto: University of Toronto Press, 71–86.

____ (2004) *Pierre Perrault and the Poetic Documentary*. Toronto: Toronto International Film Festival Group.

Cohn, Norman (2002) 'The Art of Community-Based Filmmaking', in Gillian Robinson (ed.) *Atanarjuat: The Fast Runner*. Toronto: Coach House Books, 25–7.

Comeau, Robert (1987) *Maurice Séguin, historien du pays québécois*. Montréal: VLB.

Copie Zéro (1985) 23 [Issue on Anne Claire Poirier].

Copie Zéro (1987–88) 34–5 [Issue on Denys Arcand].

Coulombe, Michel (1993) *Denys Arcand: la vraie nature du cinéaste*. Montréal: Boréal.

Coulombe, Michel and Marcel Jean (eds) (1999) *Le Dictionnaire du cinéma québécois*. Montréal: Boréal.

Daudelin, Robert (1967) *Vingt ans de cinéma au Canada français*. Québec: Ministère des affaires culturelles.

De Certeau, Michel (1990–94) *L'Invention au quotidien* [2 vols]. Paris: Gallimard.

Delaney, Marshall (1977) 'Wielandism: A Personal Style in Bloom', in Seth Feldman and Joyce Nelson (eds) *Canadian Film Reader*. Toronto: Peter Martin Associates, 279–82.

Deléas, Josette (1997) 'La quête du père dans le film *Sonatine* de Micheline Lanctôt', *Cinémas* 8, 1–2, 187–99.

Deleuze, Gilles (1985) *Cinéma 2: L'image-temps*. Paris: Éditions de minuit.

_____ (1990) *The Logic of Sense*, edited by Constantin V. Boundas, trans. Mark Lester with Charles Stivale. New York: Columbia University Press.

Deloria, Vine (1980) 'American Fantasy', in Gretchen M. Bataille and Charles L. P. Silet (eds) *The Pretend Indians: Images of Native Americans in the Movies*. Ames: Iowa State University Press, ix–xv.

Denault, Jocelyne (1981) 'Le cinema feminine au Québec', *Copie Zéro*, 11, 36–44.

_____ (1996) *Dans l'ombre des projecteurs: Les Québecoises et le cinéma*. Sainte-Foy, Québec: Presses de l'Université de Québec.

Desbarats, Carole (1993) *Atom Egoyan*. Paris: Éditions Dis Voir.

Devereaux, Leslie (ed.) (1995) *Fields of Vision: Essays in Film Studies, Visual Anthropology, and Photography*. Berkeley, CA: University of California Press.

Donohoe, Joseph (ed.) (1991) *Essays on Quebec Cinema*. East Lansing, MI: Michigan State University Press.

Dundjerovich, Aleksandar (2002) *The Cinema of Robert Lepage: The Poetics of Memory*. London: Wallflower Press.

Edwards, Natalie (1973) 'Who's Don Owen? What's he done, and what's he doing now?', *Cinema Canada*, 8, 30–48.

Egoyan, Atom (1995) *Exotica*. Toronto: Coach House Press.

Elder, Bruce (1984) 'Image: Representation and Object – the Photographic Image in Canada's Avant-Garde Film', in Seth Feldman (ed) *Take Two: A Tribute to Film in Canada*. Toronto: Irwin, 246–63.

_____ (1988) 'The Cinema We Need', in Douglas Fetherling (ed.) *Documents in Canadian Film*. Peterborough, ON: Broadview Press, 301–15.

_____ (1989) *Image and Identity: Reflections on Canadian Film and Culture*. Waterloo, ON: Wilfrid Laurier University Press.

Elder, Kathryn (1999) *The Films of Joyce Wieland*. Toronto: Toronto International Film Festival Group.

Evans, Gary (1979) 'The Politics of Propaganda: John Grierson', *Cinema Canada*, 56 (June–

July), 12–15.

_____ (1991) *In the National Interest: A Chronicle of the National Film Board of Canada from 1949 to 1989*. Toronto: University of Toronto Press.

Evans, Mary (1999) *Missing Persons: The Impossibility of Auto/biography*. London: Routledge.

Evans, Michael Robert (2000) 'Sometimes in Anger: The Struggles of Inuit Video', *Fuse Magazine*, 22, 4, 13–17.

Feldman, Seth and Joyce Nelson (eds) (1977) *The Canadian Film Reader*. Toronto: Peter Martin Associates.

Feldman, Seth (ed.) (1984a) *Take Two: A Tribute to Film in Canada*. Toronto: Irwin.

_____ (1984b) 'The Silent Subject in English-Canadian Film', in Seth Feldman (ed.) *Take Two: A Tribute to Film in Canada*. Toronto: Irwin, 48–57.

Feldman, Seth and Gene Walz (1981) 'English-Canadian Cinema since 1945', *Journal of Canadian Studies*, 16, 1, 1–2.

Fetherling, Douglas (ed.) (1988) *Documents in Canadian Film*. Peterborough, ON: Broadview Press.

Freud, Sigmund (2003 [1919]) *The Uncanny*, trans. by David McLintock, with an introduction by Hugh Haughton. London: Penguin Books.

Frye, Northrop (1965) 'Conclusion', in Carl Klinck, *Literary History of Canada*. Toronto: University of Toronto Press, 821–49.

Garel, Sylvain and André Pâquet (eds) (1992) *Les cinémas du Canada*. Paris: Centre Georges Pompidou.

Galvez, Raúl (2002) 'In Conversation: Zacharias Kunuk'. *Montage* (spring), 10–13.

Gathercole, Sandra (1984) 'The Best Film Policy this Country Never Had', in Seth Feldman (ed.) *Take Two: A Tribute to Film in Canada*. Toronto: Irwin, 36–46.

Gilmore, Leigh (2001) *The Limits of Autobiography: Trauma and Testimony*. Ithaca, NY: Cornell University Press.

Ginsburg, Faye (1995) 'Mediating Culture: Indigenous Media, Ethnographic Film, and the Production of Identity', in Leslie Devereaux (ed.) *Fields of Vision: Essays in Film Studies, Visual Anthropology, and Photography*. Berkeley, CA: University of California Press, 256–91.

Gittings, Christopher E. (2002) *Canadian National Cinema: Ideology, Difference and Representation*. London: Routledge.

Glassman, Marc (1998) 'Four Heads, One Vision: Rhombus Media at the Crossroads', *Take*

One, 7, 20, 29.

Godwin, George (1988) 'Reclaiming the Subject: a Feminist Reading of *I've Heard the Mermaids Singing*', *Cinema Canada*, 152 (May), 23–4.

Goslawski, Barbara (1998) 'An Appreciation of the Films of Joyce Wieland', *Take One*, 20.

Graham, Gerald (1989) *Canadian Film Technology, 1896–1986*. Newark, DE: University of Delaware Press.

Grierson, John (1988 [1944]) 'A Film Policy for Canada', in Douglas Fetherling (ed.) *Documents in Canadian Film*. Peterborough: Broadview Press, 51–7.

Gwyn, Sandra (1972) *Cinema as Catalyst*. St John's, Newfoundland: Memorial University of Newfoundland.

Haggard, Elizabeth (1971) *Nobody Waved Good-bye*. New York: Bantam Books.

Handling, Piers (1980) 'The National Film Board of Canada, 1939–1959', in Pierre Véronneau and Piers Handling (eds) *Self Portraits: Essays on the Canadian and Quebec Cinemas*. Ottawa: Canadian Film Institute, 42–53.

Harcourt, Peter (1977a) *Movies and Mythologies: Towards a National Cinema*. Toronto: Canadian Broadcasting Corporation.

_____ (1977b) 'Notes for an Article That Needs to be Written: Nationalism and the Canadian Consciousness', *Cinema Canada*, 37, 30–3.

_____ (1977c) 'The Years of Hope', in Seth Feldman and Joyce Nelson (eds) *Canadian Film Reader*. Toronto: Peter Martin Associates, 139–43.

_____ (1984) 'Pierre Perrault and *Le cinéma vécu*', in Seth Feldman (ed.) *Take Two: A Tribute to Film in Canada*. Toronto: Irwin, 125–35.

_____ (1995) 'Imaginary Images: An Examination of Atom Egoyan's Films', *Film Quarterly*, 48, 3, 2–14.

Hansen, Bjørn Anderson (2002) *Partition and Genocide: Manifestation of Violence in Punjab, 1937–1947*. New Delhi: India Research Press.

Harrison, Marion (1989) 'Mermaids Singing Off Key?', *CineAction!*, 16, 25–30.

Haskell, Molly (1975) *From Reverence to Rape: The Treatment of Women in the Movies*. London: New English Library.

Higson, Andrew (1989) 'The Concept of National Cinema', *Screen*, 30, 4, 36–46.

Hofsess, John (1975) *Inner Views: Ten Canadian Film-Makers*. Toronto: McGraw-Hill Ryerson.

Hoolboom, Mike (1997) *Inside the Pleasure Dome: Fringe Film in Canada*. Toronto: Gutter Press.

Houle, Michel (1988) 'Some Ideological and Thematic Aspects of the Quebec Cinema', in Pierre Véronneau and Piers Handling (eds) *Self-Portraits: Essays on the Canadian and Quebec Cinemas*. Ottawa: Canadian Film Institute, 159–82.

Houle, Michel, Jacques Leduc and Louis Hamelin (1971) Interview with Denys Arcand, in Réal La Rochelle, Michel Houle, Jacques Leduc and Louis Hamelin (eds) *Denys Arcand*. Montréal: Conseil québécois pour la diffusion du cinema, 12–31.

Igloolik Isuma Productions (1996) '*Nunavut (Our Land)*', in Peggy Gale and Lisa Steele (eds) *Video re/View: The (Best) Source for Critical Writings on Canadian Artists' Video*. Toronto: Art Metropole and V-Tape.

Jaehne, Karen (1988) '*I've Heard the Mermaids Singing*: An Interview with Patricia Rozema', *Cineaste* 16, 3, 23.

Jean, Marcel (1991) *Le Cinéma québécois*. Montréal: Boréal.

Jones, D. B. (1981) *Movies and Memoranda: An Interpretative History of the National Film Board of Canada*. Ottawa: Canadian Film Institute.

_____ (1996) *The Best Butler in the Business: Tom Daly of the National Film Board of Canada*. Toronto: University of Toronto Press.

Jones, Kent (1996) 'Review: *Dead Man*', *Cineaste*, 22, 2, 45–6.

Kalafatic, Carol (1999) 'Keepers of the Power: Story as Covenant in the Films of Loretta Todd, Shelley Niro and Christine Welsh', in Kay Armatage, Kass Banning, Brenda Longfellow and Janine Marchessault (eds) *Gendering the Nation: Canadian Women's Cinema*. Toronto: University of Toronto Press, 109–19.

King, Thomas (1990) 'Godzilla vs. Post-Colonial', *World Literature Written in English*, Fall, 10–16.

Krupat, Arnold (1989) *The Voice at the Margin: Native American Literature and the Canon*. Berkeley, CA: University of California Press.

Kunuk, Zacharias (2002) 'I First Heard the Story of Atanarjuat from My Mother', *Brick*, 70, 17–20.

La Rochelle, Réal (1981) 'Un Cinéma de defense des autochtones', *Copie Zéro*, 11, 60–6.

_____ (1986) 'Le cinéma québécois, en voie d'assimilation ou de métissage', in Jean-Paul Baillargeon (ed.) *Les Pratiques culturelles des Québécois*. Montréal: Institut québécois de recherche sur sur la culture, 215–32.

_____ (1995) 'Sound design and Music as *Tragédie en Musique*: The Documentary Practice of Denys Arcand', in Brian McIlroy and André Loiselle (eds) *Auteur/Provocateur: The Films of*

Denys Arcand. Westport, CT: Greenwood Press, 32–51.

Leach, Jim and Jeannette Sloniowski (eds) (2003) *Candid Eyes: Essays on Canadian Documentaries*. Toronto: University of Toronto Press.

Lefebvre, Jean Pierre (1964) 'Petit éloge des grandeurs et des misères de la colonie française de L'Office national du film', *Objectif*, 28.

Lejeune, Phillipe (1989) *On Autobiography*. Minneapolis: University of Minnesota Press.

Lerner, Loren (1997) *Canadian Film and Video: A Bibliography and Guide to the Literature/Film et vidéo canadiens: bibliographie analytique sur le cinéma et la vidéo*. Toronto: University of Toronto Press.

Lesage, Julia (1990) 'The Political Aesthetics of the Feminist Documentary Film', in Patricia Erens (ed.) *Issues in Feminist Film Criticism*. Bloomington, IN: Indiana University Press, 222–37.

Lever, Yves (1972) *Cinéma et société québécoise*. Montréal: Le Jour.

_____ (1995) *Histoire générale du cinéma au Québec*. Montréal: Boréal.

Levich, Jacob (1996) 'Western Auguries', *Film Comment*, May/June, 39–41.

Lind, Jane (2001) *Joyce Wieland: Artist on Fire*. Toronto: Lorimer.

Loiselle, André and Brian McIlroy (eds) (eds) *Auteur/Provocateur: The Films of Denys Arcand*. Westport, CT: Praeger.

Loiselle, André (1999) 'Despair as Empowerment: Melodrama and Counter-Cinema in Anne Claire Poirier's *Mourir à tue-tête*', *Canadian Journal of Film Studies*, 8, 2, 21–43.

_____ (2000) *Scream from Silence*. Trowbridge: Flicks Books.

Longfellow, Brenda (1984) 'The Feminist Fiction Film in Quebec: *La vie rêvée* and *La cuisine rouge*', in Seth Feldman (ed.) *Take Two: A Tribute to Film in Canada*. Toronto: Irwin, 149–59.

_____ (2001) '*The Red Violin*, Commodity Fetishism, and Globalization', *Canadian Journal of Film Studies*, 10, 2, 6–20.

Mach, Elyse (1991) *Great Contemporary Pianists Speak for Themselves*. New York: Dover.

MacKenzie, Scott (2004) *Screening Québec: Québécois Moving Images, National Identity, and the Public Sphere*. Manchester: Manchester University Press.

Magder, Ted (1993) *Canada's Hollywood: The Canadian State and Feature Films*. Toronto: University of Toronto Press.

Major, Ginette (1982) *Le Cinéma québécois à la recherché de son public: bilan d'une décennie*. Montréal: Presses de l'Université de Montréal.

Marcuse, Herbert (1964) *One-Dimensional Man: Studies in the Ideology of Advanced Industrial*

Society. Boston: Beacon Press.

Marie, Michel (1987) 'Singularité de l'œuvre de Perrault', in Pierre Véronneau, Michael Dorland and Seth Feldman (eds) *Dialogue: Cinema canadienne et québécois/Canadian and Quebec Cinemas*. Montréal: Médiatexte, 153–60.

Marks, Laura U. (1992) 'Reconfigured Nationhood: A Partisan History of the Inuit Broadcasting Corporation', *Afterimage*, 21, 8, 4–8.

_____ (1998) 'Inuit Auteurs and Arctic Airwaves', *Fuse Magazine*, 21, 4, 13–17.

Marshall, Bill (2001) *Quebec National Cinema*. Montreal/Kingston: McGill-Queen's University Press.

McLarty, Lianne M. (1982) 'The Experimental Films of Joyce Wieland', *Ciné-Tracts*, 17, 51–9.

McLeod, Neal (2001) 'Coming Home Through Stories', in Armand Garnet Ruffo (ed.) *(Ad)Dressing Our Words: Aboriginal Perspectives on Aboriginal Literatures*. Penticton, BC: Theytus Books, 17–36.

Melnyk, George (1981) *Radical Regionalism*. Edmonton: NeWest Press.

_____ (2004) *One Hundred Years of Canadian Cinema*. Toronto: University of Toronto Press.

Merleau-Ponty, Maurice (1964) *Sense and Non-Sense*, translated, and with a preface by Hubert L. Dreyfus and Patricia Allen Dreyfus. Evanston, IL: Northwestern University Press.

Morris, Peter (1965) *The National Film Board of Canada: The War Years*. Ottawa: Canadian Film Institute.

_____ (1978) *Embattled Shadows: A History of Canadian Cinema, 1895–1939*. Montreal/Kingston: McGill-Queen's University Press.

Mulvey, Laura (1975) 'Visual Pleasure and Narrative Cinema', *Screen* 16, 3, 6–18.

_____ (1989) *Visual and Other Pleasures*. Bloomington, IN: Indiana University Press.

Nadeau, Chantal (1992) 'Women in French-Quebec Cinema: The Space of Socio-Sexual (In)difference', *CineAction!*, 28, 4–15.

Naficy, Hamid (2001) *An Accented Cinema: Exilic and Diasporic Filmmaking*. Princeton, NJ: Princeton University Press.

Nelson, Joyce (1988) *The Colonized Eye: Rethinking the Grierson Legend*. Toronto: Between the Lines.

Nichols, Bill (1985) 'The Voice of Documentary', in Bill Nichols (ed.) *Movies and Methods*, vol. 2. Berkeley, CA: University of California Press, 258–73.

_____ (1991) *Representing Reality: Issues and Concepts in Documentary*. Bloomington, IN: Indiana University Press.

_____ (1994) *Blurred Boundaries: Questions of Meaning in Contemporary Culture*. Bloomington, IN: Indiana University Press.

Noguez, Dominique (1970) *Essais sur le cinéma québécois*. Montréal: Le Jour.

Nowell, Iris (2001) *Joyce Wieland: A Life in Art*. Toronto: ECW Press.

Owens, Louis (2001) *I Hear the Train: Reflections, Inventions, Refractions*. Norman, OK: University of Oklahoma Press.

Parpart, Lee (2002) 'Political Alignments and the Lure of "More Existential Questions" in the Films of Patricia Rozema', in William Beard and Jerry White (eds) *North of Everything: English-Canadian Cinema Since 1980*. Edmonton: University of Alberta Press, 294–311.

Pallister, Janis L. (1995) *The Cinema of Québec: Masters in Their Own House*. Madison, WI: Fairleigh Dickinson University Press.

Perrault, Pierre (1996) *Cinéaste de la parole: entretiens avec Paul Warren*. Montréal: L'Hexagone.

Perrault, Pierre (1992) *Pour la suite du monde: récit*. Montréal: L'Hexagone.

Pérusse, Denise (1995) *Micheline Lanctôt: la vie d'une heroine*. Montréal: L'Hexagone.

Pevere, Geoff (1988) 'Rebel Without a Chance: Cycles of rebellion and suppression in Canadian teen movies', *CineAction!*, 12, 44–8.

_____ (1992) 'La Nouvelle Vague Ontarienne', in Sylvain Garel and André Pâquet (eds) *Les cinémas du Canada*. Paris: Centre Georges Pompidou, 143–52.

Philpot, Robin (1991) *Oka: Dernier alibi du Canada anglais*. Montréal: VLB.

Pick, Zuzana. (2003) '"This Land is Ours" – Storytelling and History in *Kahnesatake: 270 Years of Resistance*', in Jim Leach and Jeannette Sloniowski (eds) *Candid Eyes: Essays on Canadian Documentaries*. Toronto: University of Toronto Press, 181–96.

Richler, Mordecai (1992) *Oh Canada! Oh Quebec!: Requiem for a Divided Country*. Toronto: Penguin Books.

Riggins, Stephen (1992) *Ethnic Minority Media: An International Perspective*. Newbury Park, CA: Sage Publications.

Robinson, Gillian (ed.) (2002) *Atanarjuat: The Fast Runner*. Toronto: Coach House Books, 25–7.

Rosenbaum, Jonathan (1996) 'A Gun Up Your Ass: An Interview with Jim Jarmusch', *Cineaste*, 22, 2, 23.

_____ (2000) *Dead Man*. London: British Film Institute.

Ruffo, Armand Garnet (2001) *(Ad)dressing Our Words: Aboriginal Perspectives on Aboriginal*

Literatures. Penticton, BC: Theytus Books.

Russell, Catherine (1999) *Experimental Ethnography: The Work of Film in the Age of Video*. Durham, NC: Duke University Press.

_____ (2002) 'Role Playing and the White Male Imaginary in Atom Egoyan's *Exotica*', in Gene Walz (ed.) *Canada's Best Features: Critical Essays on Fifteen Canadian Films*. Amsterdam: Rodopi, 321–46.

Saul, John Raulston (1997) *Reflections of a Siamese Twin: Canada at the End of the Twentieth Century*. Toronto: Penguin Books.

Seals, David (1990) *The Powwow Highway: A Novel*. New York: Plume.

Shek, Ben-Z. (1989-90) 'History as a Unifying Structure in *Le Déclin de l'empire américain*', *Québec Studies*, 9, 9–15.

Sidhwa, Bapsi (1991) *Cracking India: A Novel*. Minneapolis, MN: Milkweed Editions.

Tadros, C. (1984) '*Sonatine*: "Film maudit": A conversation with Micheline Lanctôt', *Cinema Canada*, 110, 7–11.

Tallon, Joan (2002) 'Order of Canada Promotion for Alanis Obomsawin', *Windspeaker*, 19, 10, 12.

Taylor, Charles (1993) *Reconciling the Solitudes: Essays on Canadian Federalism and Nationalism*. Montreal/Kingston: McGill-Queen's University Press.

Taylor, Drew Hayden (1998) *Funny, You Don't Look Like One: Observations from a Blue-Eyed Ojibway*. Penticton, BC: Theytus Books.

Tousignant, Isa (2001) 'Fated Possibilities: A Conversation with Robert Lepage', *Take One*, 9, 30, 14–17.

Tremblay-Daviault, Christine (1981) *Un cinéma orphelin: structure mentales et sociales du cinéma québécois, 1942–1953*. Montréal: Québec/Amérique.

Tschofen, Monique (2002) 'Repetition, Compulsion, and Representation in Atom Egoyan's Films', in William Beard and Jerry White (eds) *North of Everything: English-Canadian Film Since 1980*. Edmonton: University of Alberta Press, 166–83.

Turner, D. J. (1975) 'Historical Notes: *Whispering City* at Filmexpo', *Cinema Canada*, 21, 24–5.

Turner, D. J. and Micheline Morisset (eds) (1987) *Canadian Feature Film Index, 1913–1985/ Index des films canadiens de long métrage, 1913–1985*. Ottawa: Public Archives Canada [National Film, Television and Sound Archives].

Valaskakis, Gail (1981) *The Inukshuk ANIK-B Project, An Assessment*. Ottawa: Inuit Tapirisat.

_____ (1992) 'Communication, Culture and Technology: Satellites and Northern Native

Broadcasting in Canada', in Stephen Harold Riggins (ed.) *Ethnic Minority Media: An International Perspective*. Newbury Park, CA: Sage, 63–81.

Valaskakis, Gail and Lorna Roth (1989) 'Aboriginal Broadcasting in Canada: A Case Study on Democratization', in Marc Raboy and Peter A. Bruck (eds) *Communication For and Against Democracy*. Toronto: Black Rose Books, 221–34.

Vallières, Pierre (1968) *Nègres blancs d'Amérique*. Montréal: Parti Pris.

_____ (1975) 'Brault a manqué son coup', *Cinéma Québec*, 4, 1, 18–20.

Van Den Hoven, Adrian (1991) '*The Decline of the American Empire* in a North American Perspective', in Joseph Donohoe, Jr (ed.) *Essays on Quebec Cinema*. Lansing MI: Michigan State University Press, 145–56.

Véronneau, Pierre (1979) *Cinéma de l'époque duplessiste*. Montréal: Cinémathèque québécoise.

_____ (ed.) (1991) *À la recherche d'une identité: Renaissance du cinéma d'auteur canadien-anglais*. Montréal: Cinémathèque québécoise.

Véronneau, Pierre, Michael Dorland and Seth Feldman (eds) (1987) *Dialogue: Cinema canadienne et québécois/Canadian and Quebec Cinema*. Montréal: Médiatexte.

Véronneau, Pierre and Piers Handling (eds) (1980) *Self Portrait: Essays on the Canadian and Quebec Cinemas*. Ottawa: Canadian Film Institute.

Walz, Gene (ed.) (2002) *Canada's Best Features: Critical Essays on Fifteen Canadian Films*. Amsterdam: Rodopi.

Weber, Samuel (1982) *The Legend of Freud*. Minneapolis: University of Minnesota Press.

Weinmann, Heinz (1990) *Cinéma de l'imaginaire québécois: de La petite Aurore à Jésus de Montréal*. Montréal: L'Hexagone.

White, Jerry (1999) 'Alanis Obomsawin, Documentary Form and the Canadian Nation(s)', *CineAction!*, 49, 26–36.

Winston, Brian (1995) *Claiming the Real: The Documentary Film Revisited*. London: British Film Institute.

Wright, Judy and Debbie Magidson (1977) 'Making Films for Your Own People: An Interview with Denys Arcand', in Seth Feldman and Joyce Nelson (eds) *Canadian Film Reader*. Toronto: Peter Martin Associates, 217–34.

York, Geoffrey and Loreen Pindera (1992) *People of the Pines: The Warriors and the Legacy of Oka*. Toronto: Little, Brown.

Zucker, Carol (1980) 'Les oeuvres récentes d'Anne Claire Poirier et Paule Baillargeon', *Copie Zéro*, 11, 52–5.

Online Resources:

Archives nationales du Québec: www.anq.gouv.qc.ca

Audio-Visual Preservation Trust of Canada: www.avtrust.ca

Canadian Broadcasting Corporation: www.cbc.ca

Canadian Filmmakers Distribution Centre: www.cfmdc.org

Cinémathèque québécoise: www.cinematheque.qc.ca

Film-related websites in Canada (Queen's University): www.film.queensu.ca/links.html

National Archives of Canada: www.archives.ca

National Film Board of Canada: www.nfb.ca

National Library of Canada: www.nlc-bnc.ca

Telefilm Canada: www.telefilm.gc.ca